The Girl in the Pandemic

Transnational Girlhoods

EDITORS: Claudia Mitchell, *McGill University*; Ann Smith, *McGill University*; Heather Switzer, *Arizona State University*

Girlhood Studies has emerged over the last decade as a strong area of interdisciplinary research and activism, encompassing studies of feminism, women and gender, and childhood and youth and extending into such areas as sociology, anthropology, development studies, children's literature, and cultural studies. As the first book series to focus specifically on this exciting field, *Transnational Girlhoods* will help to advance the research and activism agenda by publishing full-length monographs and edited collections that reflect a robust interdisciplinary and global perspective. International in scope, the series will draw on a vibrant network of girlhood scholars already active across North America, Europe, Russia, Oceania, and Africa, while forging connections with new activist and scholarly communities.

Volume 5
The Girl in the Pandemic: Transnational Perspectives
Edited by Claudia Mitchell and Ann Smith

Volume 4
An American Icon in Puerto Rico: Barbie, Girlhood, and Colonialism at Play
By Emily R. Aguiló-Pérez

Volume 3
Living Like a Girl: Agency, Social Vulnerability and Welfare Measures in Europe and Beyond
Edited by Maria A. Vogel and Linda Arnell

Volume 2
Ethical Practice in Participatory Visual Research with Girls: Transnational Approaches
Edited by Relebohile Moletsane, Lisa Wiebesiek, Astrid Treffry-Goatley, and April Mandrona

Volume 1
The Girl in the Text
Edited by Ann Smith

THE GIRL IN THE PANDEMIC
Transnational Perspectives

Edited by
Claudia Mitchell and Ann Smith

berghahn
NEW YORK • OXFORD
www.berghahnbooks.com

First published in 2023 by
Berghahn Books
www.berghahnbooks.com

© 2023, 2026 Claudia Mitchell and Ann Smith
First paperback edition published in 2026

All rights reserved. Except for the quotation of short passages for the purposes of criticism and review, no part of this book may be reproduced in any form or by any means, electronic or mechanical, including photocopying, recording, or any information storage and retrieval system now known or to be invented, without written permission of the publisher.

Library of Congress Cataloging-in-Publication Data

Names: Mitchell, Claudia, editor. | Smith, Ann (Ann Lilian), editor.
Title: The girl in the pandemic : transnational perspectives / edited by Claudia Mitchell and Ann Smith.
Description: New York : Berghahn Books, 2023. | Series: Transnational girlhoods ; Volume 5 | Includes bibliographical references and index.
Identifiers: LCCN 2022053209 (print) | LCCN 2022053210 (ebook) | ISBN 9781800739505 (hardback) | ISBN 9781800739512 (epub)
Subjects: LCSH: Women—Social conditions—21st century. | COVID-19 Pandemic, 2020—Social aspects. | COVID-19 (Disease)—Social aspects. | Women—Health and hygiene.
Classification: LCC HQ1155 .G527 2023 (print) | LCC HQ1155 (ebook) | DDC 305.4209/05—dc23/eng/20230117
LC record available at https://lccn.loc.gov/2022053209
LC ebook record available at https://lccn.loc.gov/2022053210

British Library Cataloguing in Publication Data
A catalogue record for this book is available from the British Library

EU GPSR Authorized Representative
LOGOS EUROPE, 9 rue Nicolas Poussin, 17000, LA ROCHELLE, France
Email: Contact@logoseurope.eu

ISBN 978-1-80073-807-2 hardback
ISBN 978-1-83695-363-0 paperback
ISBN 978-1-80073-795-2 epub
ISBN 978-1-80073-779-2 web pdf

https://doi.org/10.3167/9781800738072

An electronic version of this book is freely available thanks to the support of libraries working with Knowledge Unlatched. KU is a collaborative initiative designed to make high-quality books Open Access for the public good. More information about the inititive and links to the Open Access version can be found at knowledgeunlatched.org.

This work is published subject to a Creative Commons Attribution Noncommercial No Derivatives 4.0 License. The terms of the license can be found at http://creativecommons.org/licenses/by-nc-nd/4.0/. For uses beyond those covered in the license contact Berghahn Books.

Contents

List of Illustrations

Introduction
The Girl in the Pandemic 1
   Claudia Mitchell and Ann Smith

Part I. Reflections

Chapter 1
Five Lessons from Past Ebola Epidemics for Today's COVID-19
Pandemic 15
   Nidhi Kapur

Chapter 2
How to Build "Meaningful Bonds" with Poor Young Women?
State Interventions during the Lockdown in Argentina 33
   Ana Cecilia Gaitán

Chapter 3
What It All Means: Young Rural Women in South Africa
Confronting COVID-19 49
   Nokukhanya Ngcobo, Zinhle Nkosi, and Ayub Sheik

Part II. Continuing Education

Chapter 4
Women Teachers Support Girls during the COVID-19 School
Closures in Uganda 69
   Christine Apiot Okudi

Chapter 5
Experiencing Care: Young Women's Response to COVID-19
Crises in Poland 86
   Anna Bednarczyk, Zuzanna Kapciak, Kinga Madejczak,
   Alicja Sędzikowska, Natalia Witek, and Faustyna Zdziarska

Chapter 6
COVID-19, Education, and Well-Being: Experiences of Female
Agriculture Students in Ethiopia   101
*Hannah Pugh, Eleni Negash, Frehiwot Tesfaye, and
Madalyn Nielsen*

Chapter 7
Exploring the Psychosocial Experiences of Women Undergraduates
in Delhi, India, during the COVID-19 Pandemic   120
Richa Rana, Poonam Yadav, and Shreya Sandhu

Part III. Vulnerabilities

Chapter 8
Lockdown and Violence against Women and Children:
Insights from Hospital-Based Crisis Intervention Centers in
Mumbai, India   139
Anupriya Singh, Sangeeta Rege, and Anagha Pradhan

Chapter 9
The Impact of COVID-19 on Child Marriage in India   156
Gayatri Sharma and Ayesha Khaliq

Chapter 10
The Impact of the COVID-19 Pandemic on Child Domestic
Workers in Ethiopia   174
Annabel Erulkar, Welela Tarekegne, and Eyasu Hailu

Chapter 11
The New Normal for Young Transgender Women in Thailand:
Unspoken Gender-Based Violence in the Time of COVID-19   190
*Rapeepun Jommaroeng, Sara Hair, Cheera Thongkrajai,
Kath Kangbipoon, and Suda Bootchadee*

Index   207

Illustrations

Figures

5.1. The slogan Women's Hell on a street in Krakow refers to the attempt during the pandemic by the Polish government to restrict reproductive rights. Photograph: Alicja Sędzikowska.   90

5.2. The slogan #stayhome on the sidewalk in Krakow. Photograph: Alicja Sędzikowska.   94

10.1. A mentor teaches girls in Addis Ababa about hygiene. Photograph: Zeleman Productions.   177

10.2. A Biruh Tesfa For All beneficiary does a job to benefit herself and her peers. Photograph: Zeleman Productions.   187

INTRODUCTION
The Girl in the Pandemic

Claudia Mitchell and Ann Smith

Time during a Pandemic

"Time is a complex and endlessly fascinating phenomenon, not simply the medium through which we do research, but an important topic of enquiry in its own right" (Neale 2010: 3). Time has been a crucial feature in the lives of girls and young women during the pandemic. Schools closed down and learning time was lost. For many girls and young women, it has not been clear that life will ever be the same, especially since extensive economic disruption can limit what is possible for any young person. While temporality is a feature of many academic publications, especially those dealing with health and humanitarian crises, there is, we think, an even greater responsibility to be aware of in writing about the lives of young people. Features of short- and long-term impact are inevitably in flux, so there is a great risk at any one time of misrepresenting the impact of crisis on young people's lives, as Claudia Mitchell (2014) and Shannon Walsh (2012) point out. See also *In My Life: Stories of Youth Activists in South Africa, 2002–2022* (Walsh et al. 2022). But time has also featured signifi-

---
Notes for this section can be found on page 10.

cantly in the process of publishing this book about girls in a pandemic. Inevitably, ironically enough, COVID-19 itself caused significant delays between our conceptualization of the book and its publication. When we first started working on it in the early days of the pandemic, we imagined that it would be a collection of chapters from around the globe that would be full of observations of what was learned. First drafts of most of the chapters of the *Girl in the Pandemic* were written months before there was any idea of a vaccine anywhere in the world, and long before terms like "variants" and "vaccine hesitancy," along with "social distancing" and "self-isolation," had entered our everyday vocabulary. Also, we need to take into account the complexity of tense when authors talk about the ever-changing present, the recurring past, and the uncertain future.

In 1722, Daniel Defoe wrote his classic *A Journal of the Plague Year: Being Observations or Memorials, of the most Remarkable Occurrences, as well Publick as Private, which happened in London During the last Great Visitation In 1665*, commonly called *A Journal of the Plague Year*. The book, about the experiences of one man, was written fifty-seven years after the last outbreak of bubonic plague, which became known as the Great Plague of London, struck the city. He did not write it from the vantage point of living through the plague, which he did only as a five-year-old child. None of the authors of the chapters in this book had the luxury of having such a perspective; they wrote about the pandemic as it was unfolding.

For this reason, we begin this introduction with reference to the challenges faced by authors in writing chapters about events as they were happening, to be published in a book that has necessarily taken several years to be completed. Sathyaraj Venkatesan and Ishani Anwesha Joshi (2022: 1) note that

> [t]he event of the pandemic has not only bifurcated our perception of time in terms of a "before" and an "after" but also complicated our awareness and experience of time. Put differently, an epochal transformation caused by pandemics has shifted our temporal experience from the calendar/clock time to a queer time situated outside of formal time-related constructions. The pandemic also implies a dismantling and rearranging of the fundamental structures of time within which human beings interacted with the world. Such a discontinuity in the linear trajectory of chronological time engenders an epistemic and ontological reconfiguration of the very sense of time itself.

They go on to argue that "a shift in the perception of time precipitates an altered spatio-temporal awareness that informs postpandemic discourses and power structures" (ibid.).

In quoting Elizabeth El Refaie (2012) that "specific situations in which we find ourselves can have an impact on our time perceptions" Venkatesan and Joshi (2022: 2) note the complexity of how we now think of the past, the present, and the future in the context of the pandemic and how this leads to and necessitates a different view of time. For example, during lockdown, we might say, or have said, in the same sentence, "We did this" and "we hope to do that," but then the lockdowns continue or are reinstituted, so the future is still the present. Or we might write about measures that are being taken as having been in the past, since at the time of writing it appears that things are improving, only for us to be hit by a new variant, so that the past is still present. While verb tense is not explicitly described as part of what Venkatesan and Joshi refer to as "pandemic time" (ibid.), we see the problematics of verb tense in pandemic time as part of academic publishing during COVID-19. As we know, academic writing is conventionally based on a long process of first developing abstracts or short proposals in response to a call, writing full drafts, having the writing submitted to peer review, and so on, and this lapse of time, coupled with the delays related directly in one way or another to COVID-19 itself, posed a dilemma in relation to the fluidity of the situation for our authors and ourselves; this allows us to recognize and acknowledge that the tenses used in these chapters might sound out of line. Unlike in more journalistic forms of writing or even the many briefing documents issued by NGOs in the early days of the pandemic on the situation of girls and young women, in writing chapters in an ever-evolving situation like this pandemic, the use of future tense might quickly become replaced by the past tense, only to become present tense. Authors were sometimes compelled to write in speculative ways and often in the language of the tentative through the use of conditional clauses. Many of the girls and young women who were involved in telephone and Zoom interviews spoke about a possible future, what they were currently doing, and what they would do if and when the pandemic ended (or would end or might end). Overall, we see this challenge of representing the past, present, and future as informing the idea of "pandemic time" and consider its impact on academic writing.

About this Book

The chapters in this book bring together work from eight countries across four continents (Argentina, Republic of the Congo, Ethiopia, India, Poland, South Africa, Thailand, and Uganda), with most of the chapters written by scholars in the Global South. Given the inequities in health and education that the pandemic has highlighted, it is *even* more critical now than ever that Southern scholarship informs what we know about the lives of girls and young women in the context of COVID-19. But beyond geography, the spaces of investigation and reporting cut across schools, hospitals, universities, and streets.

We have organized this book into three main parts: Part I: Reflections; Part II: Continuing Education; and Part III: Vulnerabilities.

Part I: Reflections

Chapter 1, Nidhi Kapur's "Five Lessons from Past Ebola Epidemics for Today's COVID-19 Pandemic," considers "how key learning from the Ebola epidemic might translate into concrete advice to enable policymakers and practitioners to actively anticipate, locate, and mitigate the evolving gender-driven consequences of COVID-19."[1] Kapur considers the disproportionate impact of the "gendered dimensions of infectious disease outbreaks . . . on girls and young women."

In Chapter 2, "How to Build 'Meaningful Bonds' with Poor Young Women? State Interventions during the Lockdown in Argentina," Ana Cecilia Gaitán, whose feminist research is based on political anthropology, focuses on a "suburban area of Greater Buenos Aires that has high rates of poverty, population density, and COVID-19 infection." She explains that, given "the lockdown enforced in Argentina to contain COVID-19 spread," the centers "in which girls and young women [found] support in facing violent situations and other restrictions on their autonomy were closed," so the state responded by "converting itself in relation to its social policies aimed at children and young people." She analyzes this response and "pose[s] questions related to the virtualization of these policies."

In Chapter 3, "What It All Means: Young Rural Women in South Africa Confronting COVID-19," Nokukhanya Ngcobo, Zinhle Nkosi, and Ayub Sheik, noting how COVID-19 intensified "the vulnerability of young women . . . living in remote rural areas of South Africa [who] face the harsh realities of inequalities and poverty," analyze the written narratives of eight South African university students (aged between seventeen and twenty-six) and the content of follow-up telephone interviews. Their findings suggest that "household chores, economic stress, and sexual violence have all been exacerbated by the pandemic" and attribute this to a "pervasive hypersexual culture and patriarchal conventions that operate as ideologically normative."

Part II: (Dis)continuing Education

This part begins with "Women Teachers Support Girls during the COVID-19 School Closures in Uganda" by Christine Apiot Okudi. This chapter points out that although the gender gap in the education of children in Uganda has narrowed, the seriously worrying conditions related to girls' education in this country are being compounded by the "COVID-19 pandemic [that] is holding back [this] development." We learn that "[i]ncreasing numbers of girls are being affected by child-with-child sexual relations and rape, both of which [may] lead to early pregnancy." Okudi points out that, as "World Vision International (2020) [has noted]," "the girls in . . . vulnerable communities like the refugee settlements are [being] seriously affected."

In Chapter 5, "Experiencing Care: Young Women's Response to COVID-19 Crises in Poland," Anna Bednarczyk, Zuzanna Kapciak, Kinga Madejczak, Alicja Sędzikowska, Natalia Witek, and Faustyna Zdziarska explore "in a multivoiced narrative . . . the grassroots initiative Dinners in the Time of Pandemic [that was] led by . . . a group of sociology students who met on an Introduction to Feminism course at the Jagiellonian University in Krakow [and who] decided to do something about the emerging cases of families and individuals who were facing food insecurity caused by the lockdown in Krakow." They use Berenice Fisher and Joan Tronto's (1990) "concept of care as a process" as their framework.

In Chapter 6, "COVID-19, Education, and Well-Being Experiences of Female Agriculture Students in Ethiopia," Hannah Pugh, Eleni Negash, Frehiwot Tesfaye, and Madalyn Nielsen examine how the COVID-19 pandemic is increasing the "preexisting gender inequalities among young women, aged between eighteen and twenty-one, who were studying at agricultural colleges in Ethiopia and who have now returned to their family homes." Their key findings from "twenty-two semi-structured interviews with female students" indicate that these young women "have suffered negative socioeconomic consequences, have lacked resources to continue their education at home, and have experienced increased mental health problems and an increased fear of being subjected to sex- and gender-based violence."

In Chapter 7, "Exploring the Psychosocial Experiences of Women Undergraduates in Delhi, India, during the COVID-19 Pandemic," Richa Rana, Poonam Yadav, and Shreya Sandhu point out that the experiences of girls and young women during the lockdown imposed on them by COVID-19 have been affected by "existing gender inequalities and social isolation" and consider "the nature of the psychosocial issues faced by women undergraduates and the coping strategies they . . . adopted." These authors conducted qualitative research that "reveals how the new normal has confined these young women to their homes and to their immediate family environment," and they discuss "how the already-gendered lives of these women undergraduates have now come under new stresses related to academic, economic, and sociocultural uncertainties."

Part III: Vulnerabilities

This part begins with Chapter 8, "Lockdown and Violence against Women and Children: Insights from Hospital-Based Crisis Intervention Centers in Mumbai, India" by Anupriya Singh, Sangeeta Rege, and Anagha Pradhan. In this chapter, the authors begin by explaining how the COVID-19 pandemic in India "overwhelmed the health system" and discuss how "the subsequent lockdown posed challenges for the adolescent girls and young women survivors of gender-based violence." This was compounded by the "suspension of court hearings and the disruption of healthcare and support services" for young girls, but we learn that in Mumbai "all Dilaasa centers (public hospital-based crisis intervention departments)" remained functional. The authors go on to recount "the experiences of girls and young women who sought support at Dilaasa centers in person or by telephone."

In Chapter 9, "The Impact of COVID-19 on Child Marriage in India," Gayatri Sharma and Ayesha Khaliq discuss the implications of the likely increase in child marriage resulting from COVID-19 for the already-vulnerable "Dalits (Scheduled Castes who rank lowest in the caste hierarchy), Adivasis (Scheduled Tribes or Indigenous people), and Muslim people who are marginalized both economically and in terms of religious discrimination." They point out that "the government's response to the massive surge in child marriage has to be targeted toward addressing the concerns of these vulnerable people" who have already "borne the brunt of the socioeconomic fallout of the COVID-19 response."

In Chapter 10, "The Impact of the COVID-19 Pandemic on Child Domestic Workers in Ethiopia," Annabel Erulkar, Welela Tarekegne, and Eyasu Hailu introduce us to the education and mentoring program Biruh Tesfa ("bright future") for All . . . that is aimed at supporting, among others, poverty-stricken children. They discuss what they learned from twenty-four telephone interviews with "project beneficiaries (including domestic workers) and mentors" after this program was suspended because of COVID-19. We learn that many girls "found themselves out of work with no income, no accommodation, and no support of any kind" and that those who remained employed "had to undertake all the household tasks that entailed exposure to the risk of COVID-19."

Finally, in Chapter 11, "The New Normal for Young Transgender Women in Thailand: Unspoken Gender-Based Violence in the Time of COVID-19," Rapeepun Jommaroeng, Sara Hair, Cheera Thongkrajai, Kath Kangbipoon, and Suda Bootchadee discuss what they learned during the twenty in-depth telephone interviews they conducted with young transgender women aged between eighteen and twenty-five. They point out that these women already "experience higher rates of gender-based violence and discrimination" and that "desperation and frustration during the COVID-19 outbreak could force them to engage in higher risk activities, like sex work, for survival." The "new normal" includes the reluctance of those requiring HIV testing and treatment, as well as hormone therapy, "to visit health facilities because of fears related to COVID-19."

So Much to Learn

We see this book as contributing to deepening an understanding of what scholars, activists, and practitioners were and are learning about girls and young women at particular moments in the evolution of the pandemic. Absent from this collection are the girl-led narratives that are so often at the center of girl-method and working with girls (Mitchell and Reid-Walsh 2008). What did it mean for the authors to do research on girlhood when it was not possible to draw on the vast repertoire of girl-led methodologies (participatory visual methods and group discussions) that youth-focused researchers typically use? Clearly the challenges of being unable to work directly with girls and young women has been a central issue, with researchers turning to document analysis and telephone interviews, and using social media, reflexive writing, and other approaches to what we describe elsewhere as "ethnography at a distance" (Mitchell et al. 2022). Discussing fieldwork in rural KwaZulu-Natal that was part of the project "Networks for Change and Well-Being: Girl-Led 'From the Ground Up' Policy Making to Address Sexual Violence in Canada and

South Africa,"[2] Relebohile Moletsane talks about the challenges posed to the ethics of doing research. She writes,

> With the arrival of COVID-19 in March 2020, and the lockdown restrictions that followed, the Networks for Change project had to suspend or postpone activities in the various research sites, including the piloting of the newly signed reporting and response protocol for addressing early and forced marriage in Loskop. Beyond complying with the COVID-19 regulations and restrictions, our view was that conditions in rural settings such as Loskop would not be conducive for research, neither would it have been ethical for us to expect our participants to continue engaging with us during lockdown, including remotely or digitally. With the onset of COVID-19, and unemployment, poverty and food insecurity at an all-time high, access to mobile phone data and the internet is almost impossible in rural communities. Thus, the much-touted alternative data generation methods are not available, particularly for participatory researchers. In essence, for us, using technology to conduct ethnography at a distance, particularly considering our participatory approach to research has not been possible. It would also be unethical for us to insist on continuing with our fieldwork in a context where issues of survival confront our participants and their families on a daily basis. We, therefore, decided to focus on the non-contact activities of the project . . . including ongoing analysis of the large data sets we have generated with the SIFs [Social Ills Fighters] since 2017. We continue to provide ongoing support to the SIFs and others in other Networks for Change sites via WhatsApp messaging. Recognizing that many people are dealing with multiple and compounding stressors during this time, we have made it very clear that the participants are in no way obliged to produce anything or respond to us in any way at this time. Through this intermittent communication, we have become aware of the challenges of accessing this technology by most of our participants, even though most, if not all of them have access to a cellphone. Unless we send them data remotely, for many, even responding to our WhatsApp messages is a challenge. (Mitchell et al. 2022: 304–5)

Crucially, the various chapters in *The Girl in the Pandemic* help to reshape what is being learned during this pandemic. Not unlike Moletsane's account above, these chapters remind us of what might be called the "why" or "under-what-circumstances" of research and some of the trade-offs when food insecurity and health-seeking behaviors must take precedence over fieldwork. They also highlight issues of risk and the possibility that mantras such as "do the least harm" in addressing ethical issues may have new meaning, where "doing most good" could become synonymous with collective care.

Finally, we come back to ideas of the passage of time and the challenge of writing in history, as it were. Perhaps it is crucial to keep in mind the broader question of what the significance is of a year or two (and more) in the life of a young person. What, for example, is the short-term impact of being out of school? What is the long-term impact of knowing that because of an unwanted pregnancy, returning to school is unlikely to ever be an option? The young women who participated in Pugh et al.'s study in Ethiopia (Chapter 6), and who at the time of the telephone interviews had been away from their colleges for several months, held some expectation that the colleges would soon be reopening and that the pandemic was just an interruption in their schooling. But we later learned that the colleges were closed for a much longer period of time,[3] and we know, anecdotally, that at least at one of the colleges many young women did not return because they were pregnant, something that they could not have known, of course, when they participated in the telephone interviews conducted in June 2020. Of course, this might simply be framed as a case of life happening, but we see this as a clear call to treat these chapters as offering the opportunity to retheorize how we think about time, in the short term, and history over the long term. As Nidhi Kapur (Chapter 1) so aptly reminds us, we have a great deal to learn from studying epidemics and pandemics in history. The chapters in this book offer a picture of how COVID-19 was playing out in seven countries early in the pandemic and, in so doing, provide a foundation for what was to come in relation to the idea of living with COVID-19.

Acknowledgments

The Girl in the Pandemic is part of the Transnational Girlhoods book series published by Berghahn Books. We are grateful to Marion Berghahn and Vivian Berghahn for recognizing the significance of publishing this collection. We very much appreciate Amanda Horn's enthusiasm and support throughout the process of publishing this and previous titles in the series. This collection emerged from a call for articles for *Girlhood Studies: An Interdisciplinary Journal* in 2020. The vast number of submissions led us to publish a Special Issue of *Girlhood Studies*, "The Lives of Girls and Young Women in the Time of Covid-19" (13:3) and now this edited book. In the Introduction to the Special Issue we noted the absence of a crystal ball to predict what a post-Covid-19 world would like and especially for girls and young women. As *The Girl in the Pandemic* goes to press uncertainty prevails.

  We thank all the contributors to *The Girl in the Pandemic*. We know that this book has been a long time in the making. There is something of an irony in the fact that a book about the impact of COVID-19 on the lives of girls and young women should at the same time be slowed down by COVID-19. We are also grateful to our reviewers for their thorough and insightful comments on the manuscript. We know that one of the huge challenges to academic publishing during this pandemic has been the endeavor of keeping everything running, with the review process a crucial component of this.

We thank Dr. Sahar Fazeli for all her assistance at the start of this project, without which we would not have been able to proceed, along with Nesa Bandarchian, Mary Lynn Loftus, and Ishika Obeegadoo, who assisted at various stages of it.

Finally we acknowledge Dr. Jennifer Thompson for inspiring the title, *The Girl in the Pandemic*.

We gratefully acknowledge the Social Sciences and Humanities Research Council of Canada, whose financial support for "Networks for Change and Well-Being: Girl-Led 'From the Ground Up' Policy Making to Address Sexual Violence in Canada and South Africa" helped support this project.

Notes

1. All unacknowledged quotations in this introduction come from the abstracts for the chapters that we had their authors provide.
2. This project, led by Claudia Mitchell (McGill University) and Relebohile Molesane (University of KwaZulu-Natal), was supported by the Social Sciences and Humanities Research Council of Canada (895-2013-3007) and the International Development Research Centre (107777-001).
3. Personal communication from Hannah Pugh, 19 August 2021.

References

Defoe, Daniel. 1978. *Journal of the Plague Year 1665*. London: Corner House.
Fisher, Berenice, and Joan Tronto. 1990. "Toward a Feminist Theory of Caring." In *Circles of Care: Work and Identity in Women's Lives*, ed. E. K. Abel and M. K. Nelson, 35–62. Albany, NY: State University of New York Press.
Mitchell, Claudia. 2014. "Fire+Hope Up: On Revisiting the Process of Revisiting a Literacy-for-Social Action Project." In *Learning and Literacy over Time: Longitudinal Perspectives*, ed. Julian Sefton-Greene and Jennifer Rowsell, 32–45. New York: Routledge.

Mitchell, Claudia, and Jacqueline Reid-Walsh. 2008. "Girl Method: Placing Girl-Centred Research Methodologies on the Map of Girlhood Studies." In *Roadblocks to Equality: Women Challenging Boundaries*, ed. Jeffery Klaehn, 214–33. Montreal: Black Rose Books.

Mitchell, Claudia, Relebohile Moletsane, and Darshan Daryanani. 2022. "The Ethics of Risk Research in the Time of COVID-19: Ethnography at a Distance in Privileging the Well-Being of Girls and Young Women in the Context of Gender-Based Violence in Rural South Africa." In *Covid-19 and the Sociology of Risk and Uncertainty: Studies of Social Phenomena and Social Theory across 6 Continents*, ed. Patrick Brown and Jens Zinn, 295–321. Cham: Palgrave Macmillan. https://doi.org/10.1007/978-3-030-95167-2_12.

Neale, Bren. 2010. "Foreword: Young Lives and Imagined Futures." In *Young Lives and Imagined Futures: Insights from Archived Data* (Timescapes Working Paper Series 6), ed. Mandy Winterton, Graham Crow, and Bethany Morgan-Brett, 4–6. Leeds: University of Leeds.

Venkatesan, Satharaj, and Ishani Anwesha Joshi. 2022. "'The Time is out of Joint': Temporality, COVID-19 and Graphic Medicine." *Medical Humanities*. https://doi.org/10.1136/medhum-2021-012357.

Walsh, Shannon. 2012. "'We Grew As We Grew': Visual Methods, Social Engagement and Collective Learning Over Time." *South African Journal of Education* 32(4), 406–15. https://doi.org/10.15700/saje.v32n4a655.

Walsh, Shannon, Claudia Mitchell, and Mandla Oliphant. 2022. *In My Life: Stories of Youth Activists in South Africa, 2002-2022*. Johannesburg: Jacana.

Part I
Reflections

Chapter 1

Five Lessons from Past Ebola Epidemics for Today's COVID-19 Pandemic

Nidhi Kapur

Introduction

Lessons learned from previous infectious disease outbreaks underscore the diversity of ways in which girls and young women can be disproportionately affected (Kapur 2020a). The experience of Ebola highlights the gendered dimensions that they will likely face as a result of the current COVID-19 pandemic. Drawing on qualitative data collected during the 2018–20 Ebola epidemic in the eastern Democratic Republic of Congo (DRC), in this chapter I examine critically five key lessons about the experiences of girls during large-scale infectious disease outbreaks.

First, understand the intersectionality and influence of age and gender.

Second, anticipate the exacerbation of preexisting gender disparities in the domestic space.

Third, navigate the economics of survival.

Fourth, acknowledge and address gender biases in scientific research and resourcing.

Fifth, pay attention to the persistent invisibility of girls.

Notes for this section can be found on page 29.

Both the immediate and secondary implications of these lessons underscore how key learning from the past can be used proactively to identify and redress the evolving gender-driven consequences of the novel coronavirus, COVID-19. Policymakers and practitioners from across the humanitarian–development nexus should use these lessons to inform the development of gender-responsive interventions at local, regional, and international levels, thus ensuring that girls remain at the center of pandemic prevention and response efforts.

The Methodological Framework

A by-product of the contagiousness of COVID-19, and the concurrent widespread mobility restrictions at the local and global level, has been a data-constrained environment for decision-makers. In the absence of conventional forms of face-to-face data collection to inform global efforts to develop responses to the pandemic, in this chapter I rely on a reflective analysis of evidence. I use primary data from consultations with Congolese girls and young women who survived the second largest Ebola epidemic in history, supplemented with publicly available statistics and information on the evolving trends of the COVID-19 pandemic. This contributes to an ever-growing body of literature that seeks to identify and draw lessons from the experiences of past pandemics, epidemics, and outbreaks around the world (Davies and Bennett 2016; Moore et al. 2020).

To better understand and address the gendered implications of Ebola, CARE International commissioned a groundbreaking gender analysis at the height of the 2018–20 crisis. Age- and gender-disaggregated focus group discussions were therefore held between October and November 2019 at the epicenter of the outbreak in the province of North Kivu, eastern DRC (Kapur 2020a). The research sample consisted of 1,008 individuals of varying ages, genders, and (dis)abilities, and included participatory consultations with 240 preadolescent girls, adolescent girls, and young women aged ten to nineteen. These were divided into two different age tranches (ten to fourteen years and fifteen to nineteen years) to allow for sufficient exploration of age-specific dynamics. To explore the impact of the Ebola crisis on the availability and accessibility of sexual, reproductive, and other health services, expectant and new mothers were also actively included, as were participants with different types of disabilities. Child-friendly, inclusive, and age-appropriate methodological tools and facilitation techniques were employed during the focus group discussions to document participants' first-person perspectives on prevention and response measures in the Ebola epidemic.

In developing the methodology, we considered the ethical implications throughout to ensure that the research teams worked respectfully and reciprocally with both children and adults. Participation was voluntary for all. Depending on the age of the participant, informed assent or consent was obtained prior to data collection. Safeguarding, anonymity, and data protection protocols were developed, and training was cascaded to all members of the research team. Enhanced safety and security measures were put in place with due consideration of the confluence of armed conflict and infectious disease outbreak in the area. Given the complex operating environment and the potential for mistrust and retaliation against perceived outsiders, it was critical that qualified enumerators were recruited in and around the research sites. They worked under the technical supervision of CARE International staff members of Congolese origin who were also either local to the area or long-time residents with a solid understanding of prevailing dynamics. As a foreigner, I limited direct interaction with research participants to interviews with key informants in the provincial capital of Goma so as not to derail the efforts of the research team further afield. Both the initial development of the research framework and later interpretation of data nonetheless benefited from my personal and professional experience of living and working in the eastern DRC and in the wider region for more than a decade.

The strength of qualitative research of this kind is that it enables the examination of the *how* and *why* questions that underpin the differential ways in which girls and young women experience a public health crisis. It draws on the expertise and insight of individuals and groups who have intimate knowledge of the crisis. However, because people experience the same situation differently, personal perspectives can vary widely between and among individuals. While this diversity of viewpoints limits the extent to which findings can be generalized, they do nonetheless offer valuable insights that, with appropriate contextualization and in complementarity with emerging evidence, can be applied to the COVID-19 pandemic.

The Experience of Ebola: Five Lessons about Girls

Endemic to the DRC, the deadly Zaire Ebola strain responsible for the 2018–20 outbreak in the eastern part of the country is known to have the highest fatality rates of all Ebola virus disease (EVD) strains (World

Health Organization 2021). The disease spread from its epicenter in a highly enabling environment characterized by armed conflict, population mobility, and community resistance. Despite aggressive efforts to stamp it out, the virus claimed 2,287 lives over twenty-two months (World Health Organization 2020b). However, these top-line casualty numbers obscure the underlying nature of the Ebola crisis. In fact, according to the World Health Organization (2020a), most of those who died were women (57 percent) and children (29 percent). Adult men constituted just 9 percent of Ebola-related deaths (ibid.).[1]

While the feminization of fatalities was a clear trend with Ebola, initial numbers in relation to COVID-19 deaths show that men appear to be more likely to succumb to the disease (The Sex, Gender and COVID-19 Project 2020). This contrast, however, does not preclude the many and varied ways in which girls and young women continue to bear the brunt, not necessarily of the coronavirus itself, but of its implications. In fact, the Ebola outbreak in the DRC had a staggeringly high case fatality rate of 66 percent (World Health Organization 2020b), while that of COVID-19 at the time of writing arguably ranges between 3 and 4 percent (Our World in Data 2020).[2] This indicates that fatalities alone do not fully demonstrate the differential ways in which individuals are exposed to, or experience, the immediate risks and longer-term consequences of an infectious disease outbreak, underscoring the necessity of looking beyond the statistics to capture the full array of secondary harms stemming from this latest coronavirus. Socially prescribed cultural norms, attitudes, and practices in relation to gender and age influence the needs, capacities, and coping strategies of individuals, ultimately dictating how they may be affected. Although these norms can and do vary across communities and countries, as well as over time, the five key lessons learned from Ebola point to the need to better understand the socio-behavioral underpinnings of disease etiology to identify the diversity of ways in which girls may be affected (Kapur 2020a).

Lesson #1: Understand the Intersectionality and Influence of Age and Gender

The experience of Ebola exemplified the extent to which the short- and long-term impacts of an infectious disease outbreak are not felt equally across all segments of the population. The ways in which girls and young women experienced the crisis were directly tied to their standing in society and their typically subordinate position within the patriarchy. Age was also an important determinant. Indeed, it was the very intersection between their age and gender that rendered preadolescent girls, adolescent girls, and young women particularly vulnerable. Accorded less social agency and decision-making power, they were also more likely to be economically reliant on male counterparts. This not only increased their vulnerability to risk, it also directly affected their help-seeking behaviors (Kapur 2020a), a trend that is becoming increasingly clear during the current pandemic as well (Pereira et al. 2020).

The risks faced by girls and young women during an infectious disease outbreak correlate, overlap, and intersect with each other. While the exact nature and prevalence of these risks will change from one context to another and will continue to evolve over the life cycle of an epidemic, the experience of Ebola is indicative of how gender and age can dictate both the immediate experience of the crisis and secondary harms well into the future (International Rescue Committee 2020), as explored in greater detail below.

Unfortunately, in both policy and practice there is a detrimental tendency toward homogeneity when it comes to questions of age and gender. At times, social discourse can misleadingly conflate girls (especially adolescent girls) and women, treating them as one homogeneous group with uniform risks, needs, and rights, as Caroline Harper and colleagues (2012) remind us. As minors, both younger and older girls face specific risks and therefore have unique needs relative to adult women. Precisely because of their status as children, girls are entitled to (but do not always benefit from) specific legislative and normative protections and provisions.

Lesson #2: Anticipate the Exacerbation of Preexisting Gender Disparities in the Domestic Space

Research shows that troubled times can exacerbate and further entrench preexisting gender inequalities, while traditional gender norms can become increasingly regressive or restrictive (Kapur 2020b). Discriminatory norms, attitudes, and expectations that are rooted in gendered beliefs and practices can amplify during crises, disproportionately affecting girls and women. One of the spaces in which this is most apparent is within the home. Socioculturally prescribed disparities in the division of domestic responsibilities and resources can be significant.

In the DRC, where girls and women already routinely take on the bulk of daily chores, their physical, mental, and logistical burden only increased at the onset of the Ebola crisis. In the context of COVID-19, this is even more pronounced. Adolescent girls especially are often expected to help their mothers or other female caregivers with household tasks, including the additional domestic demands stemming from widespread travel restrictions and school closures during the pandemic (International Rescue Committee 2020). Older girls may be required to care for younger siblings, affecting their own ability to continue their education via available distance-learning portals. Relative to boys, girls are at greater risk of dropping out of school, either temporarily or permanently (Interagency Network for Education in Emergencies and the Alliance for Child Protection in Humanitarian Action 2020).

While early fatality statistics imply, generally, that girls may be spared the virulence of COVID-19, sociocultural determinants and drivers of gender norms remain a critical factor. As was also seen during the Ebola crisis, adolescent girls and women already undertake most of the unpaid care work in the home and are therefore more likely to assume the role of caregiver to any infected family members. This makes it impossible for them to adhere to the physical distancing guidelines that protect against infection, leaving them, at least potentially, more predisposed to viral infection. This aspect cannot be underestimated in the context of COVID-19, where many authorities, in an attempt to prevent overwhelming available health services, are advising infected people to remain at home unless they require emergency care. The social isolation resulting from quarantine measures can also be significant for those with primary care responsibilities, limiting the practical and psychosocial support they are likely to receive from peers or members of their extended family (Interagency Network for Education in Emergencies and the Alliance for Child Protection in Humanitarian Action 2020).

Moreover, discriminatory gender norms often privilege the health, nutrition, and welfare of men and boys (World Food Programme 2020). In the face of increasing economic hardships and food shortages, women and girls are likely to be the last to eat. Past crises have shown that women and older girls are often the first to adopt coping strategies such as reducing the quantity or quality of food intake relative to men and younger children in the family setting (ibid.).

As with Ebola, clean water is a crucial resource in the fight against COVID-19 infection. In many contexts, gender determines the allocation of domestic tasks such as the fetching of water. During past Ebola crises, the increased need for water in the household pushed girls and women to leave their homes at odd hours of the late evening or early morning, exposing them to heightened risk of sexual violence or kidnapping as a result (UN Trust Fund to End Violence against Women 2020). One adolescent girl interviewed during the Ebola crisis in the DRC explained, "Because we need more water, we're obliged to leave our homes early in the morning or even after dark in search of water. That's when we can be raped" (Kapur 2020a: 17). The militarization of efforts to enforce infection prevention and control measures worldwide is a hallmark of the COVID-19 pandemic that cannot be overlooked in terms of its possible repercussions on the safety of girls and women as they interface between public and private spaces to carry out their domestic obligations (UN Trust Fund to End Violence against Women 2020).

Lesson #3: Navigate the Economics of Survival

The correlation between economic uncertainty and the neglect, violence, abuse, and exploitation of women and girls is well established (International Rescue Committee 2020). Past Ebola crises have provided ample evidence of the exploitative practices employed by those in positions of power, including front-line responders (Kapur 2020a). Girls and young women were reportedly extorted for financial kickbacks by those who were responsible for securing their employment. There were also indications that men in decision-making roles forced women and girls to perform sexual favors as a prerequisite to being employed or prior to receiving their salary. According to one young woman, "You must always have sexual relations with agents working on the Ebola-response, even if you have a diploma. It's very remarkable amongst women" (Kapur 2020a: 22). Healthcare providers and local authorities disclosed details of confirmed cases of pregnancies resulting from the sexual exploitation perpetrated during the Ebola crisis. One healthcare worker reported, "I've had a patient come to me to ask for an assisted abortion. She was pregnant as a result of being forced to have sex with an Ebola responder in order to get her job" (ibid.). This is indicative of more cases that were likely not reported or formally documented, as Robert Flummerfelt and Nellie Peyton (2020) point out. Collectively, this led some girls and women to abandon their posts or to avoid seeking such roles altogether, thus denying them the possibility of supplementing their income during a time of economic hardship.

The current COVID-19 crisis carries similar risks. An unexpected death in the family can pressurize children, particularly adolescents, to find ways to contribute (Interagency Network for Education in Emergencies and the Alliance for Child Protection in Humanitarian Action 2020). Girls in families already made fragile by the death of a critical breadwinner may be obliged to seek recourse in harmful coping mechanisms and survival strategies to provide for their families in impossible circumstances. Such economic insecurity can, for example, put girls at risk of being groomed for the purposes of commercial sexual exploitation, trafficking, or sale (International Rescue Committee 2020). Adolescent girls are especially at risk of resorting to transactional sex as a means of survival. During the Ebola crisis in the DRC, the sexual exploitation of girls could "be observed in local bars, and it . . . increased since the beginning of Ebola activities." Among Francophone Congolese, these girls were viewed as something of a snack to be ordered alongside drinks and were commonly called "poireaux accompagnateur de la boisson" ("leeks accompanying the drink") according to one research respondent (Kapur 2020a: 22).

Financial difficulties can also expose girls to early or forced marriage; there is growing evidence that existing drivers of child marriage are further exacerbated during times of crisis (Girls Not Brides 2020). Prior to the pandemic, one in five girls was already married before the age of eighteen (Girls Not Brides 2018). Without appropriate mitigation measures, it is reasonable to expect a surge in child marriages during both the acute and recovery phases of the pandemic (Save the Children 2020). While more research is needed, it is already clear that parents in duress will sometimes broker marital arrangements for their daughters as a perceived protective measure. In societies where a bride price is commanded, families may also view the marriage of their children as a means of generating income (International Rescue Committee 2020).

Lesson #4: Acknowledge and Address Gender Biases in Scientific Research and Resourcing

As was the case with Ebola, the future course of the current COVID-19 outbreak hinges on an effective medical response. In fact, vaccinations were developed and deployed to successfully control an Ebola epidemic for the first time during the 2019–20 outbreak in the DRC. However, the conditions necessary to receive the vaccination were unfavorable to women and children. Lactating and pregnant women were classed as ineligible, as were children under five years of age. Because of a lack of urgency in research, these population subsets were left without vaccinal protection at the peak of the crisis (Kapur 2020a).

Unequal access to vaccines is inextricably tied to gender biases evident in the ways in which empirically driven scientific research is both conceptualized and financed. Another key example of this pertains to viral transmission trends, particularly those that disproportionately affect women and young children. With Ebola, the continued presence of viral load in seminal and maternal fluids in male and female survivors was identified. Yet little was done to invest in further research to better understand the persistence of the virus after an Ebola patient had been declared recovered, despite the fact that women and babies were the most likely to be affected by secondary infections, as Sam Mednick (2019) notes.

Women and girls constitute approximately half the global population and should therefore command a proportionate investment in scientific research and resourcing. Moreover, the Director-General of the World Health Organization, Dr. Tedros Adhanom Ghebreyesus, claims that "[i]n everything we do, we are driven by science" (World Health Organization 2019). Yet the scientific underpinnings of COVID-related policy decisions risk being subject to the same partiality. It is vital to avoid a similar de-prioritization of issues directly affecting the health of women and children.

Lesson #5: Pay Attention to the Persistent Invisibility of Girls

Appropriately tailored responses that target the divergent needs of different segments of the population are possible only when there is empirical evidence to allow for this. Consistent and sufficiently detailed data disaggregation is therefore an essential first step. Yet key institutional actors, governmental agencies, and media outlets repeatedly release reports with statistics that eclipse the full picture. During the Ebola outbreak, for instance, the World Health Organization issued weekly bulletins that were widely read but lacked age disaggregation beyond adult and child, as well as sex disaggregation of children or health workers who had died of Ebola.[3] The presentation of statistics in this way can contribute to dangerous misperceptions about the homogeneity of children and increase the invisibility of girls and women.

School Closures, Home Confinement, and other Containment Measures: The Secondary Consequences for Girls

Beyond the five key lessons from past Ebola epidemics, emergent evidence from the COVID-19 pandemic demonstrates the extent to which infectious disease outbreaks transcend questions of public health alone. Attempts to contain and control virus transmission can trigger a host of secondary consequences for girls, many of which will have far-reaching implications long after the outbreak is brought under control. School closures and home confinements, in particular, can result in social isolation, removing the protective factor of schools, teachers, and peers while simultaneously increasing the likelihood of sexual and gender-based violence. Out-of-school girls may have more unstructured or unsupervised time, including that spent with men and boys. This can result in a higher probability of risky sexual behavior, as well as exposure to sexual exploitation and abuse, the impact of which can be significantly compounded by limited availability of and access to contraception and other sexual and reproductive health services during large-scale infectious disease outbreaks (World Vision 2020).

Ebola showed that the scale of the problem can be immense. Spikes in teenage pregnancies of up to 65 percent were recorded in some areas with prolonged school closures because of the outbreak of Ebola in West Africa (United Nations Population Fund 2018). Of the fourteen thousand girls who became pregnant in Sierra Leone during the 2014–15 Ebola epidemic, eleven thousand were previously attending school (ibid.). In the context of COVID-19, the issue is likely to be even more amplified. At its peak, early childhood, school, and university closures affected 90 percent of the world's student population, an estimated 1.5 billion children and young people (UNESCO 2020). Policies vary, but in many places pregnant girls or young mothers have been expelled from school, barred from sitting examinations, or face long wait times for reentry and, in addition to childcare burdens, will often face social stigmatization (World Vision 2020).

To curb the spread of COVID-19, over ninety countries were put into some form of lockdown, with billions of people facing some variation of shelter-in-place orders (Interagency Network for Education in Emergencies and the Alliance for Child Protection in Humanitarian Action 2020). While these restrictions on mobility were put into place as a protective measure against viral infection and transmission, they have also triggered an alarming spike in violence against girls and women. Homes should be safe for them, particularly during a pandemic of this nature. Yet homes, particularly those under confinement, can also be the sites of violence and abuse, often perpetrated by parents and other caregivers. It is here that children bear witness to intimate partner violence or experience physical, psychological, or sexual abuse themselves. School closures and other control measures can also mean that children are locked at home with their abusers. These risks are further exacerbated by the multiplicity of stress factors affecting parents during a pandemic of this nature, including economic uncertainty, resource scarcity, and health fears (ibid.).

The intersecting risks faced by girls and women have given rise to a "shadow pandemic" (UN Women 2020) of sexual and gender-based violence, yet widespread underreporting of abuses is commonplace because of stigma, family rejection, or lack of access to, or confidence in, the judicial process, among other factors. Community-based reporting and referral mechanisms that were available pre-pandemic may no longer be functional or accessible. Lockdowns and other movement restrictions may prevent girls from seeking support outside of the nuclear family, abruptly cutting access to teachers, neighbors, friends, and relatives, among others. This can severely restrict the safety net upon which they might normally rely. While helplines might be available in some contexts, it may be more difficult for girls under home-based quarantine to use them confidentially without fear of reprisal. Limited peer interaction can translate into delayed access to information, especially for adolescent girls who probably rely on these social networks even more (Pereira et al. 2020).

Acting in the knowledge of their impunity, many perpetrators are able to exploit the prevailing context of social isolation and limited mobility to exercise increased control over their victims, including restricting access to available services or basic necessities (Pereira et al. 2020). Research shows that stigmatization alone can prove deadly (Thompson 2015). Sociocultural norms that promote the notion that girls embody the purity of their family can add to the psychosocial trauma experienced by survivors of abuse, who are at higher risk of suicide and self-harm (Save the Children 2020).

Survivors can face a multitude of debilitating consequences, including untreated sexually transmitted infections, obstetric fistula, unwanted pregnancy, and unsafe abortion. For very young girls, the effects of physical injuries consequent upon sexual intercourse can be even worse because their bodies are not yet biologically adapted to this (Thompson 2015). Sexual and gender-based violence can have long-term implications for the educational, economic, and health outcomes of survivors as well as any future children they may bear (Plan International 2016).

Girls who find themselves pregnant as a result of sexual violence, including the rape that is endemic to forced early marriage, face potentially life-threatening complications. These can include the elevated risk of eclampsia, hemorrhage, and premature, prolonged, or obstructed labor. In fact, complications from pregnancy and childbirth are the leading cause of death among girls aged fifteen to nineteen worldwide, while girls fifteen and under have a maternal mortality rate five times higher than young women in their twenties (Kapur 2020b). In previous Ebola crises, maternal mortality rates were even higher than usual (International Rescue Committee 2019). Similar spikes can be expected in the context of COVID-19 as limited human and financial resources are diverted away from sexual and reproductive health services, as the International Rescue Committee (2020) predicts.

In addition to the provision of essential services, a localized outbreak can lead to changes in health-seeking behaviors, as evidenced by experiences with Ebola (Kapur 2020a). This can have a particularly devastating impact on girls and young women of childbearing age. Fears of inadvertently contracting the virus in addition to the possibility of forced quarantine were among the reasons most cited by research respondents to explain their avoidance of medical centers and health services during the Ebola crisis in the DRC. Girls and young women commonly indicated that family separation, social isolation, and stigmatization as a result of infection prevention and control measures pushed them to avoid seeking medical attention for other health needs during the outbreak. Those who were either pregnant or lactating reported that they preferred to forego care altogether (ibid.).

It is clear that the sexual and reproductive health of girls and women will be particularly affected as a result of such realities. Menstrual hygiene is likely to be compromised because of self-isolation, movement restrictions, and supply shortages (International Rescue Committee 2020). Preexisting differences in the source, stability, or size of income, compounded by the adverse economic conditions provoked by the pandemic, may mean that women and girls have less purchasing power to acquire items essential to their health and sanitation, such as menstrual hygiene products and soap (World Food Programme 2020). Avoidance because of the fear of infection can limit access to family-planning services, affecting utilization rates, while interruptions to contraception protocols that require routine follow up, such as intrauterine devices, can lead to unwanted pregnancies (Kapur 2020a). For girls, the movement restrictions themselves further exacerbate the preexisting dependency on adult or male peers or family members, some of whom may be reluctant to allow their daughters and wives to access services because of the fear of infection (Pereira et al. 2020).

Survivor-centered services adapted to minors, such as the provision of post-exposure prophylaxis kits designed for girls, may be even harder to source. The combination of fear and taboo, compounded with lockdown-related restrictions, can force pregnant girls to redirect themselves toward risky behaviors such as traditional medicines or underground abortions (UN Trust Fund to End Violence against Women 2020). Access to appropriate prenatal, postnatal, and safe post-abortion care are all hindered by both the physical barriers of lockdown restrictions and attitudinal shifts leading to changes in health-seeking behaviors.

Concluding Thoughts and Considerations for the Future

Lessons from the Ebola epidemic validate the need to apply a gender perspective to the analysis of public health crises. Gender analysis provides information about the relative needs, capacities, and coping strategies of girls, women, boys, and men. It reveals otherwise hidden biases among policymakers and practitioners across the humanitarian–development nexus, exposing the extent to which prevention and response efforts can be influenced by the norms of the overarching patriarchy. In this instance, gender analysis makes visible the distinct and multifaceted ways in which girls and young women are exposed to and affected by infectious disease outbreaks, creating an opportunity to close historical gender gaps in policy and practice.

Lessons from Ebola make clear that the gendered dimensions of the COVID-19 pandemic extend far beyond vulnerability to the virus itself, but must, instead, focus on the far-reaching secondary harms experienced by girls and young women. What is needed is a comprehensive consideration of the multiplicity of ways in which girls occupy spaces simultaneously related to both their age and gender. The duality of girls' experience and exposure to the short- and long-term implications of public health crises demands the judicious application of both child- and gender-sensitive approaches by actors of all stripes, including multisectoral service providers and other practitioners at local level, national policymakers, and UN agencies, international NGOs, and donors.

It is imperative, therefore, that actors engaged in prevention and response efforts identify and acknowledge the influence of socially prescribed roles and relations, including how they may have evolved over the course of a crisis. In the absence of systematized data disaggregation in data collection and reporting, it is difficult to undertake a more in-depth epidemiological and etiological analysis of infectious disease outbreaks. Actors on the ground must therefore ensure that data is "available, analyzed and actionable" (UNICEF 2020: 2).

Designing and delivering gender-responsive action in the context of COVID-19 and its aftermath is of paramount importance. It is crucial that local and international actors heed the lessons that have emerged from past practice to inform the way forward (Munnoli et al. 2020). To that end, they must anticipate and prepare for an uptick in gender-based violence in all its forms while also finding ways to mitigate the diversion of resources away from core protective services in health, education, and livelihoods (UNICEF 2020). Both child protection and the awareness of gendered norms and practices must be fully embedded in response plans, with corresponding resource allocations. While interventions must uphold the principle of *do no harm* by minimizing the risk of unintended negative consequences, they must also maximize their potential for positive impact by placing women and girls at the forefront of decision-making. Next steps must concentrate on the need to build back better in ways that substantively strengthen the ability of communities and countries to strive for greater gender equality.

Acknowledgments

This chapter draws on primary data collected during the 2019–20 epidemic of Ebola virus disease in the eastern Democratic Republic of Congo. Initial field research was conducted under the purview of CARE International. While study participants are not named to preserve confidentiality, the importance of their individual and collective insights is gratefully acknowledged. Although the COVID-19 pandemic had yet to become a reality at the time of this fieldwork, the research team and its participants were fully cognizant of the significance of gaining a better understanding of the potentially gendered implications of both present and future infectious disease outbreaks.

NIDHI KAPUR (ORCID: 0000-0003-0283-8408) is a protection, gender, and inclusion specialist with twelve years of field-based experience. Motivated by a strong interest in the complexities of programming in conflict and post-conflict zones, she has been deployed to various countries as part of emergency response teams. She has worked on many issues with and on behalf of girls and young women, including the gendered dimensions of infectious disease outbreaks. Nidhi studied international relations at the University of Toronto and at the London School of Economics. Having lived and worked around the globe, she is now based in Rwanda.

Notes

1. The term *adult men* does not include those otherwise categorized as healthcare workers, who constituted 5 percent of Ebola fatalities and for whom no sex disaggregation is publicly available.
2. The case fatality rate (CFR) is the ratio between confirmed deaths and confirmed cases. During an outbreak of a pandemic such as COVID-19, the CFR is a poor measure of the mortality risk of the disease because of the likelihood of unconfirmed cases.
3. See, for example, how data is presented in the World Health Organization's External Situation Reports on Ebola virus disease in the Democratic Republic of Congo (World Health Organization 2020b).

References

Alliance for Child Protection in Humanitarian Action. 2020. "COVID-19: Protecting Children from Violence, Abuse and Neglect in the Home." 4 May. Retrieved 13 September 2022 from https://www.alliancecpha.org/en/child-protection-online-library/covid-19-protecting-children-violence-abuse-and-neglect-home.

Davies, Sara, and Belinda Bennett. 2016. "A Gendered Human Rights Analysis of Ebola and Zika: Locating Gender in Global Health Emergencies." *International Affairs* 92(5): 1041–60. https://doi.org/10.1111/1468-2346.12704.

Flummerfelt, Robert, and Nellie Peyton. 2020. "More than 50 Women Accuse Aid Workers of Sex Abuse in Congo Ebola Crisis." *New Humanitarian*, 29 September. Retrieved 13 September 2022 from https://www.thenewhumanitarian.org/2020/09/29/exclusive-more-50-women-accuse-aid-workers-sex-abuse-congo-ebola-crisis.

Girls Not Brides. 2018. Child Marriage in Humanitarian Settings. *The Global Partnership to End Child Marriage*, August. Retrieved 7 November 2022 from https://www.girlsnotbrides.org/learning-resources/resource-centre/child-marriage-in-humanitarian-contexts/.

———. 2020. "COVID-19 and Child, Early and Forced Marriage: An Agenda for Action." *The Global Partnership to End Child Marriage*, April. Retrieved 7 November 2022 from https://advocacyaccelerator.org/resource/covid-19-and-child-early-and-forced-marriage-an-agenda-for-action/.

Harper, Caroline, Nicola Jonas, and Carol Watson. 2012. "Gender Justice for Adolescent Girls: Tackling Social Institutions. Towards a Conceptual Framework." Retrieved 13 September 2022 from http://cdn-odi-production.s3.amazonaws.com/media/documents/8746.pdf.

Interagency Network for Education in Emergencies and the Alliance for Child Protection in Humanitarian Action. 2020. "Weighing Up the Risks: School Closure and Reopening under COVID—When, Why, and What Impact." 16 July. Retrieved 13 September 2020 from https://inee.org/resources/weighing-risks-school-closure-and-reopening-under-covid-19.

International Rescue Committee. 2019. "'Everything on Her Shoulders': Rapid Assessment on Gender and Violence against Women and Girls in the Ebola Outbreak in Beni, DRC." Retrieved 22 September 2022 from https://www.rescue.org/sites/default/files/document/3593/genderandgbvfindingsduringevdresponseindrc-final8march2019.pdf.

———. 2020. "COVID-19—GBV Risks to Adolescent Girls and Interventions to Protect and Empower Them." Retrieved 13 September 2022 from http://d31hzlhk6di2h5.cloudfront.net/20200429/06/37/59/d1/a38f744a985e61a7f2a0d01e/COVID_19_GBV_AG_risks_and_Interventions.pdf.

Kapur, Nidhi. 2020a. "Gender Analysis: Prevention and Response to Ebola Virus Disease in the Democratic Republic of Congo." *CARE International*. Retrieved 13 September 2022 from https://www.care-international.org/files/files/Ebola_Gender_Analysis_English_v2.pdf.

———. 2020b. "Gender, Age and Conflict: Addressing the Different Needs of Children." *Save the Children*. Retrieved 13 September 2022 from https://www.savethechildren.ca/wp-content/uploads/2020/04/SC-Gender-Age-and-Conflict-report-final.pdf.

Mednick, Sam. 2019. "Cured but Still Contagious: How Mixed Messages on Sexual Transmission and Breastfeeding May Help Ebola Spread." *New Humanitarian*, 28 November. Retrieved 13 September 2022 from https://www

.thenewhumanitarian.org/news/2019/11/28/Ebola-sexual-transmission-breastfeeding-women-children.

Moore, Kristine A., Marc Lipsitch, John M. Barry, and Michael T. Osterholm. 2020. "The Future of the COVID-19 Pandemic: Lessons Learned from Pandemic Influenza." *CIDRAP*, 30 April. Retrieved 13 September 2022 from https://www.cidrap.umn.edu/sites/default/files/public/downloads/cidrap-covid19-viewpoint-part1_0.pdf.

Munnoli, Prakash M., S. Nabapure, and G. Yeshavanth. 2020. "Post-COVID-19 Precautions Based on Lessons Learned from Past Pandemics: A Review." *Journal of Public Health*, 4 August. https://doi.org/10.1007/s10389-020-01371-3.

Our World in Data. 2020. "Mortality Risk of COVID-19." Statistics and Research. Retrieved 13 September 2022 from https://ourworldindata.org/mortality-risk-covid.

Pereira, Audrey, Amber Peterman, Anastasia N. Neijhoft, Robert Buluma, Rocio A. Daban, Aminul Islam, Esmie T.V. Kainja, Inah F. Kaloga, They Kheam, Afrooz K. Johnson, M. Catherine Maternowska, Alina Potts, Chivith Rottanak, Chea Samnang, Mary Shawa, Miho Yoshikawa, and Tia Palermo. 2020. "Disclosure, Reporting and Help Seeking among Child Survivors of Violence: A Cross-Country Analysis." *BMC Public Health* 20: 1051. https://doi.org/10.1186/s12889-020-09069-7.

Plan International. 2016. "Girls' Education Policy Briefing." Retrieved 13 September 2022 from https://plan-uk.org/file/girlseducationpolicybriefingpdf/download?token=cEqEK_HX.

Save the Children. 2020. *The Global Girlhood Report 2020: How COVID-19 is Putting Progress in Peril*. Retrieved 13 September 2022 from https://resourcecentre.savethechildren.net/document/global-girlhood-report-2020-how-covid-19-putting-progress-peril/.

The Sex, Gender and COVID-19 Project. 2020. "Men, Sex, Gender and COVID-19: Are Men More at Risk of Infection?" *Global Health 50/50*. Retrieved 13 September 2022 from https://globalhealth5050.org/covid19/men-sex-gender-and-covid-19/.

Thompson, Hannah. 2015. "A Matter of Life and Death: Child Protection Programming's Essential Role in Ensuring Child Wellbeing and Survival during and after Emergencies." Retrieved 13 September 2022 from https://resourcecentre.savethechildren.net/library/matter-life-and-death-child-protection-programmings-essential-role-ensuring-child-wellbeing.

UNESCO. 2020. Global Education Coalition COVID-19 #Learning Never Stops Education Response, 23 October. Retrieved 7 November 2022 from https://en.unesco.org/covid19/educationresponse/globalcoalition.

UNICEF. 2020. "Five Actions for Gender Equality in the Coronavirus Disease (COVID-19 response)." Retrieved 13 September 2022 from https://www.unicef.org/media/66306/file/Fivepercent20Actionspercent20forpercent

20Genderpercent20Equality percent20in percent20the percent20COVID-19 percent20Response: percent20UNICEF percent20Technical percent20Note.pdf.
- United Nations Population Fund. 2018. "Recovering from the Ebola Virus Disease: Rapid Assessment of Pregnant Adolescent Girls in Sierra Leone." Retrieved 13 September 2022 from https://reliefweb.int/report/sierra-leone/recovering-ebola-virus-disease-rapid-assessment-pregnant-adolescent-girls-sierra.
- UN Trust Fund to End Violence Against Women. 2020. "Impact of COVID-19 on Violence against Women and Girls: Through the Lens of Civil Society and Women's Rights Organizations." Retrieved 13 September 2022 from https://untf.unwomen.org/en/digital-library/publications/2020/06/impact-of-covid-19-on-violence-against-women-and-girls.
- UN Women. 2020. "Violence against Women and Girls: The Shadow Pandemic." Statement by Phumzile Mlambo-Ngcuka, Executive Director of UN Women, 6 April. Retrieved 13 September 2022 from https://www.unwomen.org/en/news/stories/2020/4/statement-ed-phumzile-violence-against-women-during-pandemic.
- World Food Programme. 2020. "Gender & COVID-19." 14 April. Retrieved 13 September 2022 from https://www.wfp.org/publications/gender-and-covid-19.
- World Health Organization. 2019. "Second Ebola Vaccine to Complement 'Ring Vaccination' Given Green Light." 23 September. Retrieved 13 September 2022 from https://www.who.int/news/item/23-09-2019-second-ebola-vaccine-to-complement-ring-vaccination-given-green-light-in-drc.
- ———. 2020a. "Ebola Virus Disease, Democratic Republic of Congo." External Situation Report 98. Retrieved 13 September 2022 from https://www.who.int/publications/i/item/10665-332654.
- ———. 2020b. "10th Ebola Outbreak in the Democratic Republic of the Congo Declared Over; Vigilance against Flare-Ups and Support for Survivors Must Continue." News Release, 25 June. Retrieved 13 September 2022 from https://www.who.int/news-room/detail/25-06-2020-10th-ebola-outbreak-in-the-democratic-republic-of-the-congo-declared-over-vigilance-against-flare-ups-and-support-for-survivors-must-continue.
- ———. 2021. "Ebola Virus Disease: Key Facts." 23 February. Retrieved 13 September 2022 from https://www.who.int/news-room/fact-sheets/detail/ebola-virus-disease.
- World Vision. 2020. "COVID-19 Aftershocks: Access Denied—Teenage Pregnancy Threatens to Block a Million Girls across Sub-Saharan Africa from Returning to School." 21 August. Retrieved 13 September 2022 from https://reliefweb.int/report/world/covid-19-aftershocks-access-denied-teenage-pregnancy-threatens-block-million-girls.

CHAPTER 2

How to Build "Meaningful Bonds" with Poor Young Women?
State Interventions during the Lockdown in Argentina

Ana Cecilia Gaitán

Introduction

As in other countries, the COVID-19 pandemic has reinforced social inequalities in Argentina and made life in poor neighborhoods even more precarious. This exacerbation of precarity has different impacts for girls and women compared to boys and men. Since the lockdown was put in place in late March 2020, gender-based crimes remain alarmingly frequent and calls to the official hotline for assistance related to experiencing violence have ratcheted up. The data gathered from graphic and digital media from all over the country shows that during June 2020, twenty-one femicides occurred, making a total of 162 in this year at the time of writing. In 69 percent of the cases, the femicide victim was a partner or ex-partner of the perpetrator, and 70 percent of the femicides took place in the victim's home.

Notes for this section can be found on page 47.

In this chapter, I analyze the ways in which the Argentine state assists victims of violence and manages the prevention of violence against poor girls and young women, in a context in which social isolation has increased their vulnerability in specific ways and restricted the state's interventions in the areas in which these women live.

As other research in the Buenos Aires suburbs shows (Gaitán 2017; Llobet et al. 2013), prior to COVID-19, these social programs, which were implemented in child and youth centers, were places where girls and young women could access resources and find support if they were experiencing various forms of gender-based violence. Because of the lockdown, many of these places, although located in their communities, had to close their doors since neither they nor their workers were considered essential in the context of the pandemic.

Despite the closure of these state-operated centers, the lockdown did not erase the state's presence, but rather converted it (Arcidiácono and Perelmiter 2020). It suspended the regular meeting points between clients and public policies, thus demanding great versatility from officials, state workers, and community and social leaders to keep support channels open and active and to try out new responses (Heredia and Perelmiter 2020). I focus in this chapter on state actions carried out to assist poor girls and young women in the suburbs of Buenos Aires and to prevent violence aimed at them, and I review the many challenges that the state encountered during the lockdown. I address two questions: "How does the state provide care and support with limited territorial interventions?" and "How does the state maintain this bond when it must dispense with the facilities and types of interaction that are built on daily life and proximity?" To do this, I use contributions from political anthropology and feminist studies, particularly those that have problematized the state from below. These disciplines understand the state not simply as a form of centralized control over a given territory, in which power is exercised as a coherent whole, but, rather, as a contradictory articulation between and among institutions, practices, and people (Fraser 1989; Haney 1996). Both the practices, relationships, and demands of the clients on the one hand, and the regulations that are deployed to control their lives on the other, build and rebuild the state (Das and Poole 2008).

In the first section, I describe the main measures that were adopted by the national government to address gender-based violence, slow down contagion, and mitigate the pandemic's health and socioeconomic effects. Since social policies are implemented in a decentralized manner in Argentina, local governments play a key role in shaping what a given policy looks like in their territory (Rodríguez Gustá 2014). Because of this, in the second section I explore how those lines of action took shape in a commercial middle-class district that I have called Las Luciérnagas to safeguard the identity of the people who collaborated with me on this research project. Finally, I offer some preliminary reflections on the (in)ability of the state to address gender-based violence and guarantee girls' and young women's rights during the lockdown in the suburbs of Buenos Aires.

I derived the data from a qualitative research design, which was affected by the restrictions on circulation imposed from late March 2020. When the COVID-19 pandemic arrived in Argentina, I was working on qualitative research from an ethnographic perspective on the implementation of social policies for young people. The research was based in the Las Luciérnagas district of Greater Buenos Aires, where I carried out the fieldwork for my doctoral thesis (2012–17).

The public measures to contain the spread of the virus, and in particular the lockdown implemented by the national government in March 2020, placed significant obstacles to ethnographic methodological strategies, such as participant observation.

Face-to-face fieldwork became impossible, so adjustments were needed. As an alternative to meeting with interviewees in public offices and the neighborhood settings where the policies were implemented, interviews were conducted through Zoom. These were semi-structured and in-depth interviews that lasted between sixty and ninety minutes.

Online interviews were conducted with community activists and officials who worked at local, state, and federal public agencies responsible for both gender and children and youth public policies. All the interviewees were informed of the research aims and consented to participate in it. To protect their identity, I do not use their names, nor do I identify the specific districts or neighborhoods in which they work. Only the denominations of the public agencies and the state policies have been maintained.

In addition to the interviews, the analysis also encompasses the norms and official communications regulating the national lockdown, and the social media activity deployed by public agencies regarding their social policies aimed at children, youth, and women, at the local, state, and federal levels.

Facing the Pandemic Means Facing Inequalities

When the COVID-19 pandemic arrived in Argentina, the country was already facing great challenges linked to an ongoing economic crisis, increasing poverty, and difficulties in accessing international financing. The new national, provincial, and local administrations that took office in December 2019 found worrying issues regarding, for example, what could be done about the health and social protection systems, precarious working conditions, the distribution of care assignments, access to technology, and issues of violence.

In this complex scenario, and as the pandemic began to unfold, the Argentine national government implemented early measures to slow down contagion and mitigate the effect of the pandemic on health and on socioeconomic conditions. On 20 March, a lockdown was enforced throughout the country for those people who did not work in health or in essential sectors of the economy. This implied the restriction of movement for the general population, the suspension of face-to-face classes at all educational levels, the shutdown of shops, and the closure of international and provincial borders. Children were not allowed to leave their homes until 26 April when Decree 408/2020 enabled weekend recreational outings with their caregivers.

Together with the lockdown, the national and provincial governments launched a set of specific economic and social measures aimed at alleviating the impact of the crisis on the sectors deemed most vulnerable. The national state created the Emergency Family Income (IFE) for informal workers and self-employed workers with lower incomes (Decree 310/2020) and delivered special bonuses for people who received social plans and the universal child allowance (AUH) (Decree 309/2020). It also established maximum prices for basic consumer products, froze housing rental prices (Decree 320/2020), and suspended basic service cuts for nonpayment (Decree 311/2020) and home evictions.

As in other countries in the region, this crisis has particularly affected poor neighborhoods in which inhabitants live in precarious and overcrowded houses without assured access to key basic hygiene services. For them, the national government outlined a strategy called "Community isolation" and launched a program called "The neighborhood looks after the neighborhood," in which national, provincial, and local governments, in coordination with the social organizations in the communities, work to establish mechanisms for the protection of people's health and access to food. A prominent place is given to the organized work cooperatives and nonformal workers and the unemployed who make up what are known as popular economy workers. They have their own union-like structures to fight for the defense and promotion of their rights and their communities, so they assume the role of community promoters, walking through their neighborhoods to help people at risk, implement preventive measures, and work towards establishing hygienic safety in the community. Assuming that the lockdown makes women, girls, adolescents, and LGBTI+ people even more vulnerable to gender-based violence, those preventative measures also include providing information about national and local hotlines that deal with reports of violent situations. In these unusual circumstances, these vulnerable people are often forced to live with their aggressors and with more restricted possibilities for leaving their homes and seeking help.

Although there are no official and public statistics on the occurrence of femicide during the lockdown, in public statements made three weeks after it began, the National Minister for Women, Genders and Diversity indicated that, while the rate of general crimes had decreased, reports on what were most likely to have been gender-based murders showed a steady high rate. In addition, she specified that after the lockdown began, the daily average of requests seeking assistance for gender-based violence through the national 144 hotline was 39 percent higher than in the previous days (Frontera and Alcaraz 2020).

A few months before, in December 2019, the brand-new government created the National Ministry of Women, Genders, and Diversity, a space whose creation the local feminist movement had demanded historically. In line with this national decision, Buenos Aires provincial state also created its own women's ministry. Both are led and coordinated by feminist activists from the fields of human rights, trade unionism, and popular organization. The lockdown found them still under construction, with no buildings or offices of their own and with officials yet to be named in their positions. Faced with this in an unforeseen health situation, the national ministry promoted many measures related to gender and diversity. Specifically linked to addressing gender-based violence were three lines of action: comprehensive assistance; interinstitutional and intersectoral articulations; and the strengthening of community and solidarity ties. These same lines, with their nuances, guided the provincial ministry's work in coordination with the district offices dedicated to gender and diversity.

Among the comprehensive assistance measures, the 144 hotline was declared an indispensable service and its service channels were reinforced.

This line provides information, advice, and support throughout the country, 24/7, and can call on 911 in emergency situations.[1] In addition, other communication channels were generated through email along with a direct contact line through WhatsApp, and a free downloadable application complementary to a hotline was set up. A guide was also uploaded on the web pages of both national and provincial ministries with the geolocated resources with which the 144 hotline works. Two weeks after the lockdown started, the national ministry issued Resolution 15/2020, which clarified that instances of gender-based violence are included among its force majeure exceptions, thus allowing women and LGBTI+ people to leave their homes.

The national ministry, like the provincial one, promoted intersectoral and inter-ministerial articulations with the offices of Security, Social Development, and Justice; with other state entities such as the Public Prosecutor's Office, the Supreme Court, and its Women's and Domestic Violence offices; and with universities and trade unions. Actions aimed at strengthening community and solidarity ties were initiated; the #CuarentenaEnRedes (#LockdownInSocialMedia) communication campaign was launched and, at the provincial level, the slogan *Seguimos Conectadas* ("we stay connected") was adopted. In the same way, the directorates of territorial approaches and articulations worked on strengthening the networks of community accompaniment in situations of gender-based violence.

However, among the main national measures to assist victims and to address and prevent gender-based violence, there is nothing specifically directed toward girls and young women. No explicit inter-ministerial links have been found in the wide array of state agencies responsible for guaranteeing the rights of children and adolescents. Facing existing doubts among the population regarding the transfer of children and adolescents between parents who do not live together, the national ministry promoted Resolution MDS 132/2020, which establishes exceptions to social isolation in cases of duty of assistance to children and adolescents by their parents or guardians, in accordance with Decree 297/2020. Meanwhile, with regard to the provincial women's office, although there are also no specific initiatives with the Provincial Agency for Children and Adolescents, there are links to the Ministry of Education. Together with social organizations and trade unions, both ministries distribute brochures and materials that address gender-based violence, along with food bags from the School Food Service and booklets for the pedagogical continuity of students lacking digital connectivity.

Other offices have deployed various kinds of digital or virtual lines of action targeting girls and young women. For example, within the framework of the National Plan for the Prevention of Unintentional Pregnancy in Adolescence (ENIA), the National Ministries of Health, of Social Development, and of Education have tried to guarantee the online continuity of spaces for comprehensive health counseling in secondary schools in some provinces. The aim is to adapt these to counseling on sexual and reproductive health, gender-based violence, and legal termination of pregnancy in a virtual way to guarantee a listening channel. The ENIA inter-ministerial plan also works with the provinces to provide and guarantee children and adolescents' access to contraceptive methods and the legal termination of pregnancy in health centers, free of charge. Following the recommendations of the World Health Organization, these two sexual and reproductive health services were declared essential by the national government.

Through the National Secretariat for Children and Adolescents and the Family (SENAF) of the Ministry of Social Development, the state provides a free and confidential hotline (the 102 hotline) that offers a service for listening, support, and guidance for boys, girls, and adolescents. Through it, SENAF coordinates, in conjunction with other state agencies, possible interventions needed in cases of the violation of their rights. Unlike the 144 hotline its scope is not national, and some provinces have their own lines. For this reason, the Ministry of Justice and Human Rights national 137 hotline, aimed at dealing with situations of family or sexual violence, is crucial. This is also free and provides 24/7 containment, assistance, and accompaniment, 365 days a year. During the lockdown it incorporated service channels by email and WhatsApp. The Ministry of Health has a nationwide specific line (0800-222-3444) for consultation on sexual and reproductive health matters. It provides information and advice and removes obstacles to accessing sexual and reproductive health goods and services. In addition, the Youth Institute of the Ministry of Social Development, through its institutional website *hablemosdetodo* ("let's talk about everything") and its social media accounts, produces content and disseminates relevant recommendations for young people who are going through violent situations.

Reflections on the state by feminists and political anthropology experts have warned that to understand how state programs operate, it is not enough to study their formal designs, and we need, rather, to analyze how they are implemented and anchored in the daily and concrete lives of their clients. These contributions have indicated the importance of incorporating a vision of the state as a network of relations between those who implement the policies, the territorial networks, and their clients (Haney 1996). Therefore, in the next section, I explore the actions deployed by both the national and provincial governments during the lockdown in the Buenos Aires metropolitan area when it came to guaranteeing rights, assisting victims, and preventing gender-based violence against poor girls and young women. Taking Las Luciérnagas district as a reference, I analyze how the resources aimed at the social inclusion of children and young people—which, prior to COVID-19, allowed poor girls and young women to access help and find support when they were facing violent situations—indicate how the state converted itself in relation to these actions aimed at continuing to assist these groups.

Updating Challenges in Building "Meaningful Bonds"

Inaugurated due to political concern about the impacts of poverty and educational and labor exclusion in the last two decades, a set of programs and centers have emerged in Latin American countries for children, and especially young people with what are known as violated rights or those who are at risk of exclusion. In Argentina, the emergence of these centers and programs was framed in the context of the institutionalization of children's and adolescents' rights, so specific procedures and arrangements were deployed to affirm the formal statements of human rights and social inclusion. These arrangements orbited around definitions of children's participation and voice (Llobet et al. 2013). Although their objectives usually revolve around integrating adolescents into the educational system and the labor market, they could also be places where poor girls and young women could access resources and find support when facing violent situations (Gaitán 2017).

As a way of reestablishing the relationship between the state and children and young people in poor neighborhoods, while distancing themselves from repressive state agents like the police or the judiciary, these social programs are intended to be a space of contentment and listening. To this end, they follow the actions and knowledge of other actors like social activists, community leaders, and volunteers. Thus, their deployment in poor neighborhoods and in being part of the intervention with the knowledge of community leaders, these programs build their own identity

(Llobet et al. 2013). Their workers are also dedicated to carrying out an affective and physical hands-on intervention (Gaitán 2017) that may be especially valuable at a time in children's or young people's lives that is institutionally understood as vulnerable and filled with potential harmful exposures. In these hands-on interventions, state agents are personally and affectively involved and committed. Their professional careers, technical knowledge, and ethical-political positions are intertwined in bonding with adolescents. In this quest to bond, many workers have managed to get children and young people to open up and provide sensitive information about their lives, something that can allow them, in some way, to guarantee or protect their rights. Although all the workers were attentive to achieving this bond with their clients, it was the neighborhood actors who were most successful in forging these relationships, which were characterized by their availability, mutual affection, and trust, since they knew and walked through the neighborhood in a different way to the outside workers with a technical profile. These actors also had another relationship with the clients and their families and could even influence their personal actions through the mobilization of interpersonal relationships that existed prior to the arrival of the program in the neighborhood (Gaitán and Paz Landeira 2020). In their relationships with some of the state agents, many clients were able to solve temporarily some of the situations resulting from the intersectional oppressions they experienced because of being female, young, and poor. These institutional contexts and these attentive workers connected the clients to the possibility of expanding their possibilities for making decisions about themselves (Gaitán 2017; Llobet et al. 2013).

These child and youth centers were not considered essential by National Decree 297/2020, so they had to close their doors when the lockdown began. This happened in spite of what some local authorities in Las Luciérnagas felt. A member of the Youth Policy Directorate in Las Luciérnagas said,

> It is clearly a reference space for the kid. Also, understanding that in there [the neighborhood] the quarantines are not inside the houses, they are communal, so the kids are circulating. So, it seemed important to me that they can have that point [youth centers] of reference because in the houses they may live [in] some complex situation of violence, because they are locked up, because they need to relax, because they need a space like the one we made, more pleasant for those who live in daily life, with people who are much more empathetic than their family. I mean, there is a lot of things that make these devices relevant and essential for boys and girls, understanding that quarantine is not inside their home.

After losing that battle, these youth centers and support structures in Las Luciérnagas had to transition, partly, to a virtual mode. As a first step, efforts were made to ensure follow-up via WhatsApp and telephone by the technical team (social workers and psychologists at the center) in the situations with which they had already been working. These workers are in charge of articulating remotely with the rest of the children's and adolescents' rights protection system as part of the Local Service and the Secretariat of Comprehensive Policies on Drugs of the Argentine Nation (SEDRONAR).

Currently, an offer of online activities has been added to the personalized virtual follow-up. These range from a space for comprehensive sexual health counseling and access to legal abortion under the ENIA plan to school support, vocational guidance service, and workshops (rap, physical training, drawing, and so on). With the community centers having moved to a virtual mode of action, most of the state agents' work is done remotely from their homes, far from the neighborhoods. As expressed by the municipality's Childhood, Adolescence, and Young People officials, actual visits and interventions are carried out only in what are called urgency situations, when there is suspicion or certainty that the clients' rights are being violated.

As the Las Luciérnagas Youth Director told me in our last communication while he was in quarantine, he and four of his workers had had to preventatively isolate themselves after attending an emergency in the poor neighborhood La Estrella, which was what he called a "worrying point of contagion" for the district. A sixteen-year-old adolescent had fled from the Shelter House where he was temporarily staying to visit and stay with one of his older brothers in the neighborhood.[2] Faced with this situation, the workers went with the technical team to look for him so that he could have at least a first approach from the neighborhood's youth service. They wanted him to have this as a reference structure even though it would be implemented remotely. After the intervention, the teenager tested positive for COVID-19 and was isolated in a hotel for his recovery. The workers and the official, although they did not test positive, had to comply with the fourteen days of preventative quarantine in their own homes.

The fact that the official had to step publicly into the territory and perform tasks that, in another context, the technical team probably would have solved by themselves, exemplifies what Mariana Heredia and Luisina

Perelmiter (2020) note—in the current circumstances, the task divisions and hierarchies within the state structure have become more flexible, with more porous boundaries.

The local authorities took office in December 2019. In March 2020, the Childhood, Adolescence, and Young People Office was only at the beginning of its reorganization and planning process when the pandemic hit the country. In addition, the changing phases of the lockdown meant constant restructuring of the forms and distribution of work. During the first fifteen days of the lockdown only the highest-ranking officials attended the central offices, and the street-team workers circulated in some central areas of the district but, after a while, as the Director of Children Policies told me, they "could not take it any more with their body." Faced with these limits, rotating guards were organized to deal with Local Service situations with the workers who live closer to the central offices and do not have to take public transportation to get there. (Without the pandemic, the offices of the Local Services would have operated in the territories and not at the headquarters of the Undersecretary for Children and Youth, located in the center of the municipality of Las Luciérnagas.) In the event that people from the community cannot reach the central offices, if sexual abuse or mistreatment cases are reported, teams, although restricted, restructured, and with hygiene protocols, are deployed in the territories.

The eruption of the virus during the planned work of the new administration entailed reinventions and new strategies. In addition to fueling uncertainty regarding the possibility of achieving the basic goals set, it reactivated some challenges that transcend the particular context. As the Undersecretariat for Children and Youth in Las Luciérnagas put it,

> It is not enough to open an Instagram [account] and communicate through it to reach boys and girls. There is a challenge and an obligation and a permanent responsibility to think about how we may create the conditions to bond effectively and meaningfully with the kids. Well, there we have to offer public policy proposals and forms of communication that are meaningful to them and to which they can be receptive. It seems to me that this forces us to think because there is also great heterogeneity. That is why we talk about youths, there are inequalities that we have to consider: economic, cultural, and generational inequalities. Not only in the universe of young people, but between the actors who try to enter into communication, the state actors in their various forms and the youths in their diverse varieties. It is a permanent challenge to see how we find ourselves, how we bond, how we communicate.

"When You Do Not Have the Voice of Children You Have to Trust and Articulate with Actors"

As noted, the phases of lockdown restructured the children's and adolescents' rights protection system, posing restrictions that in many cases have been adjusted and resignified by the workers in order to guarantee their goals and prevent the violation of rights, or restore them. The halting of face-to-face school classes and the closure of the children's and adolescents' community centers placed serious obstacles in the communication channels with them. The virtualization of all communication meant that local childhood and youth workers had to try new articulations with state and nonstate actors and to trust in old ones, in order, as the Director of Childhood policies told me, "to reach their voices."

Although the first stage of lockdown found these actors primarily dedicated to guaranteeing food assistance, coordinating with the Social Action Ministry, and trying to rebuild relationships with families neglected by the previous administration, over the course of weeks, their actions began to expand. This involved a strengthened link to other local, provincial, and national state areas in which they worked to prevent mistreatment of, and gender-based violence against, children and adolescents and to deal with situations involving sexual abuse. As the Director of Childhood Policies commented, since they do "not have the voice of the children and young people," they must trust and establish links with other actors that mediate with them. Among these actors are the schools, the Primary Health Care Centers, and the women's police stations, from which the largest number of complaints came.

Las Luciérnagas's Gender Area (the local government's office in charge of designing, assessing, and implementing public policies on gender and diversity, with a transversal approach to all other areas of government) has also been a relevant actor, not only through the local gender violence assistant resource, but also through the work that the district promoters of gender equality carry out in the communities. Women workers from this Gender Area went out to the territories to advise their neighbors that the local gender violence assistant center was working and to inform them about the hotlines. These brief conversations and the handing over of brochures continue to take place within the framework of other national programs such as "The neighborhood looks after the neighborhood," either in health post or in supplying daily food through popular dining rooms.[3]

These actions by the local Gender Area are also part of broader initiatives promoted in the territories by the Buenos Aires provincial Ministry of Women, Genders, and Diversity. From the beginning of its administration, this new ministry deployed and articulated work with the local gender offices, which were convened together with political, feminist, social, and union organization leaders to build networks of companions in the face of situations of gender-based violence. This was implemented first in the framework of "The neighborhood looks after the neighborhood" and then within the provincial program Bonaerenses Solidarios ("solidarity of the people of Buenos Aires"). The goal is to incorporate rights promoters who have the skills to detect situations linked to obstacles in access to sexual and reproductive health and gender-based violence. As a coordinator at the provincial Ministry of Women, Genders, and Diversity pointed out about these promoters and the changing lockdown rules,

> [w]e were not going to be able to work on raising awareness—for example, I mean, they will have to be with the neighbors with their gender stereotypes such as they were—but to quickly bring tools that allow network construction and a dialogue with the state so that, in situations of vulnerability, particularly of gender violence, there could quickly be a communication channel.

In relation to the last relevant actor in the children's and young peoples' assistance programs, which are the social organizations at the community level, it is worth noting that these are not a new element within the social bureaucracies of the Argentine state, but, rather, a long-standing one that assumes greater importance in this special context. As Heredia and Perelmiter (2020) point out, the role of social organizations in guaranteeing the "capillarity of the state presence" (n.p.) has been enhanced during the pandemic.

As indicated by one of the Evita Movement activists in Las Luciérnagas, if their "task has always been to have eyes and tools to bring the state to the territory," during this crisis their "main task is to keep the bonds alive and to ensure food supply for the neighbors." Referring to the harsh lessons learned during the four years of government by the right-wing Cambiemos Alliance, which gravely increased poverty, the activist explained that "now it is time to hold on tight, we already know how to organize ourselves, we are not going to leave anyone behind."

Like other organizations and social movements with territorial anchorage, the Evita Movement's focus is not only on guaranteeing food and hygiene supplies, but on working toward women, children, girls, and

LGBTI+ people having violence-free lives. This work is done through networks and community centers of their own, established prior to the pandemic, which are now articulated with COVID-19-specific programs such as "The neighborhood looks after the neighborhood."

Open Reflections

Before COVID-19, social programs implemented in child and youth centers were places where girls and young women could access resources and find support when they experienced gender-based violence. Because of the lockdown, these resources in the suburbs of Buenos Aires, many of them located in the communities, had to close their doors. Neither the support centers nor their workers were considered essential in the pandemic context, so they had to transition, partly, to a virtual mode. This transition took place in a context in which access to electronic devices and internet connectivity is still far from being a fundamental right securing the lives of children and adolescents.

Although workers in the childhood and adolescence office in Las Luciérnagas appraise work virtualization favorably, they are aware that because the pandemic and lockdown took place in a context of preexisting inequalities, any remote work presents many obstacles; it makes access difficult for those children and adolescents with disabilities, since not everyone has internet at home or on their cell phones, or even a device with which to connect. Many may actually have to share devices with the people with whom they live, so these conversations are exposed to adults who regulate their use. As indicated by the local Director of Childhood Policies, virtual work with children is even more complex than with adolescents, because many of them do not have their own devices. Given this situation, the house-to-house visits to the children's houses carried out by one of the territorial leaders who worked at the support resource were crucial. These "small acts allow life to be knitted pair by pair" (Das 2012: 139); these care practices, core to the social production and reproduction of life in common (Rosen 2019), are carried out mainly by territorial actors and precede the lockdown (Franco Patiño and Llobet 2019; Gaitán and Paz Landeira 2020). At present, they seem to have doubled their efforts. These territorial actors and social leaders are the ones who were attentive to food management and hygiene aspects from the beginning of the lockdown, and they are also in charge of giving the warning notice not only of COVID-19 contagion, but also of gender-based violence situations or cases of police brutality.

When the analytical lens is directed to the territories, where policies are actually embodied, it is evident that the protection of girls and young women's rights, as well as their assistance in situations of gender-based violence in the pandemic context, rest mainly on the informal arrangements and norm adjustments that state workers make. They rest more on the actions of territorial networks and social organizations than on formal work moved to some kind of virtual mode.

ANA CECILIA GAITÁN (ORCID: 0000-0002-7972-9034) has a PhD in Anthropology from the University of Buenos Aires (UBA). She is currently an Assistant Researcher at the Technical and Scientific National Council (CONICET) and a professor at UBA and the National University of San Martín (UNSAM), teaching feminist and gender studies. She has carried out postdoctoral studies at the College of the Northern Border of Mexico (COLEF).

Notes

1. This is an emergency assistance telephone number.
2. According to Provincial Law 13,298, Shelter Houses are the first instance of an "inside-institution" protective measure for children and adolescents. They host them until the implementation of other measures has been evaluated.
3. These health posts distribute basic supplies such as bleach, soap, sanitizers, and masks. People working in these posts also provide services and information on healthcare issues and gender violence situations. They also trigger the assistance protocol for people with symptoms compatible with COVID-19.

References

Arcidiácono, Pilar, and Luisina Perelmiter. 2020. "Assistance in Remote Mode: One Hundred Days that Shook the State." [In Spanish.] *Anfibia*. Retrieved 13 September 2022 from http://revistaanfibia.com/ensayo/cien-dias-que-sacudieron-al-estado/.

Das, Veena. 2012. "Ordinary Ethics: The Perils and Pleasures of Everyday Life." In *Companion to Moral Anthropology*, ed. Didier Fassin, 133–49. New York: Wiley Blackwell.

Das, Veena, and Deborah Poole. 2008. "The State and its Margins: Comparative Ethnographies." [In Spanish.] *Cuadernos de Antropología Social* 27: 19–52.

Franco Patiño, Sandra, and Valeria Llobet. 2019. "The Child Development Centers and the Processes of Institutionalization of Childcare in the Province of Buenos Aires." In *Marches and Countermarches in Local Gender Policies: Territorial Dynamics and Citizenship of Women in Latin America* [in Spanish], ed. Ana Rodríguez Gustá, 59–86. Buenos Aires: CLACSO.

Fraser, Nancy. 1989. *Unruly Practices: Power, Discourse and Gender in Contemporary Social Theory*. Minneapolis: University of Minnesota Press.

Frontera, Agustina, and Florencia Alcaraz. 2020. "Sexist Violence and Covid-19: 'Between March 2019 and 2020 There is Almost No Variation.'" [In Spanish.] *Latfem*, 9 April. Retrieved 13 September 2022 from https://latfem.org/pandemia-y-perspectiva-de-genero-entrevista-con-la-ministra-elizabeth-gomez-alcorta/.

Gaitán, Ana. 2017. "Youth and Motherhood in the Neighborhood: Ethnography of the Negotiations of Meanings and Practices in the Implementation of Social Policies in the Buenos Aires Suburbs." [In Spanish.] PhD dissertation. University of Buenos Aires. Retrieved 13 September 2022 from http://repositorio.filo.uba.ar/handle/filodigital/4596.

Gaitán, Ana, and Florencia Paz Landeira. 2020. "Relationships, Experiences and Commitments: Territorial State Workers in the Implementation of Social Policies for Children and Youth." [In Spanish.] *Ciudadanías* 7. Retrieved 13 September 2022 from http://revistas.untref.edu.ar/index.php/ciudadanias/article/view/863/702.

Haney, Lynne. 1996. "Homeboys, Babies, Men in Suits: The State and the Reproduction of Male Dominance." *American Sociological Review* 61(5): 759–78. https://doi.org/10.2307/2096452.

Heredia, Mariana, and Luisina Perelmiter. 2020. "IDAES Talks: Where Do We Start? The 5 Lives of Social Policies." [In Spanish.] *Anfibia*. Retrieved 13 September 2022 from http://revistaanfibia.com/ensayo/las-5-vidas-las-politicas-sociales/.

Llobet, Valeria, Ana Cecilia Gaitán, Marina Medan, and Gabriela Magistris. 2013. "'This Space is for You to Speak': The Legitimation of Intervention in Social Programs." In *Senses of Social Exclusion: Beneficiaries, Needs, and Practices in Social Policies for Children and Young People* [in Spanish.], ed. Valeria Llobet, 129–60. Buenos Aires: Biblos.

Rodríguez Gustá, Ana. 2014. "The Same Social Policy, Three Dissimilar Gender Effects: The Local Implementation of a Conditional Cash Transfer Program in Argentina." [In Spanish.] *Trabajo y Sociedad* 22(6): 559–76.

Rosen, Rachel. 2019. "Poverty and Family Troubles: Mothers, Children, and Neoliberal 'Antipoverty' Initiatives." *Journal of Family Issues* 40(16): 2330–53. https://doi.org/10.1177/0192513X18809745.

CHAPTER 3

What It All Means
Young Rural Women in South Africa Confronting COVID-19

Nokukhanya Ngcobo, Zinhle Nkosi, and Ayub Sheik

Introduction

We are a team of three researchers from varied social, cultural, and linguistic backgrounds. We are two African women, one from a deeply rural location and the other from a peri-rural area, and an urban Indian man of South African origin. For this study, having team members whom we could all consider insiders strengthened our position as researchers, since qualitative research generally strives to understand social life from the viewpoint of those who live it, so, as insider researchers we were in a good position to access participants and to generate trustworthy data with relative ease (see Reeves 2010). Furthermore, team members had engaged in other research projects that dealt with rurality, sexuality, and gender-based violence previously. We have a lot of empathy for students and understand the hardships many of them experience daily. Our priority is the empowerment and emancipation of students through our teaching, research, and community activism.

We became interested in how young women from rural areas attending university navigated their lives in the context of COVID-19 restrictions, since all activities at university were halted, residences were closed, and students were compelled to return to their homes in order to mitigate the devastating effects of the pandemic. The rural areas in KwaZulu-Natal are characterized by severe poverty, a lack of essential healthcare services, poor infrastructure, and inadequate education facilities, and are still under the stewardship of tribal chiefs and customary law. Noting the unprecedented challenges facing these rural students, we were prompted to inquire into how they would cope in circumstances of precarity heightened by the restrictions and psychosocial challenges brought on by the pandemic.

The South African government's diversion of already-scarce resources to attempts to mitigate the effects of the pandemic led to a dire situation. The unprecedented crisis of the COVID-19 pandemic in South Africa has seen increased levels of unemployment and widespread salary cuts that have aggravated economic hardship and coupled with corruption related to the distribution of food aid, it has contributed to collective despair and suffering since many families have been forced to rely on emergency social relief programs for their survival. Being confined to already-constrained and ill-equipped living spaces given the restrictions of lockdown has made social distancing impossible in many cases, and this has led in turn to an increase in gender-based violence (GBV), and to higher rates of infection among this population given the gendered role of caregiving to the ill.

Routine medical care was reduced as hospitals prioritized victims of the pandemic. In addition, social services for the reproductive health of women and girls, counseling services, and shelters for victims of abuse either had their activities severely curtailed or stopped altogether. Shelters that remained open are often inaccessible to women whose movements have been severely restricted by stay-at-home regulations. The pandemic has also instilled a generalized fear and sense of anxiety in the population as it continues to take its deadly toll on human life. The fact that there is no known cure for the COVID-19 virus, coupled with the fact that its etiology is poorly understood, has heightened fears, as has the frequent publication of fake-news articles, reports, and advisories. All this is testing the resilience of people as never before.

We contend that while lockdown, quarantine, and school closures were in place to prevent the spread of the contagion, measures should have been put into place to protect young women at this time of increased vulnerability. Instead, young women continue to be faced with numerous challenges that have become extremely pressing, and nowhere else is this as acute as it is in rural areas. Consequently, our focus in this study was on the experiences of young female rural students sent home as university residences were closed during the lockdown.

Female Rural Students' Precarity during COVID-19

Given the conditions imposed by the pandemic, we sourced a literature review from online newspapers, websites, e-journals, and available electronic books since all libraries were closed. Over the past months, as the world has sought desperately to deal with the medical impacts of the virus and to prepare a response to its many secondary effects, research on COVID-19 has accelerated. However, more research on the social impacts of COVID-19 and on their consequences for young rural women who are students at a university is required. This is particularly so because the scale of the pandemic has affected young rural women in all aspects of their daily lives, including their safety, well-being, education, economic security, health, nutrition, and access to technology. In fact, all preexisting inequalities have been made worse by COVID-19 ("How Will COVID-19 Affect . . . ?" n.d.). The rural areas of Ulundi, Nkandla, and Nongoma in KwaZulu-Natal, in which this study was located, are characterized by small-scale farming and an already-high unemployment rate. Since rural homesteads are located in clusters, physical contact between people is inevitable and this accentuates the impact of the contagion on an already-vulnerable population (Ogunkola et al. 2020).

COVID-19 and Gender-Based Violence

While the government's response to COVID-19 (the imposition of national lockdown) may have helped mitigate the spread of the disease and reduce its effects (Amaechi et al. 2021), it seems to have enabled an unwelcome surge in other social ills, such as GBV, especially in rural areas and informal settlements (Rauhaus et al. 2020; Taub 2020). Being forcibly quarantined to their homes with their abusers made victims of domestic violence even more vulnerable and more exposed to violent abuse. In other words, while helping delay the spread of the virus, the lockdown enabled an upsurge of "intimate terrorism (Amaechi 2021). Domestic violence in the rural areas was exacerbated by conservative social relations that entrenched patriarchal boorishness as the norm. Deeply ingrained perspectives socialize men into believing in necessary relationships between masculinity, violence, and hegemonic control and, therefore, perpetuate violence against women.

Early or Forced Marriage

Early or forced marriage, a phenomenon driven chiefly by poverty and underdevelopment (Musa et al. 2021), is more than twice as likely to occur in rural areas and over three times more common among the poorest demographic. Shuttered universities and schools, isolation from friends and support networks, and rising poverty and pregnancy rates in lockdown resulted in a corresponding increase in early and forced marriage. The university closures meant that several protective functions of university were lost, exposing students to amplified teenage pregnancies, increased domestic chores, increased early marriage, and increased transactional sex (Addae 2021).

Financial and Psychosocial Stress

Students' lives have also been disrupted by increased levels of unemployment, hardship, and stress in families during the pandemic. As resources are diverted toward fighting the pandemic, reproductive healthcare in many countries has been compromised. A further layer of suffering is imposed on girls with disabilities and those from marginalized communities ("Implications of the Covid-19 Crisis . . ." 2020.)

The United Nations has described the worldwide increase in abuse as a shadow pandemic alongside COVID-19. Anurag Chaudhary (2020) also points to the increase in the amount of unpaid work at home that has had the corresponding effect of increasing pressure on young women confined to their homes. Ameena Goga et al. (2020) observe that young women, given their crucial stage of biological, cognitive, psychological, behavioral, and social development, place greater value on social interaction and face-to-face peer contact. Consequently, the psychosocial stress on young women is exacerbated by the pandemic.

The pandemic has also seen a surge in school dropout rates and in the number of adolescent girls engaging in child labor (De Hoop and Edmonds 2020). In addition, girls and young women also experience greater food insecurity and malnutrition ("COVID-19 Could Condemn Women . . ." 2020). Community-based organizations such as "Women Win" (committed to the unique needs of adolescent girls) are also no longer able to organize sport, recreation, and feeding programs for indigent girls since their operating expenses go unfunded and such events are prohibited by the rules of physical distancing (Women Win n.d.).

A review of available resources suggests that the pandemic has exacerbated preexisting gendered violence and related vulnerabilities. This is compounded by the lockdown, which compels female students to return to their homes in rural areas.

Methodology

For this case study, we used a qualitative research approach within an interpretivist paradigm. A case study was appropriate since we sought to enhance our understanding of the experiences of rural students sent home during the pandemic. The undergraduate female student participants ranged in age from seventeen to nineteen and the postgraduate female students from twenty-three to twenty-six. We used linear snowball sampling to get access to these participants. We talked to a student who had asked for food assistance and who explained the challenges she was facing at home during the COVID-19 outbreak. We told her that we planned to conduct a study to obtain an understanding of students similarly afflicted, and she said she wanted to be the first to participate in it, so she set in place the process of obtaining another seven participants. As already mentioned, their written narratives, based on how they experienced the COVID-19 lockdown as young women, were one of our sources of data generation. We requested that the participants remained anonymous in their narratives by using pseudonyms and that they detailed their experiences during the COVID-19 lockdown. We asked them to create email addresses that would not reveal their identities, and to append their cell phone numbers to their narratives in case we needed to call them should any elaboration be necessary, and also to enable us to conduct telephone interviews with them for the purposes of triangulation. In the telephone interviews we asked probing questions based on their individual narratives—sometimes for clarification, but always to ensure thick, rich data.

Our aim was to understand the subjective experiences of these students who had to return so abruptly to their homes in the rural areas of KwaZulu-Natal when the South African government declared lockdown in an effort to contain the pandemic. We employed qualitative data analysis methods and used thematic analysis. This started with data coding, from which the themes emerged.

All ethical considerations were met according to standard ethical protocol. In addition, since each participant had her own cell phone, we felt reassured regarding her safety and the confidentiality of her communication. We also emphasized that these were sensitive matters that required the utmost discretion and that the participants should take every precaution against contact with potential abusers. For example, if they could not speak for some reason or perceived a threat to their safety during the call, they were to tell us to call back later and stop the call immediately.

Research indicates that it is crucial to create fieldwork relationships that effectively engage participants in useful collaboration (Pezalla et al. 2012). This enhances the validity of research, since the relationship with respondents inevitably affects what the researcher is allowed to observe or is told. Additionally, as researchers we need to be conscious of how our ontological and epistemological assumptions are tempered, first as educators, and second as researchers, in a context in which gender inequalities are deeply entrenched.

Findings and Discussion

Three key themes emerged from the data, from which we extrapolated subthemes. The themes that we go on to discuss are experiences in relation to the home environment, societal experiences, and personal experiences.

Experiences in Relation to the Home Environment

Unconducive Living Conditions

Participants noted that requirements such as quarantine rules, self-isolation, and physical distancing were impossible since some of them shared beds or sleeping mats. These participants, given that they stayed at home, were at risk of contracting the disease. As Nomzamo stated,

> I live with my grandmother, my siblings, and cousins. We are seven in total in my household, my grandmother, four girls, and two boys. We have two rondavels; one is used as a kitchen and the other one as a bedroom. There is one bed on which my grandmother sleeps, with two of my youngest cousins. We sleep on the sleeping mats on the floor. If one get[s] sick, how can we survive? We will all be infected because we won't be able to quarantine.

In such constrained spaces, privacy is impossible and the potential for interpersonal conflict and abuse is also high. In their telephone conversations, which elaborated on the written narratives, the participants' feelings came through much more explicitly. In these conversations they spoke about their frustration and their sense of shame regarding their economic stress, along with their fear of contracting the COVID-19 virus.

Gender-Based Violence

Already treated as second-class citizens in many countries, most women have suffered abuse and violence at home during the COVID-19 lockdown. Some have reported being trapped at home with their abusers, while others have witnessed gender-based violence at home, with its attendant trauma. Long after the scars of physical abuse have healed, the psychological wounds persist. Some participants witnessed their fathers abusing their mothers and older sisters. Some were themselves abused. Cynthia said,

> Watching parents fight is traumatizing, let alone when you are also the victim [of abuse]. I was compelled to take my mom's side and assisted her to fight my dad... It was not for the first time... So traumatizing!

Maria commented,

> My experience with this virus is that I have been the victim of gender-based violence. I was sexually abused by my stepbrother. I depend on him for money and everything, but luckily, I managed to escape before he could penetrate me.

Happiness added,

> COVID-19 brought pain to a number of families. The truth of the matter is that some people do not talk about these things, but it really happens. My sister was beaten to [a] pulp by our older brother, but she did not report the case to the police, for... fear of my brother and the whole family. So sad.

These narratives provide a snapshot of instances of gender-based violence exacerbated by the restriction on mobility during the lockdown. Much of the gender-based violence stems from the legacy of the deeply engrained patriarchal culture that still prevails as a normative cultural standard in the rural areas of South Africa. The fact that women and girls are now trapped with their abusers in the same households puts them in serious danger. Added to this is the fact that, in the rural areas, there are few, if any, places of shelter, and these are beyond the reach of most victims. Additionally, many victims of gender-based violence are silenced by fear and the stigma of shame that being a victim carries in this cultural context.

Taking Care of the Sick in the Home Environment

Since the number of COVID-19 cases increases every day, female students are also affected in that they necessarily become healthcare givers in their families. As the Plan International report "Living under Lockdown: Girls and COVID-19" (2020) makes clear, disease outbreaks increase girls' and young women's duties of care to elderly and ill family members, as well as to siblings who are out of school. For example, Nompilo said, "Everyone at home expects that I am the one who must take care of my mother who has been sick for some time. I am scared but I can't reveal that to others." Jo-Anne added, "It is frightening to provide care to the sick [family] members at home, not knowing if they are infected with COVID-19 or not. It is not safe." Happiness commented, "I have to look after my older sister and my younger brother, both of them who are sick." Thembile lamented, "My dad died of COVID-19 about four weeks ago, and I also got infected because I was in contact with him every day, also being the one who was taking care of him as he always refused to go to hospital."

As can be seen, young women face the challenges of being the caregivers in their families and are increasingly exposed to contagion. This is the result of the gender stereotypes that see women and girls necessarily taking on the role of caregiver. There was no indication that the participants' older or younger brothers were tasked with the same duties. The girls and young women who find themselves playing a crucial front-line role in caring for the sick are at high risk of contracting the disease. These findings echo those of Sara Casey and Giselle Garino (2020), who note that gender norms relegating women to the realm of care work and fulfilling these roles put them on the front lines in times of crisis, and this results, of course, in a greater risk of exposure.

The Home Environment as an Unconducive Space for Studying

Poor home environments were seen to be unconducive to studying. For example, household chores include cleaning the house every day, fetching water, cooking, dishing up food for family members followed by the washing of dishes, ironing, and caring for young siblings. Along with having to complete these chores, many participants were not offered any support by their parents. This is why some decided to go back to work on campus. Cynthia, for example, commented, "I cannot tell how parents think we are able to study and expect a pass at the end of the day, while they know they are the ones who do not give us time to do our university work." Maria added, "My parents did not receive higher education, so it is difficult to get support from them. I wish I could go back to the university and get all the support I need." For Nompilo, "Home chores that are four times more than my brothers' leave me stressed and short-tempered."

In agreement with these participant observations, a UNICEF (2016) report reveals that girls spend 40 percent more time, or 160 million more hours a day, on household chores such as cooking, cleaning, collecting firewood, and caring for family members than do boys of the same age. The report notes that this overburden of unpaid household work begins in early childhood and intensifies as girls reach adolescence. Further, girls are often made to start working from as early as five to nine years of age, spending 30 percent more time than boys of their age on chores. This disparity increases dramatically as children reach the age of fourteen, with more than 50 percent of household labor being assigned to girls. In addition, Christian Gollayan (2019) reports on a study by the Pew Research Center, carried out from 2014 to 2017, that found that girls spent thirty-eight minutes more doing daily housework than boys, who spent about twenty-four minutes cleaning around the house.

Societal Experiences

Fake News

There is a lot of misinformation about the new coronavirus (Rall 2020), from conspiracy theories ("Conspiracy Theories on Covid-19 . . ." 2021) and hoaxes to dangerous cures and false evidence. Emma Sadleir, a social media expert cited in Rall (2020), states that anyone sharing fake news about COVID-19 may be fined or jailed for six months. People who forward unverified news articles could find themselves in trouble as well. It is a warning that "[e]very single person who presses forward is committing a criminal offence if they are intending to deceive" (ibid.). Sadleir urges residents to presume that every voice note or message about the coronavirus is fake until proven otherwise and advises people to verify the information they receive. Sarah Smit (2020) writes that South Africa is among the countries—after the United States, Brazil, and the Philippines—in which politicians were seen to have an even higher responsibility for online misinformation than in other countries.

A lot of fake news has been reported in South Africa and, luckily, some of it has been identified as such by the South African government (n.d.) in an online piece called "Stop Fake News." However, before many of these fake news items reach the attention of the authorities, they have already had a deleterious effect in communities. Such news items included, for example, "Vaccines for COVID-19 Are Designed to Kill Africans as Part of a Population Control Plan," "Big Pharmaceutical Companies Created the Virus to Profit Billions from Supplying the Vaccine," and "Covid-19 Comes from 5G Towers" (all from the *Independent Online*).

In response to the prevalence of fake news in South Africa, Happiness said, "You can imagine . . . you are infected, people joke about your illness and there is a lot of fake news making rounds [on] every social media platform. The pain is immeasurable."

Maria added,

> There is nothing that is so traumatizing like fake news about COVID-19. They look for old videos and make you believe they are about COVID-19. For example, COVID-19 patients sleeping on the hospital floors because there are no beds for them. I don't know what needs to be done to make people realize the pain they cause to others.

Nompilo commented, "They will circulate fake news about it [the coronavirus] and you already have symptoms. They make you count yourself among the dead. It is so traumatizing and senseless."

Closure of Hair Salons

The closure of hair salons during the lockdown was a challenge to many of the participants. This is because to them, a new look and beauty generally are, to a large extent, defined by a hairstyle, whether it is a haircut, braid, or hair color. For many participants, the closing of the hair salons has been stressful since they feel that a good hairstyle is a necessity for looking good and boosts their self-esteem and confidence. Merle, for example, stated, "I have been ridiculed for my hairstyle because I cannot go to the salon to do my hair the way I used to." Cynthia explained,

> I am shy to go [out in] public with my hair. I don't need someone to tell me my hair is untidy, my hairstyle is worn out, my hair is coming out, all this and that. It is a pain I will never forget. I use[d] to go to the salon after every two weeks. What do I do if people laugh at me for my worn-out hairstyle . . . being ridiculed, and told my hair is like that of a para [vagrant] who lives on the street. I see no need to close the salons, having [a] good hairstyle is our right.

Martha responded, "I feel like I have not washed myself when I look at my hair. [I am] just wondering how long it will take for the government to ease regulations regarding salons."

These statements show the importance of grooming to these young women. Jenni Bipat (2020) reported in the *South Coast Herald* on an online petition calling for the opening of hair salons during the COVID-19 lockdown. The salon industry wanted to be recognized as an essential service. Philani Nombembe (2020) reported that hairdressers and beauticians took the government to court for prohibiting their operations. However, they were unsuccessful; the court rejected their petition.

Being Ridiculed for Being a Government COVID-19 Grant Recipient

In April 2020, the Minister of Social Development, Lindiwe Zulu, announced a Special COVID-19 Social Relief of Distress Grant to all deserving South African Social Security Agency (SASSA) recipients. The criteria for qualifying for the grant included being an unemployed South African citizen, permanent resident, or refugee registered with Home Affairs who was not receiving any social grant and who was eighteen years old or above (Department of Social Development n.d.).

For Merle, "Being ridiculed for the R350.00 government grant did not sit well with me. I don't know why on earth if you are financially struggling, people just get something to talk about, and make sure you feel the pain."

In relation to receiving the food parcels organized by the government, Nompilo commented,

> I was very embarrassed [at] being laughed at by neighbors for being in the queues to receive food parcels, even those unemployed just like me. I was relieved when the government changed the strategy of giving food parcels, instead [giving] vouchers. That sounded better. I had told myself I will never go there [to receive the food parcels] ever again.

Social Stigma and COVID-19 Infection

According to the girls who participated in the study, the stigma of being infected with COVID-19, be it themselves or a family member, creates a rift between them and the people they regard as neighbors or friends. They told us that if they or a family member tested positive, they became the talk of the day because people would gossip about them and sometimes laugh at them. Of course, the death of a family member was even worse. The fear of being ridiculed, shamed, or discriminated against was the reason some opted not to reveal their positive COVID-19 status.

This was corroborated by Bongi, who said,

> I have not been infected but two of my family members have. I went for testing, and I was negative. Thank God for my results because were it not for my negative status, everyone would be gossiping about me, as if I [had] committed a crime.

Martha said,

> My aunt got tested and her results were positive. Everyone in the village knew, and we were avoided by everyone, even our neighbors. That was [the most] terrible experience ever. You do not expect this sort of treatment while you are faced with this deadly disease. Instead, you expect people to give you support.

In addition, Belinda commented, "I'd better hide my status rather than reveal it, for the fear of being treated like a murderer who is supposed to go to jail."

According to a World Health Organization (WHO) report (2020),

> Social stigma in the context of health is the negative association between a person or group of people who share certain characteristics and a specific disease. In an outbreak, this may mean people are labelled, stereotyped, discriminated against, treated separately, and/or experience loss of status because of a perceived link with a disease. Such treatment can negatively affect those with the disease, as well as their caregivers, family, friends and communities. People who do not have the disease but share other characteristics with this group may also suffer from stigma.

The WHO report also states that the current COVID-19 outbreak has provoked social stigma and discriminatory behaviors against people of certain ethnic backgrounds, as well as anyone perceived to have been in contact with the virus. What is of concern is that this can first drive people to hide the illness to avoid discrimination; second, it can prevent people from seeking healthcare immediately; and third, it could discourage them from adopting healthy routines to mitigate the effects of the pandemic.

Personal Experiences

Alcohol Ban

Some of the young girls who participated in the study felt that even though alcohol has many disadvantages, it helps young people to socialize. Some expressed boredom because of the ban on alcohol and felt that their happiness was being compromised. Belinda commented, "I don't understand why this alcohol lockdown." Nompilo added, "I don't drink too much but it is just for socializing purposes. Alcohol regulations should be eased because having a sip of alcohol makes me forget about all my bad experiences." Yesmien commented, "They may say alcohol is banned but people know where to get it if they really want it. Just one glass will make a difference to me."

Cynthia said,

> I cannot tell why it is so bad to drink if you are a girl. Did you see how many girls joined the queues to the liquor stores on the day we moved to level 3? I was there as well. Hahahaha!!!

Maurice Smithers (2020) writes that for some people in South Africa, one of the tougher restrictions in the COVID-19 lockdown is the lack of access to liquor and the frustration of those who drink regularly. Nonetheless, the Southern African Alcohol Policy Alliance in South Africa (SAAPA SA) fully supported the initial State of Disaster Regulations that ruled that all liquor outlets—for both onsite and offsite consumption—had to close at 6 p.m. on weekdays and Saturdays and 1 p.m. on Sundays and public holidays.

Unhealthy Lifestyles

Having an unhealthy lifestyle was mentioned by the participants as a bad experience during COVID-19. While these girls had tried to adopt a healthy lifestyle before the COVID-19 outbreak, this was now fruitless. Eating habits, eating times, and the type of foods they now consumed were all affected. Bongi noted, "I eat more than three times a day . . . I can open the fridge as much as I can. If there is something I like, I just grab and eat." Cynthia commented, "Sitting at home the whole day means eating a lot, and less exercising." Nompilo added,

> I eat so many times each day, but less exercise. This is the reason I am gaining weight. Before the COVID-19 outbreak, I had lost six kilograms within two months, but those kilograms are now back, because I eat junk, take a lot of food,

and I do not take any body exercises. This makes me feel bad. I am not doing justice to myself.

Laura Di Renzo et al. (2020) report that eating habits and lifestyle modification may threaten our health. Maintaining the correct nutritional status is crucial, especially during a period in which the immune system cannot be compromised. These researchers mention that those with severe obesity have a higher risk of COVID-19 complications. From the data, we infer that COVID-19 has adversely affected dietary routines and general health for many of our participants since they have been confined at home and their mobility has been restricted.

Financial Difficulties

Young girls from low-income families have become the victims of abuse during the COVID-19 lockdown. Some participants found themselves having love relationships with older men because of the need for money that their families could not provide. For example, Yesmien commented,

> I have not told anyone, even my friend, [that] it happened I slept with an old man, whom I don't even love, simply because I wanted him to give me money to buy data bundles, food and everything I needed. I know he too did not love me. It was no rape, I must admit.

Nompilo added, "A harsh reality is that we find ourselves having to sleep with men we don't even love, for the sake of getting money." The need for money drives young girls to engage in sexual relationships, trading their bodies for cash. UNICEF (2020) corroborates this fact, claiming that there is sufficient evidence to support the view that economic insecurity leads to sharp rises in intimate partner violence and the exposure of adolescent girls to sexual exploitation, harassment, and other types of GBV.

Conclusion

These young rural women's experiences in the context of COVID-19 and the resulting lockdown and restriction measures suggest that they have experienced unprecedented emotional, psychological, physical, financial, and socioeconomic pressures. The young women perceived the rules and regulations put in place to prevent the spread of COVID-19 as detrimental to them in a number of ways, as we have shown. While governments ensured that measures to curb the spread of the pandemic were in place, setting up protocols to protect women under these conditions was neglected. Thus, we argue that women's interests were not taken into consideration and that this led to an escalation of the already-chronic trends of sexual exploitation and hardship.

Carrying out this research has shifted our perceptions about our students. We recognize the need for increased empathy, since we cannot teach in a bubble divorced from the everyday reality of our students. We now also appreciate the value of positioning ourselves as a community of care by trying to be much more constructive in helping our students not only achieve academically, but also survive the unprecedented crisis of COVID-19.

Nokukhanya Ngcobo (ORCID: 0000-0002-1738-6195) is a lecturer in the School of Education: Languages and Arts Education, University of KwaZulu-Natal. Her research focuses on language and gender, critical literacy, youth, health, sexuality, gender-based violence, HIV and AIDS in education, cultural identity, and mother-tongue-based bilingualism.

Zinhle Primrose Nkosi (ORCID: 0000-0001-6086-3252) is a senior lecturer in the School of Education: Languages and Arts Education, University of KwaZulu Natal. She teaches IsiZulu, supervises postgraduate research, and is invested in community projects for mother-tongue revitalization.

Ayub Sheik (ORCID: 0000-0002-8633-3740) is an associate professor in the School of Education: Languages and Arts Education and Deputy Academic Leader at the University of KwaZulu-Natal. He was an Andrew Mellon Postdoctoral Fellow and a DAAD scholar at the University of Essen, Germany. He supervises research in English education and his research preoccupations are academic literacy, poetry, and African folklore.

References

Addae, Evelyn Aboagye. 2021. "COVID-19 Pandemic and Adolescent Health and Well-Being in Sub-Saharan Africa: Who Cares?" *International Journal of Health Planning and Management* 36(1): 219–22. https://doi.org/10.1002/hpm.3059.

Amaechi, Kingsley Ekene, Tsoaledi Daniel Thobejane, and Raymond Rasalokwane. 2021. "Feminist Reflections on the Impact of the South African National COVID-19 Lockdown on the Upsurge of Gender Based Violence in

Mahwelereng Township of Limpopo Province, South Africa." *Gender and Behaviour* 19(1): 17186–203.

Bipat, Jenni. 2020. "Online Petition Calls for Soft Opening of Hair Salons after Covid-19 Lockdown." *South Coast Herald*, 19 April. Retrieved 14 September 2022 from https://southcoastherald.co.za/402128/online-petition-calls-for-soft-opening-of-hair-salons-after-covid-19-lockdown/.

"Big Pharmaceutical Companies Created the Virus to Profit Billions from Supplying the Vaccine." 2021. *Independent Online*.

Bissoonauth, Rita. 2020. "Addressing the Impact of Covid-19 on Girls and Women's Education in Africa." *The Global Partnership for Education (GPE)*, July 10. Retrieved 14 September 2022 from https://www.globalpartnership.org/blog/addressing-impact-covid-19-girls-and-womens-education-africa.

Casey, Sara, and Giselle Carino. 2020. "Gender-Based Violence in the Covid-19 Pandemic." *EurekAlert*, 20 April. Retrieved 14 September 2022 from https://www.eurekalert.org/pub_releases/2020-04/cums-gvi042020.php.

Chaudhary, Anurag. 2020. "Women in Covid Pandemic: Beyond Morbidity and Mortality." *Indian Journal of Cardiovascular Disease in Women* 5(3): 274–77. https://doi.org/10.1055/s-0040-1716133.

"Conspiracy Theories on Covid-19 Vaccine Can Be as Deadly as Virus Itself." 2021. *Independent Online*, 29 Jan. Retrieved 14 September 2022 from Retrieved 7 November 2022 from https://www.iol.co.za/news/opinion/conspiracy-theories-on-covid-19-vaccine-can-be-as-deadly-as-virus-itself-8adf871e-2d9e-4d6a-8e43-ae188308ac52.

"Covid-19 Comes from 5G Towers." 2021. *Independent Online*.

"COVID-19 Could Condemn Women to Decades of Poverty: Implications of the COVID-19 Pandemic on Women's and Girls' Economic Justice and Rights." 2020. *CARE International UK*. Retrieved 14 September 2022 from https://reliefweb.int/sites/reliefweb.int/files/resources/CARE_Implications_of_COVID-19_on_WEE_300420.pdf.

De Hoop, Jacobus, and Eric Edmonds. 2020. "Why Child Labour Cannot be Forgotten during COVID-19." *UNICEF*, 14 May. Retrieved 14 September 2022 from https://blogs.unicef.org/evidence-for-action/why-child-labour-cannot-be-forgotten-during-covid-19/.

Department of Social Development. n.d. "Special COVID-19 Social Relief of Distress Grant." Retrieved 14 September 2022 from https://www.sassa.gov.za/Pages/COVID-19_SRD_Grant.aspx.

Di Renzo, Laura, Paola Gualtieri, Francesca Pivari, Laura Soldati, Alda Attina, Giulia Cinelli, Claudia Leggeri, Giovanna Caparello, Luigi Barrea, Francesco Scerbo, Ernesto Esposito, and Antonino De Lorenzo. 2020. "Eating Habits and Lifestyle Changes during COVID-19 Lockdown: An Italian Survey." *Journal of Translational Medicine* 18: 229. https://doi.org/10.1186/s12967-020-02399-5.

Goga, Ameena, Linda Gail Bekker, Philippe Van de Perre, Wafaa El-Sadr, Khatija Ahmed, Mookho Malahleha, Trisha Ramraj, Vundli Ramokolo, Vuyolwethu Magasana, and Glenda Gray. 2020. "Centring Adolescent Girls and Young Women in the HIV and Covid-19 Responses." *Lancet* 396(10266): 1864–66. https://doi.org/10.1016/S0140-6736(20)32552-6.

Gollayan, Christian. 2019. "Teenage Girls Do More Homework and Household Chores than Boys: Study." *New York Post*, 5 March. Retrieved 14 September 2022 from https://nypost.com/2019/03/05/teenage-girls-do-more-homework-and-household-chores-than-boys-study/.

"How Will COVID-19 Affect Girls and Young Women?" n.d. *Plan International*. Retrieved 14 September 2022 from https://plan-international.org/emergencies/covid-19-faqs-girls-women.

"Implications of the Covid-19 Crisis on Girls and Young Women." 2020. *Plan International*, 20 July. Retrieved 5 November 2022 from https://hivdev.gn.apc.org/library/documents/implications-covid-19-crisis-girls-and-young-women.

"Living under Lockdown: Girls and COVID-19." 2020. *Plan International*. Retrieved 14 September 2022 from https://www.planusa.org/docs/Plan_Living_Under_Lockdown_Report.pdf.

Musa, Shuaibu Saidu, Goodness Ogeyi Odey, Muhammad Kabir Musa, Samar Mohammed Alhaj, Blessing Abai Sunday, Suleiman Maimuna Muhammad, and Don Eliseo Lucero-Prisno. 2021. "Early Marriage and Teenage Pregnancy: The Unspoken Consequences of COVID-19 Pandemic in Nigeria." *Public Health in Practice* 2: 100152.

Nombembe, Philani. 2020. "It Could Get Ugly: Lockdown Ban on Hairdressers, Beauticians in Court Today." *Times Live*, 12 June. Retrieved 14 September 2022 from https://www.timeslive.co.za/news/south-africa/2020-06-12-it-could-get-ugly-lockdown-ban-on-hairdressers-beauticians-in-court-today/.

Ogunkola, Isaac Olushola, Yusuff Adebayo Adebisi, Uchenna Frank Imo, Goodness Ogeyi Odey, Ekpereonne Esu, and Don Eliseo Lucero-Prisno III. "Rural Communities in Africa Should Not Be Forgotten in Responses to COVID-19." *The International Journal of Health Planning and Management* 35(6): 1302–5.

Parry, Bianca Rochelle, and Errolyn Gordon. 2020. "The Shadow Pandemic: Inequitable Gendered Impacts of Covid-19 in South Africa." *Gender, Work & Organization*. https://doi.org/10.1111/gwao.12565.

Pezalla, Anne E., Jonathan Pettigrew, and Michelle Miller-Day. 2012. "Researching the Researcher as Instrument: An Exercise in Interviewer Self-Reflexivity." *Qualitative Research* 12(2): 165–85.

Rall, Se-Anne. 2020. "Covid-19: Separate the Facts from the Fake News, Warns Social Media Expert." *IOL*, 29 March. Retrieved 14 September 2022 from https://www.iol.co.za/news/south-africa/kwazulu-natal/covid-19-separate-the-facts-from-the-fake-news-warns-social-media-expert-45738550.

Rauhaus, Beth M., Deborah Sibila, and Andrew F. Johnson. 2020. "Addressing the Increase of Domestic Violence and Abuse during the COVID-19 Pandemic: A Need for Empathy, Care, and Social Equity in Collaborative Planning and Responses." *American Review of Public Administration* 50(6/7): 668–74. https://doi.org/10.1177/0275074020942079.

Reeves, Carla L. 2010. "A Difficult Negotiation: Fieldwork Relations with Gatekeepers." *Qualitative Research* 10(3): 315–31. https://doi.org/10.1177/1468794109360150.

Smit, Sarah. 2020. "Fake News Fears as Covid-19 Highlights the Dangers of Misinformation." *Mail & Guardian*, 16 June. Retrieved 14 September 2022 from https://mg.co.za/coronavirus-essentials/2020-06-16-fake-news-fears-as-covid-19-highlights-the-dangers-of-misinformation/.

Smithers, Maurice 2020. "Alcohol, Alcohol Harm and Alcohol Dependency: Putting Things in Perspective." *Daily Maverick*, 13 April. Retrieved 14 September 2022 from https://www.dailymaverick.co.za/article/2020-04-13-alcohol-alcohol-harm-and-alcohol-dependency-putting-things-in-perspective/.

South African Government. n.d. "Stop Fake News." Retrieved 22 September 2022 from https://www.gov.za/covid-19/resources/fake-news-coronavirus-covid-19.

Taub, Amanda. 2020. "A New COVID-19 Crisis: Domestic Abuse Rises Worldwide." *New York Times*, 6 April. Retrieved 5 November 2022 from https://www.nytimes.com/2020/04/06/world/coronavirus-domestic-violence.html

UNICEF. 2016. "Girls Spend 160 Million More Hours Than Boys Doing Household Chores Every Day." 7 October. Retrieved 14 September 2022 from https://www.unicef.org/media/media_92884.html.

———. 2020. "COVID-19—GBV Risks to Adolescent Girls and Interventions to Protect and Empower Them." Retrieved 14 September 2022 from https://www.unicef.org/documents/covid-19-gbv-risks-adolescent-girls-and-interventions-protect-and-empower-them.

"Vaccines for COVID-19 are Designed to Kill Africans as Part of a Population Control Plan." 2021. *Independent Online*

Women Win. n.d. "Covid-19: Protecting Adolescent Girls and Young Women." *Women Win*. Retrieved 14 September 2022 from https://www.womenwin.org/news/girls-empowerment-through-sports/covid-19-protecting-adolescent-girls-and-young-women/

World Health Organization. 2020. "A Guide to Preventing and Addressing Social Stigma Associated with COVID-19." 24 February. Retrieved 14 September 2022 from https://www.who.int/publications/m/item/a-guide-to-preventing-and-addressing-social-stigma-associated-with-covid-19.

PART II
Continuing Education

CHAPTER 4

Women Teachers Support Girls during the COVID-19 School Closures in Uganda

Christine Apiot Okudi

Introduction

Schools in Uganda closed indefinitely on 20 March 2020. Several attempts to open them have so far been unsuccessful. In Uganda, school is a haven for girls; the presence of the Senior Woman Teacher (SWT) protects girls and encourages attendance, retention, and the completion of their education, as Okudi (2016) notes. The girls receive adolescent and reproductive health information, as well as guidance and counseling. They are also taught skills for life after school and are provided with an advocate, a mentor, and a role model to whom they can look up. All this was put on hold by the closure of schools in March.

At home, the girls now lack support systems that strengthen their skills and protect them from deterrents to progress in their education. For example, the Ugandan government has noted increasing cases of domestic

---

Notes for this section can be found on page 83.

violence against women and girls during the COVID-19 lockdown (Katana et al. 2021).

In the trying circumstances of the COVID-19 pandemic, the members of many vulnerable groups will be put at even greater risk. In Sierra Leone, by way of example, temporary school closures and the lack of economic opportunities during the Ebola outbreak in 2014 drove girls who did not have access to girls' clubs to spend time with men. This resulted in increased early childbearing and had long-term implications for the education of those girls who dropped out of school permanently. According to an International Federation of Red Cross and Red Crescent (IFRC) report (2020), key among those at risk are young girls from low-income backgrounds, who risk falling into circumstances that will prevent their future education. This crisis is also likely to put them at higher risk of sexual violence and exploitation, trafficking, child marriage, forced labor, and social exclusion. Girls in Uganda are already faced with a host of barriers to education that result in substantial gender disparities.

In the Education and Sports Sector Strategic Plan (2017/18–2019/20), the Ministry of Education and Sports (MoES) reaffirms its commitment to promoting gender equality, in part by addressing gender-specific barriers that undermine girls' education, including the management of sexual maturation. In this regard, the SWTs have been assigned the role of guiding learners to handle some of these challenges. These SWTs occupy a position recognized by the MoES as one of the basic requirements and minimum standards for operation of schools in Uganda (MoES 2017). This position is acknowledged in the National Strategy for Girls' Education (NSGE) 2015–19 as playing a key role in guiding learners' transition from childhood to adulthood (MoES 2013).

During the COVID-19 lockdown girls out of school did not have this support mechanism to guide and counsel them, provide them with facts on issues related to adolescent health, and teach them the skills of being assertive to protect themselves from any dangers in the community that might eventually have an impact on their education. Post-COVID-19, the girls will need to be supported to return to schools when these reopen, and barriers like the lack of school fees (for instance) must be dealt with. Child mothers and pregnant girls must be taken care of through the enacting, for example, of laws that will support them to return to school.

Methods

In my study, I aimed to establish the role of SWTs in a community setting and to identify the prevailing issues affecting girls during the COVID-19 closure of schools.

Exploratory Study

This is an exploratory study designed with the difficulties occasioned by the COVID-19 pandemic in mind. Since this study offers a snapshot or cross section of the population, I carried it out in the two districts of Luweero and Wakiso to cover both a rural and a peri-urban area in Uganda. This enabled me to obtain an overall picture of conditions at this time that will allow for further research in the future.

Safety Protocols

I obtained a letter of permission to do this research in the community from the Local Council 1 (LC1) chairperson. I had to take into consideration the COVID-19 restrictions in relation to the planned activities, so I put into place all the necessary Special Operating Procedures (SOPs) to ensure the safety of the girls and the SWTs. This included taking the SWTs through a session on how to administer the questionnaire and ensure that they knew how to keep themselves safe and protect the students with whom they met.

Participating Senior Women Teachers (SWTs)

These teachers guide, counsel, and support girls with both survival and developmental skills. They advocate for the girls in the school setting, act as role models to them, and provide all the necessary information on adolescent health as indicated in the policy guidelines for a SWT in Uganda (MoES 2020).

The SWTs in this study were selectively identified because all ten of them are in active service as class teachers in primary schools in Luweero and Wakiso. The SWTs are all female teachers with more than three years of service each. They doubled as respondents and research assistants because they had to support the girls and also administer the questionnaires to them. The SWTs were therefore taken through the SOPs for the COVID-19 period, which included maintaining physical distancing, putting on masks, and sanitizing or washing hands regularly.

Participating Students

The eighty-nine girls, aged between eleven and eighteen, were randomly selected from fifteen private and government primary schools in both Wakiso and Luweero districts. Of the students, 61 percent were from peasant families, 37 percent were from the business community, and 2 percent were from civil servant families.

Participating LC1 Women Representatives

The LC1 woman representative holds a political position at village level in Uganda. This representative, appointed in every village in line with the affirmative action clause within Uganda's new constitution of 1995, is mandated to ensure that women's issues are highlighted in all discussions. Ten LC1 women representatives were part of this research, because they speak for the girls too. All were selected because they were then sitting LC1 women representatives in the villages in which the schools are located and in which the girls and SWTs reside.

Questionnaires and Interviews

The first activity at the start of the research study was the development of the data collection tools. These included the questionnaires for the students and interview guides for the SWTs and LC1 women representatives.

Given the COVID-19 lockdown, the data collection was pegged to the two methods of questionnaires and interviews. The SWTs and the LC1 representatives were interviewed by phone, while the girls were provided with a questionnaire with both closed-ended and open-ended questions. The closed-ended questions offered predefined answer options from which the respondent had to choose, while the open-ended questions allowed them freedom and flexibility in providing their answers.

The issues discussed during the interviews were related to those currently affecting girls living through the COVID-19 pandemic and the ways in which the SWTs could support them to protect themselves and stay safe during this period. The SWTs took the opportunity to encourage the girls to study during this break to ensure that they are not left behind when schools reopen.

Research Questions

The research questions were as follows:

1. What is the importance of the SWT's role in schools?
2. What issues do the girls in the community face during the COVID-19 school closure?
3. What kinds of activities can the SWT do to support girls in the communities during this school closure?

Data Collection and Analysis

The data was analyzed using a mix of both descriptive and inferential statistics, qualified through open-ended questions for students and phone conversations with the SWTs and LC1 women representatives. I undertook to interview the SWTs and LC1 women representatives.

During the data collection phase, phone briefing meetings were held at the end of each day to triangulate and ensure that good-quality data was being obtained. Discussions were also held on newly emerging issues.

Results

Community Support

All the girls reached were aware of the position of SWTs in school and were able to identify their roles, as listed above, and recognize that it is through the enactment of these roles by these teachers that they benefit as students. All the LC1 women representatives, too, were aware of the role of SWTs in schools and were able to describe them.

The girls were asked to identify three main people who provided them with support in the community. The LC1 woman representative was mentioned by 44.5 percent, NGOs by 32 percent, and the LC1 chairman by 16 percent. Relatives were listed by 7 percent and parents by 2.3 percent. None of the girls identified the police as people they would approach for help. The SWTs also identified the LC1 woman representative as their ally in working on supporting girls in the community, while 85 percent of the LC1 women representatives appreciated the support of the SWTs and indicated their willingness to work with them. The LC1 women representatives acknowledged working on issues related to girls who need referrals from the school to the community. Of these, 21 percent mentioned having worked with the SWTs in handling cases from school that had needed referral to a girl's community.

Heavy Domestic Chores

The current issues and challenges identified by the girls included heavy domestic chores; 66.3 percent of them made this claim. Of the girls from peasant backgrounds, 78 percent brought up heavy domestic chores as an issue that affected them greatly during the COVID-19 school closure. Related to these chores, the girls mentioned the lack of time to do any schoolwork and requested the support of the SWTs in asking their parents to give them the opportunity to study and also provide them with materials for learning and lighting. Of the SWTs, 57 percent identified heavy domestic chores as a challenge, while 49 percent of LC1 woman representatives did so.

Socioeconomic Factors

Of the girls, 12.5 percent mentioned that they were not able to access learning materials because their parents were unable to provide them. The government has provided revision notes for students and copies of these materials can be found at the subcounty level, but parents or guardians must access these copies and photocopy them for their children. However, the parents or guardians have not done so because they do not have the money for photocopying.

While guidance and counseling from SWTs was, at 91 percent, the most requested, 81 percent of the girls indicated the need for sanitary pads and for support from the SWTs in providing them with skills related to making reusable sanitary pads. More girls requested this materials-based service from the SWTs than any other.

The survey also tried to identify the best possible ways for the SWTs to gain access to the girls, and it emerged that 89 percent of the girls were to be found in places where they supported their family income and livelihood. These jobs included selling wares in shops and at stalls, giving support in gardens, caregiving, and doing domestic chores in the home.

Seventy percent of the girls indicated that they would love the SWTs to regularly visit their homes to advise and speak with their parents so that the latter can understand them better, give them time to revise their schoolwork, and provide them with learning materials and sanitary pads. Of these girls, 67 percent also indicated that they would love to have the SWTs visit them and help them with their studies.

Health Information, Domestic Violence, and Sex-Based Concerns

Of the girls from the peri-urban setting, 59 percent said that the need for adolescent health information and support was the main challenge they were experiencing, while 31 percent of the girls from the peri-urban areas pointed out that they lacked adolescent health information, and 11 percent were faced with domestic violence as a problem. However, none of the girls pointed to either early marriage or sexual harassment as an issue in their communities. However, 20 percent of the LC1 chairpersons cited early marriage and 75 percent cited sexual harassment, stating that they had received several reports of early marriages and defilement of girls in their communities.

Discussion

This study aimed to establish the role of the SWTs in a community setting and to identify the prevailing issues affecting girls during the COVID-19 school closure. This will help identify ways through which the SWTs could continue to support girls' education by providing girls with the services they would otherwise have been accorded at school if not for the closures. Schools have been a haven for all girls, and more so for vulnerable ones given that the government of Uganda has ratified various policies that support and protect children and has put into place the National Strategy for Girls' Education 2014–19 (MoES 2013).[1]

The Ugandan government has suggested that having SWTs is one way of overcoming gender discrimination and helping girls to deal with the challenges related to this. The SWTs were assigned to primary schools and, later, to secondary ones. This was part of the Basic Requirements and Minimum Standards (BRMS) in Education Institutions (MoES 2020) document in Uganda, revised in 2009.[2]

This placement of SWTs is one of the contributing factors to the safety that girls experience in Ugandan schools, which enables them to attend regularly, complete their schooling, and get good examination results. However, as part of coping with the COVID-19 pandemic, Uganda closed schools on 18 March 2020, and six months later, at the time of writing, schools are still closed, as is the case in many other countries. This has created the problem of how to support the girls and protect them from defilement, early pregnancy, and early marriage and ensure that they can return to school when these reopen.

Reports from the Ebola crisis in Liberia in 2014 indicated that girls faced several challenges during the crisis, including early pregnancy and marriage. It was clear that most girls were unlikely to return to school at the end of that crisis. Most of the child protection cases during the COVID-19 pandemic in Uganda are related to child labor, defilement, child marriage, and domestic violence, all of which have a devastating impact on the welfare of children, as reported by Hope Ejang Muzungu (2020).

The government of Uganda used the article "Lessons from Sierra Leone Ebola Pandemic on the Impact of School Closures on Girls" (2020), published by *The Conversation* on 20 May of that year, to guide its policies on girls' safety and education during the lockdown. These policy responses, which prolonged the school break for girls, point to the need for interventions and alternative safe spaces within the community to support pregnant girls to continue their education. For example, interventions could include supporting young women through virtual mentoring or phone-based group chats, or any other feasible group activities that take up time that might otherwise be spent on unproductive activities. Such support could also help girls build and maintain their social networks, enabling them to be more resilient during the crisis.

In stories about COVID-19 narrated by youth from northern Uganda aged between eighteen and twenty-four, Save the Children (2020) found that the youth ended up engaging in risky behavior that led to unwanted pregnancies and child marriages because they were idle and did not have opportunities to participate in social networks, like sports galas, community dialogues, and religious activities.

My study reveals that there are hardly any support systems for girls in the community. The LC1 woman representative was mentioned by the SWTs and girls as the person in the community to whom they turn. However, this position is a political one, introduced in Uganda as part of the affirmative action plan to ensure that women are represented administratively, politically, and financially in society. But the woman representatives have varying levels of education, are from different professions, and have different experiences, so they may not be trained to support girls and may not have time to juggle women's and girls' issues in the community in a way that enables them to deal with both adequately.

The SWT is a dedicated resource who already works with the girls and is trained to guide, counsel, and work with children. The government of Uganda has been able to make some strides in supporting girls, not only through affirmative action but also through laws and regulations that protect them. These structures and regulations are more easily monitored and implemented at school level than in the community. This could be because of local culture and tradition and the lack of a referral and follow-up system in communities similar to the one that exists in the school setting, which makes it a safer place for girls, given the resource of the SWT.

The argument for the work of the SWT in the community is further strengthened by the experience in Sierra Leone, which indicated that over the course of the Ebola epidemic, out-of-wedlock pregnancy rates for girls aged twelve to seventeen increased by 7.2 percent at the onset of the crisis. The report, by Imran Rasul et al. (2020), goes on to state that this was entirely reversed for girls who had had access, prior to the epidemic, to the safe space of one of the girls' clubs. This justifies having the SWTs continue with their roles and provide these clubs in the communities to help ensure that girls continue to be empowered to keep away from the temptation of early marriage and sexual relations that can lead to pregnancy, and in the long run, lead to their dropping out of school.

The girls mentioned the LC1 chairperson as their other support mechanism, but this is a political position and is mainly male dominated. As noted in the research findings, slightly fewer than half of the girls mentioned the person in this position, yet they are the first point of arbitration in the community. The police were not identified by the girls as a resource to whom they could go for help. On inquiry, the girls mentioned that they did not feel they would get any support from the police, and they feared approaching them.

It is not surprising that heavy domestic chores ranked the highest among the girl's challenges, with 66.3 percent of the girls mentioning this. In Uganda, the COVID-19 lockdown coincided with the planting season. Of the respondent girls, 60 percent were from peasant homes that depend on subsistence farming for their livelihood. Children generally make up the labor in small farms. It is not surprising that 55 percent of the 67 percent of girls who mentioned heavy domestic chores as an issue came from peasant homes, since this was an opportune time for parents to take advantage of their children's availability. Family livelihoods have been shaken by the effects of the COVID-19 pandemic and everyone must work doubly hard to ensure the sustainability of these livelihoods. However, heavy domestic chores constitute the price paid by girls.

The survey also tried to identify the best possible way for the SWT to gain access to the girls, and it was found that 89 percent of the girls were in places where they helped support their family income and livelihood. The advantage of finding these girls at their workplaces is that they will be with either their parents or caregivers or their employers, who could then join in the conversations with the SWT. This presents the opportunity for the SWT to advise both the girl and the caregiver or employer about the importance of education and about how these adults can protect the girls and provide them with time to study during the long school break.

The need for the girls to contribute to the family livelihood undermines the need to encourage remote learning; the family considers the latter a luxury because they are not able to afford even the most basic necessities. A report by Joining Forces Coalition (2020) points out the importance of continued learning during this period and goes on to explain that the longer children stay out of school, the higher the risk of their never returning. Girls who are not learning during this period will lag behind their peers when school resumes.

Heavy domestic chores are thus affecting girls during the pandemic. Cultural demands mean that girls and their mothers must fall into prescribed gender roles and perform all the chores in the home, including caregiving to the young and the elderly. The Global Partnership for Education (GPE 2020) reports that especially in rural areas, with their high poverty rates, girls are usually expected to work to increase the family's income. In cases where the family is unable to manage with its meagre income, local tradition dictates that girls be married off in exchange for bride price to help offset financial insecurity.[3]

Having access to adolescent health information is important to the girls in peri-urban settings. This could indicate the higher risks they may be facing, in that they are less engaged in domestic chores and so more easily lured into sexual behavior in exchange for money. The SWTs have been instrumental in providing confidential counseling and guidance in this respect and in telling girls where they can get referrals if they need any help on issues related to sex and adolescent health. Many health centers have been forced to close because of the strict government lockdown. As pointed out by Peer to Peer Uganda (PEERU) (2020), only one or two youth-friendly centers have remained open, and only in the larger urban centers that are far from rural and peri-urban areas. This leaves girls with no one to turn to for the adolescent health information that the SWTs can readily provide.

Being faced with domestic violence was listed as a challenge by 11 percent of the girls. This does not come as a surprise, with so many reports of increasing gender-based violence taking place in homes during the COVID-19 lockdown. Julius Omona (2020) states that people are undergoing stress, fatigue, and depression linked to insecurity and worries about diminishing income, and that this has fueled domestic violence. From 31 March to 14 April 2020, 328 cases of domestic violence were reported to the police nationwide (ibid.).

In relation to the girls' failure to identify the police as one of their referral points in the community, there was no mention of early marriage or sexual harassment as an issue in their submissions. This is surprising because of the increasing number of media reports of defilement and early pregnancy in girls. In the article "191 Defilement Cases Reported in Albertine Region During Lockdown" (2020), the *Independent* reported that the police had raised a red flag over the escalation of defilement cases in this region since COVID-19 struck.

This study provided a clear message from 81 percent of participants that the girls lack sanitary pads and that their parents and guardians are not providing them with any. They were also able to identify the support they usually expected in school from the SWTs, who teach them how to make reusable ones. Girl Up,[4] an NGO in Uganda, recognizes this need and explains the risk that adolescent girls face during COVID-19 regarding accessing menstrual products. Girl Up goes on to explain the dynamics of COVID-19's effect on family income and supply chains around the world, resulting in sanitary pads being more costly and less prioritized by heads of households during the current crisis. The SWT could play a great role in supporting girls by having subcounty and village girls' clubs emulate the clubs in schools, where girls are taught to make reusable sanitary pads (Girl Up n.d.).

Guidance and counseling, both for girls and their parents, is another part that the SWTs can play in their role in the community; 72 percent of the girls indicated that they would love regular visits by the SWTs to their homes, and 67 percent indicated that what they would appreciate about visits by the SWT is that she would be able to bring the girls and their guardians together and go through a variety of issues related to supporting girls, as well as mediate on any issue related to bringing up an adolescent girl that arose.

Agnes's Story

I offer Agnes's story here by way of illustrating the role that an SWT played in a young girl's life.

Agnes is a fifteen-year-old girl in primary 7 who lives in Masaka district with her mother and three siblings in a peasant family that depends on subsistence farming for a living. Like any other teenage girl, Agnes has dreams, and she wants to be a nurse. However, when the COVID-19 pandemic resulted in the closure of all the schools, Agnes's mother took her to Kampala to help her aunt with household chores.

In the house to which Agnes was taken, there was a male visitor who set up a routine of defiling her. When she was asked about him, Agnes said, "I do not know the man and I do not even know his name. I do not know where he came from. He was a visitor in that home, and I could not tell anyone that he was defiling me."

Agnes came back to Masaka to find that school had reopened and that her classmates were in school and preparing to take their primary leaving exams, but Agnes was sick and was then found to be pregnant. The school contacted Agnes's mother and explained to her the importance of having her daughter take the primary leaving examinations. Since Agnes was to give birth before the exams, the school was willing to support her in taking her exams after she had had her baby.

Agnes went through a very difficult labor and gave birth to a healthy baby girl. Unfortunately, after only two days she was unable to manage caring for the baby's umbilical cord and the child bled to death. Agnes, still only a child herself, underwent the kind of trauma through which no young girl should ever have to go. The SWT began making routine visits to Agnes at home and helped her with her studies while providing her with counseling and guidance. The SWT ensured that Agnes was sufficiently stable emotionally and psychologically to take her exams, which she managed to do.

Agnes's mother was her only support system during this hard time, but given the family's limited finances, education, and information, she could only try to support her daughter within the given circumstances of her poverty and illiteracy, which limited her ability to seek justice for her. She also did her best to guide and counsel her daughter as she went through these hard times. Here, the SWT played an important role in supporting the family with information about the laws and referrals for the support for teenage mothers.

Today, Agnes is still traumatized by this experience, but with the continued emotional and psychological support provided by the SWT, she is now awaiting her primary leaving examination results and looking forward to progressing with her education.

Recommendations on How to Engage SWTs in Communities to Support Girls

Using the already-existing structures, the SWT role could easily be supported by the probation and gender offices at district level. Through these offices the SWTs could receive guidance and support as they undertake their roles, and they could get the necessary support and information on training and any supplies available to girls from government and nongovernmental organizations. According to the Uganda Violence against Children in Schools (VACIS) survey conducted by the Ministry of Gender, Labor, and Social Development (2018), the SWT would maintain the reporting procedures and ensure that the most vulnerable girls receive support.

The SWT would work with the existing structures to set up a referral system for any cases of violence against the girls in the community, as recommended in the guidelines for the roles of SWTs (MoES 2020). The LC1 chairperson, police, probation, and gender offices would all be available to support the work of the SWT and would be aware of her roles. By linking up with these referral points the SWT would be able to provide some services to the girls beyond her jurisdiction, for example in instances where a girl is defiled, since this would require immediate intervention by the police.

The SWT, together with the women representative, could set up days on which girls could come to the subcounty headquarters for counseling sessions. There could also be group sessions like the girls' clubs at school where girls can be registered in groups of no more than fifteen to attend sessions on adolescent health, COVID-19, and skills and finance sessions.

Joining Forces Coalition (2020) recommends supporting teacher networks with apps such as WhatsApp and other social media platforms. The article points to the potential of bringing teachers together in virtual groups to share resources and methods for teaching remotely. This could be very helpful to the work of the SWT in the communities. Through social media platforms they could provide connectivity for the girls and set up virtual clubs, provide information, and share learning with them. Their fellow teachers and other staff members, too, could be helped to understand how better to support girls and where to get referrals for different problems experienced by the girls.

The SWTs would not only be serving girls from the schools to which they are attached, but all girls in the community area within their localities, so it is important that each be identified and introduced as the SWT in a specific locality.

Conclusion

The fact that the government has institutionalized the position of the SWT and included it as one of the basic requirements and minimum standards in schools means that every school that has girls at both primary and secondary level is required to have a SWT (MoES 2009). This is an indication that there are at least as many SWTs as there are girls' schools in each village or subcounty. This is a trained workforce with the ability to support girls. Since the SWTs could cover girls from different schools, there will be a need to set up an association to coordinate their efforts under the gender unit of the district local government. The SWT is already part of the VACIS reporting procedure and so can maintain this role in the community to cover all issues affecting girls.

The activities of the SWT in the community could mirror what they have already been doing at school level. This would include offering guidance and counseling, advocacy, adolescent health advice, role modeling, and skills development. However, because of the current lockdown and the fact that students will be at home and in the community, home visits would be needed along with group sessions. Radio and television messaging could be used to reach as many girls as possible. In this way the value of the SWTs would be maximized to the advantage of hundreds of girls.

CHRISTINE APIOT OKUDI (ORCID: 0000-0002-7772-7588) has more than twenty-five years' experience as an educationalist, starting as a secondary school teacher. For the last fifteen years, in support of child development, she has worked with Save the Children Norway, Promoting Equality in African Schools, Bridge International Academies, and Cotton On Foundation in Uganda. She holds a bachelor's degree in Education and a masters in Development Studies, and recently completed a residency at the Brookings Institution focusing on the rights of girls to education. She initiated guidelines for the strengthening of the role of Senior Women Teachers in Uganda.

Notes

1. The National Strategy for Girls Education (NSGE) provides for a national implementation framework, laying out strategies to achieve the goal of narrowing the gender gap in education, and in this way to accord the girl child the right to equal access, an equal chance to take part and share in the education system, and equal educational results and outcomes. The prioritized areas of focus in the NSGE are: an effective policy implementation framework for girls' education; harmonization of education sector programs in this area; commitment of requisite resources to girls education; institutionalized/routine research in this area; and capacity enhancement and involvement for all critical actors in girls' education.
2. In 2001 the MoES issued the Basic Requirements and Minimum Standards Indicators for Education Institutions (BRMS) to schools and other relevant stakeholders to guide the organization and management of educational institutions.
3. According to MIFUMI, an NGO and women's rights agency that worked with Gill Hague and Ravi Thiara (2009), bride price consists of a contract by virtue of which material items (often cattle or other animals) are handed over or money is paid by the groom to the bride's family in exchange for the bride, her labor, and her capacity to produce children. This usually results in girls being married off early, domestic violence, and these girls being reduced to slaves whom the husband and his clan feel they have bought as a labor resource to add to their community.
4. Girl Up Initiative Uganda launched the "COVID-19 Survive and Thrive Fund" to help families in our communities to purchase basic necessities, and important among these were sanitary pads for girls. The schools serve as meeting places for parents and girls to collect supplies, and the Girl Up staff are on hand to talk to girls if they need counseling or support.

References

"191 Defilement Cases Reported in Albertine Region During Lockdown." *Independent*, 4 July. Retrieved 15 September 2022 from https://www.independent.co.ug/191-defilement-cases-reported-in-albertine-region-during-lockdown/.

Girl Up. n.d. "Major Challenges Faced by Our Girls and Young Women During Covid-19." Girl Up Initiative website. Retrieved 15 September 2022 from https://www.girlupuganda.org/covid-19.

GPE (Global Partnership for Education). 2020. *2020 Results Report*. Washington, DC: GPE Transforming Education. Retrieved 15 September 2022 from https://www.globalpartnership.org/sites/default/files/docs/results-report-2020/2020-09-GPE-Results-Report-2020.pdf.

Hague, Gill, and Ravi Thiara, with MIFUMI. 2009. *Bride-Price, Poverty and Domestic Violence in Uganda Final Report*. Retrieved 5 November 2022 from https://www.academia.edu/38542969/Bride_Price_Poverty_and_Domestic_Violence_in_Uganda_Professor_Gill_Hague_Dr_Ravi_Thiara_with_MIFUMI

International Federation of Red Cross and Red Crescent Societies. (2021). 2020 ANNUAL REPORT. Geneva. Retrieved June 7th, 2021, from https://www.ifrc.org/sites/default/files/2021-09/20210902_AnnualReport_ONLINE.pdf.

Joining Forces Coalition. 2020. Keeping Children Safe in Uganda's COVID-19 Response. Kampala: Global Social Service Workforce Alliance. Retrieved 15 September 2022 from http://socialserviceworkforce.org/system/files/resource/files/Keeping-Children-Safe-in-Uganda.pdf.

Katana, Elizabeth, Bob Mod Amodan, Lilian Bulge, Alex R. Ario, Joseph Nelson Siewe Fodjo, Robert Colebunders, and Rhoda K. Wanyenze. 2021. "Violence and Discrimination among Ugandan Residents during Covid-19." *BMC Public Health* 21: 467. https://doi.org/10.1186/s12889-021-10532-2.

"Lessons from Sierra Leone Ebola Pandemic on the Impact of School Closures on Girls." 2020. *The Conversation*, 20 May. Retrieved 15 September 2022 from https://theconversation.com/lessons-from-sierra-leones-ebola-pandemic-on-the-impact-of-school-closures-on-girls-137637.

MGLSD (Ministry of Gender, Labor, and Social Development). 2018. *Uganda Violence against Children in Schools Survey*. Kampala: UNICEF.

MoES (Ministry of Education and Sports). 2009. *Basic Requirements and Minimum Standards Indicators for Education Institutions*. Kampala: MoES. Retrieved 15 September 2022 from http://www.education.go.ug/utsep/wp-content/uploads/2020/03/Final-Copy-BRMS.pdf.

———. 2013. *National Strategy for Girls Education (NSGE) in Uganda 2015–2019*. Kampala: Government of Uganda. Retrieved 5 November 2022 from https://scorecard.prb.org/wp-content/uploads/2018/05/National-Strategy-for-Girls%E2%80%99-Education-in-Uganda-2015-2019.pdf

———. 2017. *Education and Sports Sector Strategic Plan 2017/18–2019/20*. Kampala: Government of Uganda. Retrieved 5 November 2022 from http://npa.go.ug/wp-content/uploads/2018/11/EDUCATION-AND-SPORTS-SECTOR-STRATEGIC-PLAN.pdf.

———. 2020. *Guidelines for the Implementation of the Roles and Responsibilities of the Senior Men and Senior Women Teachers in Uganda*. Kampala: Government of Uganda. Retrieved 15 September 2022 from https://www.ungei.org/sites/default/files/2021-02/Guidelines-Implementation-Roles-Responsibilities-Senior-Teachers-Uganda-2020-eng.pdf.

Muzungu, Hope Ejang. 2020. "A Matter of Life and Death: A Case of the Uganda Child Helpline; An Essential Service during COVID-19." *UNICEF*,

12 May. Retrieved 15 September 2022 from https://www.unicef.org/uganda/stories/matter-life-and-death-case-uganda-child-helpline.

Okudi, Christine Apiot. 2016. "Policies for Senior Women Teachers to Improve Girls' Secondary Education." *Brookings*, 2 December. Retrieved 15 September 2022 from https://www.brookings.edu/research/policies-for-senior-women-teachers-to-improve-girls-secondary-education/.

Omona, Julius. 2020. "COVID-19 and Domestic Violence in Uganda." International Society for Third-Sector Research (ISTR). Retrieved 15 September 2022 from https://www.istr.org/blogpost/1851131/348623/COVID-19-and-Domestic-Violence-in-Uganda.

PEERU (Peer to Peer Uganda). 2020. "Youth Impact and Response to COVID-19 in Uganda." 18 May. Retrieved 15 September 2022 from https://peertopeeruganda.org/youth-impact-and-response-to-covid-19-in-uganda/.

Rasul, Imran, Andrea Smurra, and Oriana Bandiera. 2020. "Lessons from Sierra Leone's Ebola Pandemic on the Impact of School Closures on Girls." *The Conversation*, May 20. Retrieved 5 November 2022 from https://theconversation.com/lessons-from-sierra-leones-ebola-pandemic-on-the-impact-of-school-closures-on-girls-137837.

Save the Children. 2020. "Uganda Youth Speak out on the Impact of COVID-19." *reliefweb*, 15 May. Retrieved 15 September 2022 from https://reliefweb.int/report/uganda/ugandan-youth-speak-out-impact-covid-19.

CHAPTER 5
Experiencing Care
Young Women's Response to COVID-19 Crises in Poland

Anna Bednarczyk, Zuzanna Kapciak, Kinga Madejczak, Alicja Sędzikowska, Natalia Witek, and Faustyna Zdziarska

> Remember, care is a dimension of love,
> but simply giving care does not mean we are loving.
>
> —bell hooks, *All about Love*

Introduction

In this chapter, we aim to document and explore, as a case study, a grassroots initiative based on the concept of care that we founded during the pandemic in Poland. As five female sociology students, we created Dinners in the Time of Pandemic to facilitate supporting people in urgent need of food by connecting them with individuals who were willing to share their supplies. We seek to facilitate collaborative knowledge production so that, as coauthors and as creators of this initiative, we can contribute to sociological reflection on the pandemic. We discussed the experiences of going through the pandemic, gathered individual narratives, and decided to use the concept of care as our analytical tool. Following Sarah Wall (2008), we were inspired by autoethnography as a research method because it allows us to reflect on our own experience. From the start, we would like to underline that Dinners in the Time of Pandemic had been operating for only four months at the time of writing, with almost three of these spent in self-isolation, with us communicating only through social media. This chapter constitutes our first attempt to structure our experience of building a grassroots initiative and is also an account of how we adapted to the new reality. It is a case study of this particular initiative in a very particular time frame. These first months of the pandemic were marked by uncertainty but also an intense wave of mobilization. During this time of *doing*, it was important to document and reflect on what was happening on the local level with the COVID-19 pandemic, but also on the global level. As mentioned above, this chapter was inspired by the notion of autoethnography. However, because of the extreme time limitation, lack of personal contact, and the high level of commitment to the work of the initiative, we decided to frame the analysis of Dinners in the Time of Pandemic as a case study. An autoethnography would have required engagement in a much longer research process with more space for reflecting on and presenting a critical approach to the group dynamic, care practices, and interactions with the local environment. With the framing of a case study, we began by reconstructing the origin of the initiative in the political context of Poland. Then we analyzed two levels of narrative—the collective and the individual—about Dinners in the Time of Pandemic so that our case could be seen as a collective entity and an individual experience connected to each other by the concept of care.

We elaborate on the theoretical framework of care in the first part of this chapter. In the second, we present, briefly, the context of Poland, focusing on the actions the government took during the pandemic. In the third section, we present our multivoiced narrative about the initiative. The data was gathered during two online group meetings and four individual interviews with the cofounders of the initiative.

The Framework of Care: An Initiative Led by Young Women

The concept of care we are using is characterized by the two features of voluntarism and reciprocity. It distinguishes this concept from the practices of care forced upon women by the gender-based division of labor. The capitalist system inherently benefits from the unpaid care work of women (Federici 1975, 2012; Fraser 2013; Titkow et al. 2004). The neoliberal system has had an effect on care. For Victoria Lawson,

> Under neoliberal principles, care is a private affair, occurring in homes and families. In the privatization of care, we construct certain sorts of people as in need of care—the infirm, the young/elderly, the dependent, the flawed—ignoring the fact that we, all of us, give and need care. (2008: 3)

We follow Berenice Fisher and Joan Tronto's theory of care and define it as a social process that "speaks ultimately to our survival as a species rather than isolated individuals" (1990: 40). We use the notion of care as a concept focused on the process and on interactions with the involved actors rather than the actors themselves. Care as a process involves the following components: caring about; taking care of; caregiving; and care-receiving (Fisher and Tronto 1990).

The process of care starts with the caring about that is a stage of becoming preoccupied with the needs of others and formulating a caring approach on the level of thoughts and attitudes. In the case of the initiative Dinners in the Time of Pandemic, we, the second and subsequent authors of this chapter, started to worry about the potential effects of the pandemic on society. Our attitude toward the issue was formed; we cared about what would happen with people who were most affected by the lockdown. As the situation was developing and the imagined concerns were becoming factual with the introduction of protective measures, obligatory quarantine, social distancing, and massive layoffs, the process of care transformed into the next stage, that of taking care of. Individually, we all searched for what could be done and decided to set up our own initiative to address the problem of food shortages. What Fisher and Tronto (1990) called caregiving is an act of care that uses available resources to sustain or improve a situation. For Dinners in the Time of Pandemic, this caregiving was the facilitation and organization of food deliveries in the first months of the pandemic. Currently, these acts of care have expanded to supporting people in the search for jobs. The recipients of this care are positioned in the last stage of the process of care, which is care-receiving.

The framework of the process of care was later expanded by Tronto (2013) to include the stage of caring that touches on the relationship between democracy and care. She writes, "This final phase of care requires that caring needs and the ways in which they are met need to be consistent with democratic commitments to justice, equality, and freedom for all" (ibid.).

In the relatively short time of our activities, we reflected on the state of care in the democratic system and addressed this in our discussions and interviews. We noticed how unprepared Polish public institutions were, and we also noted that asking for help is linked to feeling shame and even to humiliation. We saw evidence of how mutually caring communities have become scarce under the capitalist system.

The Context of Poland

The initiative Dinners in the Time of Pandemic emerged in a very particular political context in Poland. Since 2015 Poland has been ruled by the national-conservative party, Law and Justice, which holds a majority in Parliament. In the 2019 election, it received the highest popular vote since the system's transformation in 1989. The first cases of COVID-19 were detected in early March 2020 and the pandemic state was officially introduced on 20 March of that year. The series of events that occurred afterward are illustrative of Law and Justice governance. The pandemic completely disrupted the presidential campaign and the election that fell on 10 May 2020. The party's president, Andrzej Duda, was a front-runner for reelection when his popularity started to decrease as the pandemic slowly exposed how underfinanced, unprepared, and lacking in supplies Polish healthcare was. Not wanting to lose any more supporters, Law and Justice avoided declaring and delayed introducing the state of natural disaster that would postpone the election date. Instead, they proposed prolonging the current presidential term for two years or organizing voting by post. The public health crisis was overshadowed by political games. Finally, just three days before the date that was originally selected, the election was postponed until 28 June.

In addition to this, the government used this time of national crisis to focus attention on the planned reform aimed at restricting women's and girls' reproductive rights. Poland has one of the strictest abortion laws in the European Union. Abortion is illegal except in cases of rape, when pregnancy presents a threat to the women's life, or if the fetus is irrepa-

Figure 5.1. The slogan Women's Hell on a street in Krakow refers to the attempt during the pandemic by the Polish government to restrict reproductive rights. Photograph: Alicja Sędzikowska.

rably damaged. Since 2016 the Law and Justice government has pushed for removing the third clause. This would result in almost completely restricting a woman's or a girl's right to an abortion (see Figure 5.1). Besides restricting women's rights, the current government has been developing an anti-LGBTQ+ public discourse that intensified during the presidential campaign coinciding with the beginning of the pandemic and resulted in a significant increase in homophobia.

The concerns about the political situation in Poland were evident in an interview with Alicja, conducted by the first author. She said,

> I am afraid of [the] elections, that Duda will win, the reelection will bring aggression, division, we are worried about LGBT+ people. I don't want to out anyone but there are many people in the initiative from the LGBT+ community and the fact [that] they face more discrimination is worrying for us. There was the photo [taken] of a sign on a wall that said "fuck LGBT" with the arrows pointing at someone's window. There were people beaten up in front of the LGBT-friendly club [that] was not even a gay club. Lately, there were girls from the climate strike beaten up as well. They were at the campaign rally [for] Duda. I talked with one of these girls and she was under the impression that when she was being pushed Duda looked at her and he did not react. I am afraid of aggression, calling some people not Polish, I am afraid of people I love and care about.

We Are the Initiative: The Collective Narrative

The initiative Dinners in the Time of Pandemic began on 1 April 2020 at the Institution of Sociology at the Jagiellonian University in Krakow. Following the decision of the rector, all classes at the Institute of Sociology were moved online on 25 March. Inspired by the various social initiatives emerging across Poland and with the support of the leading professor, a group of students in the Introduction to Feminism classes set up an online group called Visible Hand-Sociology. The group aimed to gather information on the current situation of the students at the Institute of Sociology and to search for ways to help them. Alicja put out an announcement about setting up an initiative that would connect people in urgent need of food with those willing to help. She recalls the origin of this idea.

> I was reading posts on this grassroots-helping group for Krakow citizens on Facebook and I noticed posts that someone lost their job, and they were asking for food. Very unpleasant comments started to appear as a response, asking how it was possible that the person could not afford food. I thought it would be great if there was a group where those people [could] announce their needs and I could just watch over it so there [was] no hate.

She was immediately joined by four other girls, Zuzanna, Kinga, Natalia, and Faustyna, her fellow authors from the Introduction to Feminism class, and they set up a Facebook group to facilitate food delivery for those affected by the lockdown.

It is crucial here to acknowledge the role of the gender studies professor, since all the core members of the initiative were aware of and appreciated her caring approach during the lockdown. What might be called a chain of care was set in motion. The professor redesigned the classes by prioritizing the well-being of the students and giving them time to process the lockdown. Then students used this space and created their own initiative and started acting outside the university. Zuzanna explained,

> The professor really cares about us, when she did the first online classes with us we did not talk about the course content, she asked everyone how they feel, in what condition we are, if we have any strength, and what we can do for each other to support each other. Then, I don't remember exactly who, [someone] came up with the idea to start a support group for sociology students, and we did, and it is cool.

Alicja added,

> Thanks to the professor this support group was created because she knew that we are dispersed, at family homes that sometimes can be hostile, that we lost the support from the university and we feel detached, so this support group was supposed to be a prototype of the community and the initiative Dinners in the Time of Pandemic also became a community. And I think it helped us much more than it helped Krakow in general. We had an opportunity to meet many of the first-year students who then joined us.

Faustyna said,

> I joined the team of Dinners in the Time of Pandemic one week after Alicja started it. At the beginning of April, when coronavirus was spreading more rapidly, I was looking for a place for myself among many initiatives that started emerging. I wanted to feel needed, [make] a contribution to the community. I liked Alicja's idea because other support groups were focused on shopping for someone or walking a dog for people in quarantine or in groups at risk. It seems no one thought about the problems generated by losing a job because of coronavirus. After all, losing a job means losing income. Lack of income means using savings and thinking of what expenses can be cut? How can one survive on lower costs? You can try but it cannot be done forever. At some point, hunger will appear. And it did in many families—in Krakow and other places.

From the beginning, the initiative developed rapidly; at its highest point it gained between two hundred and three hundred members per day, made up of people willing to help and those in need, as well as drivers who connected both sides. At the time of writing, there are 1,100 people using the Facebook group and approximately 30 acting in operative and administrative activities. As is clear in the collective narrative about the initiative's trajectories that we go on to offer, the constant themes are the relations between us and reflection on the leadership style. This initiative carried the huge potential of defining feminist self-organizing and practicing more inclusive leadership. We were dealing with extraordinary circumstances in confronting the urgent needs of people who asked for support, coordinating food deliveries, and, equally importantly, dealing with online studying. In such a demanding context it was a challenge not to fall into a vertical, leader-centered decision-making structure. Given that we started studying sociology only recently, it is interesting to revisit our auto-reflection on this topic. Alicja, as an initiator of Dinners in the Time of Pandemic, noticed how difficult it was to coordinate a group in a nonhierarchical way. She said,

> We were never in favor of, like, a hierarchical structure but somehow it happened on its own. I think I have always had this characteristic that I talk, and I think it happened naturally. I am often worried that I am bossy or dominating,

but I asked the others a million times if I should "manage" and the feedback was that if I didn't do it nothing would happen. Maybe it is because we are taught from kindergarten that there is somebody above us and now we cannot act in groups. On Mondays, we have meetings to vent about or talk through all the issues. We did not have these meetings at the beginning, but we are very overstretched by this work [that] affects your mental health, that is why I came up with the idea to have such a meeting, then I got feedback that there is a need to discuss issues regularly and we set up one day. When it comes to the mental burden, I had to organize the psychologist [who] offers support once a week. As far as I know not everybody is using her service but sometimes she is needed, sometimes there are situations in the group that we cannot solve and she helps.

Since the initiative is slowly moving toward formalization, we will need to do further research on how it is going to transform from this grassroots initiative led by young women into a formalized nongovernmental entity. The narrative about the initiative's horizontal and collective character has been the subject of conversations with other core members from the start. Alicja explained,

> At the very beginning, the initiative was not structured, and even though our legal status is still not regulated, we are a thriving, hardworking team where everyone has her/his role. There is no hierarchy, we [listen] to each other and [treat] each other on the basis of partnership. As Dinners in the Time of Pandemic, we are one organism.

Zuzanna said,

> There is one thing I always underline; we, the girls, are doing a lot but we are not doing it alone and we always depend on others, and it is awesome that we can organize as a society. I always put attention on that because I am very grateful that there are people who want to do this.

Natalia added,

> I would mention how big the support [of the] team is for each other. The community was created, the group of people who share not only the joy and difficulties of working in Dinners in the Time of Pandemic, but the initiative is open for discussion about literally every topic. In times when group meetings are threats, something like that can save your life.

Individual Histories

As much as the initiative has become a space for testing community-building and care practices, each of the girls spent the lockdown resulting from the pandemic physically isolated.

Figure 5.2. The slogan #stayhome on the sidewalk in Krakow. Photograph: Alicja Sędzikowska.

Some of us went back to our family homes and just a few stayed in Krakow in rented apartments. As part of the explorative nature of this chapter, we tried to analyze how experiences of this pandemic and having acted in a grassroots initiative translated into the practices of care. The topic that occurred in most of our conversations was mental health. The initiative Dinners in the Time of Pandemic cooperates with the above-mentioned psychologist, who is willing to support us on an individual basis. Nevertheless, the stress and anxieties related to losing a job, coming back to a toxic family environment, or even handling the exam sessions had a huge impact on the mental health of some of us. So we decided to share personal stories together with accounts of the role the initiative played in keeping us in balance at that time.

For Zuzanna,

> Well now I will go into a tough topic, I mean I am in a comfortable situation because the financial situation of my family is ok, but, so to speak, emotionally it is not easy. During this pandemic I am focusing on surviving with my parents, sometimes I completely forget that there is a pandemic because I have trouble with my stepdad, and I am focusing on not escalating the conflict. I am very happy that the initiative happened because I have a commitment and it helps me function.

Natalia said,

> I felt extremely isolated, it was more difficult for me than the fear [of] being infected. But taking into consideration my partners' health I knew I [could not] leave isolation. My support was my family and my best friend. I can honestly say that if not for the isolation I would not have met a person I am very close with. I knew that it was a privilege to stay at home and not worry about food or income. I felt obligated to do something. And the initiative gave me this opportunity.

Alicja said,

> The pandemic has a good side for me. What had stopped me from going to a psychologist before, not only being under pharmacological treatment, was a financial barrier. I tried the therapy offered by the public health system, but it was so bad that my problems only got worse. So, I found my current psychologist because she offered help for people who hit a rough stretch during the pandemic, she offered a few sessions for free. Later on, when she found out about my financial situation, she offered me therapy for half price. It was a huge relief for me because normally I could not afford it. I started therapy with her, and she recently told me that I have started recovering. I feel stronger.

One of us reported,

> Additionally, lately I feel worse, for eight months I have been with my depression in the care of a psychiatrist and now I am going through a more difficult time when it is hard for me to find a new meaning in activities, it is hard to fight off the waves of thoughts about the magnitude of suffering that is in the world, it is hard to feel myself in all of that.

There is an interesting juxtaposition of struggling with personal mental health challenges and building a grassroots initiative. Self-care is intertwined with care about the community, which makes these modes of caring complementary. In the Polish context, coming forward with mental health challenges is still rare, but this group of girls made the issue visible, starting with involving the psychologist who supports the group and its members in sharing the stories of their personal struggles. The group strives to care about each other while building a support system for people affected by the pandemic. In this context, care has a multilayered character, from self-care and care in the informal group to taking care of others. In the process of reflecting on the personal stories we also pose a question about the relationship between care and feminism. Although the call to join the initiative was posted on the general group of sociology students at the Institute of Sociology, the core group members were students in the Introduction to Feminism class. As mentioned above, the professor leading this course expressed care for her students. We could see the sensitivity to gender equality along with the formation of a feminist identity going beyond the university course. Two of the girls decided to share their experiences. Zuzanna said,

> I always felt/defined myself as a feminist but I didn't have basic knowledge so I decided that this course would [be] a basis for developing my knowledge. In addition, the course is taught by this professor, so it was obvious that it [was] going to [be] an awesome course. My parents do not have progressive political beliefs, we rarely speak about politics. I have built my beliefs by searching the internet and reading what other people wrote. To be honest I cannot point [to] one moment when I became a feminist, but I think in high school I already called myself a feminist. I had a really cool class in high school because all girls were feminists, most of the class was leftist, and even our teachers took part in [the] Black Protest [protests against restricting reproductive rights in 2015] with us in R. [a midsize Polish city].

Alicja said,

> The first thing I organized was a Gothic clothes market, but it was more capitalist than charitable. In general, I did everything on my own, now this initiative is the first time I do something in a group. Before I also organize[d] a campaign, Draw Vagina, it was a feminist campaign teaching about the female body. Unfortunately, our sexual education is very poor. So, I always acted alone and now this task of managing people is new for me, I was never part of students' governments or things like that, that is why I often ask people about feedback [on] whether I am not too much. I think [some] classes had an impact, the professors put a lot of attention on group work. During both courses, Introduction to Feminism and Climate Crises, we talked a lot about what we can do as a community, as a group. We talked about sisterhood, what comes from mutual support. I think these classes made me realize that I am not alone. I started to listen to others, it was a novelty for me, I started to listen to what other people have to say. Studying has changed me a lot.

She added,

> Feminism is different in each country, feminism in Poland can be also divided into groups. There are middle-class women fighting for reproductive rights, but they don't see other issues. We should not be dividing ourselves. In our group we try to cooperate. My generation stopped believing in public institutions like my mother's generation. We are starting institutions from the ground.

Groups Supported by the Initiative

This chapter has revolved around the experiences of young women, but the groups it supports are at the core of the initiative. This is why we go on to outline the main challenges we have been encountering since the beginning of the initiative.

Alicja explained,

> I know that people wait for seven to eight weeks for help from the state. They go to social services in the city saying they have nothing to eat and they are told to wait seven weeks. They have to wait for our help for around two weeks and I feel remorse. Those who had experiences with social services are taught to say everything about themselves right away, even their worse sides and how bad their situation is so that someone pays attention. So, we get to know at the beginning about all the illnesses, histories about partners abandoning mothers with children, lost jobs. Usually, it is like an entire essay in the first message. I want to make it clear that this is not our only target group. Our target group also spread to people who cannot find support from family (for various reasons) or from their friends, because they are in a similar situation and cannot share food or offer a bed.

Natalia said,

> The big challenge is the relation[ship] between the help coordinator and the help receiver. It happened a few times that the supported person emotionally blackmailed the coordinator, talking about attachment or sharing very personal stories. It is very difficult because we are not trained as social workers, so we don't know how to approach [this] and we are also prone to a lot of stress. My main motivation is the hope that a few days after getting the food the situation will be better and they can focus on searching for a job, not worrying about food.

She went on to say,

> What really moved me in this cooperation is [the] enormous gratitude for help but also [the] timidity when they have to remind us that another food package is needed because when you have six people in the family the supplies shrink at an alarming pace.

The initiative operates between two groups of people: those who need support and those who offer support. The supporters emerged at the beginning of lockdown. When they realized their privilege of working from home and having a regular income, they started to look for organizations they could support. As one of the girls recalls, Dinners in the Time of Pandemic was set up to facilitate systems of neighborhood assistance, but in the context of strict safety measurements this became a complicated task.

Faustyna explained,

> At the beginning, we were just five coordinators. When I joined the team I recruited some volunteers. With time the demand for more members was grow-

ing, more and more people in need were contacting us. And then the logistic challenges emerged. There were more people willing to help in districts where we did not have many people in need. So, we had to figure out the way of transporting the food supplies from one end of Krakow to the other, [which] was really difficult under the lockdown because we didn't want to put anyone at risk by using public transportation. That is how the idea to form a group of drivers was born, they are volunteers who deliver food from donors to people in need. As a matter of fact, our activities have been developing with time, and with time we figure out where we should put more attention.

Alicja added,

After a month and a half of our activities we were contacted by a woman who works in HR and she asked if she could help us and it started to make sense, that we could help with a job search. We had a few meetings with the HR group, that consists of three people, and we [thought] about how to help. We decided we wanted to give people autonomy in job searching. We noticed that it does not make much sense to send them particular job offers, we rather help them to look for good websites or mobile applications where they search for a job. The HR group helps with writing a cover letter or even an email, it is not so easy for everyone.

The majority of people who are donating are in their forties, often have children on their profile pictures on Facebook, 90 percent are women, men rarely engage. By the photos we can say they are middle-class, they are not from poor districts. Recently one of our donors organized an action in her local shop. She left the box for people to donate food, with information about our initiative. She did it twice and it was a huge success. Now we are thinking about how to expand this action because some people don't want to do shopping anymore, so we want to ask in [a] local chain of grocery shops if we can place boxes for donations there.

The three cases described above put into perspective how the initiative operates. It creates a space for testing different ideas, which come not only from the core members and coordinators but also from the donors and recipients of support. We want to adapt the initiative to the post-pandemic reality. Even though Dinners in the Time of Pandemic emerged as a response to the crisis, we want to continue our work. We are going to face more structural issues going beyond day-to-day neighborhood assistance.

Conclusion

We mentioned at the beginning that this chapter is a space for us—young, female undergraduate students of sociology and a postgraduate student researching feminist activism in cities—to explore our experiences of the pandemic. It is a sort of experimental academic text in which our narrative is at the center, and which builds on the concept of care. Putting our experiences into this theoretical framework resulted in a few conclusions.

First, the pandemic made visible the academic community's role in providing care for students, not only in the form of financial and emotional support but also in teaching responsible responses to social crises. In the case of the Institute of Sociology, only a few professors accommodated themselves to the challenging teaching context, and these classes were a starting point for self-organizing.

Second, the social effects of lockdown redefined the sources of support and care in people's lives. In many cases, the traditional family was not a safe space in which to seek shelter, nor could it provide the necessary resources. Dinners in the Time of Pandemic tried to reach beyond the division between care provided in the private sphere and care provided by state institutions.

The third important conclusion concerns the impact of the pandemic on our mental health and that of young women generally. The members of the initiative faced a huge amount of stress and anxiety, and they underlined on multiple occasions how important the mutual care within the initiative was. They also shared their experiences of seeking professional mental healthcare. We know that self-care is a crucial element of collective care, not only in terms of an individual's well-being but also in relation to the initiative as a whole.

Anna Bednarczyk is a PhD student researching feminist activism in cities. Zuzanna Kapciak, Kinga Madejczak, Alicja Sędzikowska, Natalia Witek, and Faustyna Zdziarska are students in the first and second years of BA programs in sociology. They are the initiators of the grassroots organization Dinners in the Time of Pandemic.

References

Federici, Silvia. 1975. *Wages against Housework*. Bristol: Falling Wall Press.
———. 2012. *Revolution at Point Zero: Housework, Reproduction, and Feminist Struggle*. Oakland, CA: PM Press.
Fraser, Nancy. 2013. Fortunes of Feminism: From State-Managed Capitalism to Neoliberal Crisis. Brooklyn, NY: Verso Books.

Fisher, Berenice, and Joan Tronto. 1990. "Toward a Feminist Theory of Caring." In *Circles of Care: Work and Identity in Women's Lives*, ed. E. K. Abel and M. K. Nelson, 35–62. Albany, NY: State University of New York Press.

hooks, bell. 2000. *All about Love: New Visions*. New York: HarperCollins.

Lawson, Victoria. 2007. "Geographies of Care and Responsibility." *Annals of the Association of American Geographers* 97(1): 1–11. https://doi.org/10.1111/j.14 67-8306.2007.00520.x.

Titkow, Anna, Danuta Duch-Krzystoszek, and Bogusława Budrowska. 2004. *Women's Unpaid Labour: Myths, Reality, Perspectives*. [In Polish.] Warsaw: IFIS PAN.

Tronto, Joan. 2013. *Caring Democracy: Markets, Equality, and Justice*. New York: New York University Press.

Wall, Sarah. 2008. "Easier Said Than Done: Writing an Autoethnography." *International Journal of Quantitative Methods* 7(1): 38–53. https://doi.org/10.|1 177/160940690800700103.

Chapter 6

COVID-19, Education, and Well-Being
Experiences of Female Agriculture Students in Ethiopia

Hannah Pugh, Eleni Negash,
Frehiwot Tesfaye, and Madalyn Nielsen

Introduction

The purpose of this study was to gain insight into gender-specific challenges facing female students during the pandemic and to provide sound recommendations for change to improve their situation. We thought that this information might also be useful in future pandemics or similar events that necessitate home-based learning. Research questions included "What are the social effects that the COVID-19 pandemic has on young women studying at agriculture, technical, vocational, education, and training (ATVET) colleges in rural Ethiopia?" and "What are the effects on education that the COVID-19 pandemic has on young women studying at ATVET colleges in rural Ethiopia?"

The COVID-19 pandemic has had a significant impact on the health and well-being of people around the world (Gilbert et al. 2020). In Ethiopia, the first case of COVID-19 was diagnosed on 13 March 2020. The government of Ethiopia implemented various measures including a five-month state of emergency, border closures, and periods of mandatory quarantine. Large institutions were closed, meetings were prohibited, and physical distancing measures were imposed.

On 16 March 2020, four agriculture, technical, vocational, education, and training (ATVET) colleges, where many female students between the ages of seventeen and twenty-eight are enrolled, closed under federal government mandate and all the students were sent home. At the time of writing, staff members have had no contact with them since the onset of the pandemic, and colleges are unlikely to open fully until March 2021 at the earliest. This raises concerns about the effects of pandemic closures on the daily lives, well-being, and access to education of female students.

As Jewel Gausman and Ana Langer (2020: 466) note, "It is urgent that we adopt a gender lens to study the pandemic and its effects . . . This may be especially important in disadvantaged populations and resource-poor communities, where women are especially vulnerable." This is, of course, timely and relevant since women and girls in Africa are considered to be among the most vulnerable to the effects of this pandemic (Chuku et al. 2020). In addition to health impacts, COVID-19 is having serious socioeconomic consequences that disproportionately affect women, youth, and people employed in the agriculture sector (United Nations Ethiopia 2020).

While confined to their homes, many of these women are without access to the internet, as Alemayehu Geda (2020) reminds us. This restricts their ability to continue their education, makes them feel even more isolated, and may increase their vulnerability to sex- and gender-based violence (SGBV). It is evident that further research linking pandemics to an increase in violence against women in Ethiopia is needed (Peterman et al. 2020; United Nations Ethiopia 2020). As Tilahun Mengistie (2020) points out, attempts to continue education for students at home have been limited, sporadic, and focused mainly on students in the university sector who live in urban environments.

Ethiopia offers a unique situation given that over 69 percent of the population is under twenty-nine years of age (WHO n.d.). This means that the disruption of the routine of daily instruction, and of the general momentum of education, is likely to affect the well-being of many young people enrolled in post-secondary studies. Effects include depression, anxiety, and an overall decrease in their current quality of life (Kaparounaki et al. 2020). Although most of the international research findings in this area are from Europe and Asia, mental health effects from this pandemic are expected to be significant among higher education students in Ethiopia (Negash et al. 2020) and further research in this area is vital if we are to provide evidence that increased interventions and policy changes at government level are needed.

Methodology

In this study, we interviewed female students from four ATVET colleges in rural Ethiopia. These are supported by the Agricultural Transformation through Stronger Vocational Education (ATTSVE) project, which is funded by Global Affairs Canada and led by Dalhousie University and partner organizations and was designed to develop agricultural education at four ATVET colleges across Ethiopia to ensure that students and graduates are equipped with competencies to support Ethiopia's policy priority to shift from subsistence to market-based agriculture. The ATTSVE project, through a gender mainstreaming approach, established and initially funded gender offices at each college. These provided a range of services including counseling, mentoring, training, day-care centers, and small financial grants to needy female students to ensure that they could continue with their education and afford food and sanitary supplies. We were interested in the views of these female students on how the COVID-19 pandemic has changed their daily lives, affected their overall well-being, and affected their access to education and other resources. Semi-structured interviews were conducted using a list of thirteen predetermined open questions.

Study Population

The study population for this research was made up of young women students at four ATVET colleges in Ethiopia that, as mentioned above, are supported by the ATTSVE development project. The colleges supported are Maichew in the Tigray region, Nejo in Oromia, Woreta in the Amhara region, and Wolaita Soddo in the Southern Nations Nationalities and Peoples' Region (SNNPR). This spread represents the four major regions of Ethiopia and includes rural and semi-urban students. The four colleges then had 3,095 full-time students in total, of whom 38 percent were female, so this sample represents 2.4 percent of the female student population pre-COVID. All these students are now living in their family homes with one parent or two, one or more siblings, and, in many cases, additional extended family members.

As research team members, we selected, from student lists, twenty-eight participants who then had cell phone access in their homes; this was the only way of contacting students given the COVID-19 restrictions, since the majority do not have access to the internet. Although twenty-eight female students between the ages of eighteen and twenty-seven were interviewed, for the purposes of this chapter, given its focus on girls' experiences, only the twenty-two interviews with students between eighteen and twenty-one have been used. We also thought it important to use the input of students based in both rural and semi-urban areas so as to represent both geographical categories.

Ethical Considerations

There were several ethical considerations that influenced the direction of this research, including some concern about using college and, in particular, project staff to conduct the interviews. It could have been argued that students might feel coerced into participating, since their refusal to do so might affect their being provided with services from the ATTSVE project or by the gender-focal staff, lecturers who in addition to their teaching responsibilities, are responsible for coordinating and managing gender-related issues on campus, when they return to the colleges post-COVID-19. However, the available interviewers were limited because of language barriers and COVID-19 restrictions. A discussion in the preliminary call with students about the different roles played by the providers of project services and by the researchers attempted to mitigate any power imbalances between students and interviewers.

As a mixed group of researchers from the Global South and Global North and from different socioeconomic backgrounds, we considered our own feminist positionality in relation to different cultural imperatives, such as gendered norms, as well as evaluator assumptions and biases, as we designed the questions and interpreted the data in the social and cultural context of the study. This involved detailed discussion among all four of us as researchers when we coded the results to ensure that the data was being interpreted without cultural bias.

Data Collection

Each student was given a preliminary call to check that she was interested. Following the Dalhousie Research Ethics Board Approval process, participants were asked to provide verbal consent to their participation in the study. Since there are many different local languages spoken across the sample population, college interviewers were given informal training by researchers to cover the aims of the study, to provide interview techniques, and to discuss ethical issues.

Semi-structured interviews were then conducted over the phone; these lasted between thirty and forty-five minutes and used a predetermined list of open-ended questions intended to encourage lengthy answers that would provide detailed qualitative information and allow the researchers to seek clarification when necessary.

Changed Scope

An important initial aim of the study was to identify whether female students were experiencing increased SGBV as a consequence of the pandemic, as is happening in many countries (United Nations Ethiopia 2020). However, we were concerned about discomforting students or putting them at additional risk by asking such questions, since during the isolation period they were likely to lack privacy during the interview calls, being, as they were, in small homes with other family members present. Therefore, we changed the focus to asking students about their general well-being and giving them the opportunity to direct their responses as openly as possible (see the third question below).

Key Qualitative Questions

The main qualitative questions asked were as follows:

> What are the effects of the COVID-19 pandemic on your daily life?
> How is COVID-19 impacting your education?
> How has COVID-19 impacted your overall well-being (health, safety, comfort)?
> Are you looking forward to returning to your ATVET education?

In addition, one quantitative question was asked: What do you miss about being at the ATVET college? Interviewees were given a range of responses from which to choose; we list these below in our discussion of the replies to this question. This gathering of quantifiable data was designed to draw some measurable conclusions to complement or contrast with the qualitative data.

Ten interviews were conducted in the Ethiopian national language, Amharic, by the team of researchers. The remaining interviews were conducted by gender-focal officers from the colleges in their local languages, and the transcripts were then translated by the researchers into English. The translations were carried out by two members of the research team based in Ethiopia and known to the Canadian members of the team as being competent to do this. Transcripts were reviewed by the researchers as a group and any that were particularly difficult to understand were discussed.

Data Analysis

All interviews were transcribed and translated into English. Although researchers had some deductive ideas that influenced their broad areas of interest in the study and the interview questions, inductive coding was used to ensure that themes emerging from the research came as directly from the findings as possible, even though this is more complicated when one is using translated transcripts. A first round of open coding followed by some focused coding allowed us to narrow down the themes emerging from the responses. These were validated through discussion among all of us to ensure that findings were not lost in translation. We also conducted a small statistical analysis to calculate percentages of quantitative responses about the main things that students missed from before the pandemic struck and the main challenges they have faced during the pandemic.

We used comparative analysis to determine whether female experiences were different between regions and colleges or between rural and semi-urban students.

Findings and Discussion

Most students interviewed experienced significant negative changes to their daily lives. We recognize that our research does not reflect the experiences and views of all female college students in Ethiopia, but it does give us detailed insight into gender-specific challenges that some female students are facing during the pandemic. It also provides us with sound recommendations for change as the worsening pandemic affects teaching and learning in the country.

What Are the Effects of the COVID-19 Pandemic on Your Daily Life?

Most students experienced increased responsibilities in relation to supporting family businesses or contributing to household labor (or both). One student assisted her sister with her community cafeteria business as an essential service. While some students interviewed were working externally during the COVID-19 pandemic as agricultural laborers, maids, or cleaners, many others faced economic hardship, since most students normally have to work both while at college and during vacations to earn enough to stay at college. Many could not work because of the government directive to stay at home, the lack of employment, workplace closures or reductions, and, for some, the fear of leaving their homes.

One participant noted that the cost of living had increased, and it was more difficult for her and her family to pay rent. It was also mentioned that the cost of goods and public transportation had increased significantly in Ethiopia since the pandemic was declared, with general inflation rising at that time by 23 percent and food inflation by 26 percent (Geda 2020). It was clear to us that financial concerns were significant for many study participants.

In Ethiopia, female representation in the labor force is unequal, with 68.5 percent of employed women working as unpaid family workers and 24.8 percent in informal jobs. Consequently, women and girls face a larger informal care burden in the household compared to their male family members or male partners (UN 2013).

Students reported that before COVID-19, living on campus freed them from the household labor they were expected to do while at home, although they were still expected to do most of the cooking and cleaning for themselves and the male students (ATTSVE 2019). After returning to their homes, female students were faced with the responsibility for household work, against which they had to balance what they needed to do with regard to their education. Domestic labor and caring for younger siblings had become equal or almost equal in terms of hours to an unpaid full-time job for most study participants. Male students in Ethiopia are expected to do agricultural work or engage in business, and to be involved in politics outside of the home, but this is not, in general, as time-consuming as the domestic labor expected of female students, as an article in *Ethiopia Forum* ("Gender Roles in Ethiopia" 2013) observes.

Women and girls face a larger informal care burden within the household compared to their male family members or male partners (Wenham et al. 2020), which is represented in this study. They are often expected to balance their work or education with an increased demand for contribution to household or family responsibilities. One can see from this study how women have been affected differently in their typical routines because, as the young women pointed out, men and boys have not experienced the same increase in household responsibilities and the pressure to stay in the home. This balance during the physical distancing associated with the COVID-19 pandemic could become difficult or unpredictable, potentially leading to negative implications for women's mental or physical health (ibid.). The effects on women's mental health are discussed in more detail later in the chapter.

Ethiopia has many multiethnic and multicultural groups whose diverse cultural and gender roles affect women and girls differently (UN 2013). The rural respondents in our study from the northern Amhara, Oromia, and Tigray regions had to engage in low-paid, time-consuming employment (often informal) with very long hours, as waitresses, maids, and coffee sellers. In comparison, most of the female students in the SNNPR studying at Wolaita Soddo college, the only one of the four situated in a small town, appeared to have higher economic status, since they reported that they were now expected only to care for relatives in the home, rather than work externally as well, and this gave them more free time, and, therefore, more chance to study.

Although most changes to daily life for study participants were negative ones, there were some positive social and economic effects. One participant mentioned that she had increased her level of personal hygiene through additional hand and body washing and had had the opportunity to become more physically active through exercise inside her home compound. One student from Maichew was able to start her own business preparing and selling coffee because she had more free time than usual. This gave her valuable entrepreneurial experience and increased her income.

How is COVID-19 Impacting Your Education?

Everyone interviewed had her education significantly affected by COVID-19. The interviewees were in various combinations of the four levels of diploma education, with approximately 50 percent of them originally intending to graduate in July 2020 had the pandemic not intervened. All students will have to return to their campuses if they want to finish their programs and complete their final examinations. Remote continuation of their programs has not been an option. Several students mentioned that they were attempting to reread old notes, but in most ways their education had ceased. One student told her interviewer, "My goal is to complete my education to support my family and the community. I am not attending class because of the virus, so it affects my whole life.

I miss my friends who are supportive during my studies through sharing materials and mutual support."

The loss of educational support from the ATTSVE project was of major concern to many students. Of significance was their feeling that they still needed access to many of these services in their home-based context; this indicates that educational support is still of great need for young women in Ethiopia to have the opportunities afforded to their male counterparts.

How Has COVID-19 Impacted Your Overall Well-Being (Health, Safety, and Comfort)?

The COVID-19 pandemic, and the social distancing resulting from it, caused participants in this study to experience changes in their mental health and their overall well-being. Some of these changes relate to their daily lives, in that participants have had to change their normal routines as a result of physical distancing and have had to cope with increased responsibilities in the home. These factors have caused feelings of sadness and isolation and have increased their stress levels.

The reduction in their social interactions led several participants to mention feeling sad, since their typical social interactions with family members outside the home, and with friends and neighbors, ceased because of the pandemic. Increased fear of death and worry about illness along with anxiety about being able to access health services during an outbreak of disease were experienced by our participants, and these emotions are known to lead to undue stress and poor mental health (IASC 2020).

An increase in fear and worry was common among some female students, who said that they feared dying or falling ill from COVID-19. Four students explained that they were worried about the poor health infrastructure in their area given the pandemic, six stated that services providing sanitary materials and contraceptives were not currently operating and that this concerned them, and two students mentioned that they would be uncomfortable accessing health services if they were to become sick. This is in line with other studies that have found that women in particular have difficulty accessing sexual health, prenatal, and maternal care services during COVID-19 (see Wenham et al. 2020) and that this can cause additional worry.

Many studies have demonstrated the negative impact of infectious disease outbreaks on public mental health, including SARS in 2003 and the

2009 novel influenza A epidemic (see, for example, Yeung et al. 2017). Research shows that airborne epidemics are likely to lead to members of the public, especially young people, experiencing psychological problems such as post-traumatic stress disorder, depression, and anxiety (see also Liang et al. 2020).

It was evident that most of the participants in this study experienced some level of deterioration in their mental health because of the pandemic, starting with significant negative feelings about the interruption of their education and not being able to graduate in 2020. One participant stated that she will not feel comfortable until life returns to how it was prior to the pandemic. Another noticed that her anger was easily triggered because of these feelings of frustration at having to stay home.

Key terms mentioned in the interviews included "feelings of frustration and hopelessness," "loss of goals" and "feelings of sadness," especially about delayed graduation, "disappointment" from their families, and "feelings of depression." Several students used the phrase "mental health difficulties." However, mental health support services are limited in Ethiopia generally, and especially in rural areas. This is an area of concern, especially since college and university students in Ethiopia are generally the ones who present with the highest level of mental health issues (Negash et al. 2020).

The reasons behind these negative mental health effects seem to be multifaceted and included financial worry about supporting themselves at home and completing their education, loss of employment, and not being able to graduate and support their families or become independent. Students feared the unknown. Heavy domestic workloads for most of them, and the pressure of working externally for some, were stressful. For a smaller number, feeling bored and the inability to socialize were important factors. These findings are similar to those of a recent study in Brazil that indicated that school closures led to feelings of helplessness, worthlessness, and heightened insecurity among youth (Ornell et al. 2020). As one of our study participants said, "Everyday life is getting difficult and disgusting. I can't do the things I was doing at the college like reading, studying, and conversing with friends. Now I am assisting my family at home, and I can't go out."

Have Female Students Been Feeling Safe during the Pandemic?

While the findings above have been arranged under the key questions asked during the interviews, we offer here the responses to the overall question we asked about the students' general well-being, rather than the one planned originally about their experiences of SGBV (as explained in the section titled "Changed Scope" above). No students mentioned experiencing serious SGBV themselves, although examples of being subjected to verbal harassment were provided by a few students. One said that many of the interviewed students, in order to survive financially, worked in cafeterias where male customers harassed them by saying, for example, that now that there was no education at all, they should marry them and have children. The Ethiopian interviewers and researchers reflected that these types of comments showed that the expectation for girls from rural and semi-urban environments to marry a breadwinner and have children was still current, at least in some regions.

However, we were surprised that in response to being questioned about their well-being, and about working and traveling outside the home, many students spoke about their increased fear of SGVB, and some respondents reported incidents of such violence among their friends and in their communities. This led us to question our own positionality in assuming that the students would not be comfortable discussing these issues, since they were much more forthcoming than we had expected and, of course, this enriched our findings.

Ethiopia has among the highest rates of SGBV against students ranging from those in secondary school to those in higher education in sub-Saharan Africa (Beyene et al. 2019). SGBV is an ongoing and documented challenge for female college students. A recent study conducted at the same four colleges before the pandemic struck revealed that rates of prevalence are high, although significant variance exists between colleges (Starr and Mitchell 2018). We do not know exactly how much this has changed for these students because of the restrictions imposed by the pandemic. As mentioned above, students were not asked directly about SGBV because of privacy concerns, and no student mentioned having directly suffered a serious incident, but some examples of verbal harassment they had endured were provided. However, 70 percent of students mentioned that SGBV had happened to someone they knew or to someone in their communities and that their own fear of it had increased.

The fear of SGBV emerged from the research findings and was mentioned by almost all students interviewed. This affected the young women's daily lives. One student from a rural area told her interviewer, "My parents are worried and scared about me being exposed to SGBV and now my mom directly pushes me to marry somebody that she would like to be her near neighbor." One student from a semi-urban area was aware that there had been more SGBV incidents, including rape, unwanted pregnancy, and abduction, among members of her local community during the pandemic. This had affected some of her friends and other community members and led to forced marriages encouraged by family members after the victims became pregnant. These events are not being reported to the police. She said,

> I know now the situation is worse and I pay much [more] attention to protecting myself from exposure to SGBV. I feel scared going to [the] market, traveling to work, having medical appointments, and it makes me want to avoid these places.

Most of the students discussed incidents in their communities that led to their increased fears regarding SGBV, and the way that this was affecting them and, in some cases, their families. However, one student mentioned her involvement in the creation of an awareness and sensitization campaign in her district and said that she had advised some of the survivors to report the cases to the Department of Women's Affairs and the police. We are hopeful that women-led change has begun and that, in the future, more cases will be reported, and that it will be easier for young women to access support.

The local Ethiopian interviewers based at the colleges expressed some surprise that the young women were comfortable discussing SGBV at all, especially on a phone call. They speculated that the students may have been more comfortable mentioning these issues because of greater exposure to training and resources from the ATTSVE project.

The findings show that the daily lives of female students have changed significantly because of the pandemic, and most of these changes are negative. They can be categorized by four thematic concerns that emerged from the interviews: negative socioeconomic consequences; inability to continue their education at home; increased mental health problems; and an amplified risk of (or fear of) sex- and gender-based violence.

What Do You Miss about Being at the ATVET College?

For us to quantify how most of the participants were feeling, they were asked what they missed most about being able to attend college. The options were: attending classes; engaging in self-study; spending time with friends; continuing with previous living situations; having access to gender clubs (extracurricular gatherings of students to address issues such as gender equity, gender-based violence and so on); and getting support from gender-focal offices. They were also encouraged to think of other options.

Of the respondents, 82 percent selected attending classes as the aspect they most missed, which supports our thematic finding that missing education, given its significance to these young women, has been hugely upsetting to them. They highlighted their desire to be able to use library services, the internet, and learning materials to which they had had access before the campuses closed. Access to all this would have allowed them, at least potentially, to continue their education from home. One student from a rural area said, "I miss the support from the gender office, such as pocket money, sanitary materials, and advice, which is very important to strengthen me morally and psychologically." Given what this student said, the ATTSVE project has perhaps underappreciated the strong importance of gender-focal support and club activities to female students in this educational context.

The most popular second choices in response to this quantitative question, at 36 percent each, were getting support from gender-focal offices and spending time with friends. These findings show that students were missing not only educational opportunities, but also vital extracurricular support in relation to their well-being, along with financial help that would enable them to participate in and benefit fully from their education. One student in the final year of her program said, "My gender club provided skills training like leadership, self-awareness, and assertiveness. This helps me to face challenges, and the financial support and sanitary materials from the gender office helps [me] to continue my education."

Are You Looking Forward to Returning to Your ATVET Education?

Every single student said that she was looking forward to returning to her education, which, given the worsening COVID-19 situation in Ethiopia (WHO n.d.), is likely to be delayed until at least March 2021. Although they are extremely keen to return to their education, female students are also afraid of returning to campus because of the lack of the previously supplied sanitary products, uncertainty about hygiene protection from COVID-19, increased exposure to SGBV, and financial issues.

Limitations and Recommendations

Limitations

Since only students with cell phone access could be interviewed, all interviews were necessarily conducted by phone. Of the female students over the four colleges, 70 percent had access to a basic cell phone, so the sample necessarily excluded the experiences of students who have no access to a cell phone, some of whom may well have been more vulnerable.

Recommendations and Implications

We recommend that the government increase funding to ATVET colleges so that they can provide much-needed services and resources for students at home, including grants, sanitary materials, and access to distance tutoring and mental health support. Phone calls from ATVET staff to keep in contact with students would be useful and would allow the students to receive current and reliable information. Improving internet access for rural students is desirable, but we realize that this would require not just infrastructural improvement but major shifts in educational and agricultural policy.

Research shows that female Ethiopian students may experience more challenges in completing their education than male students because of factors including high expectations regarding domestic labor and the lack of teaching support (Demise et al. 2002). Therefore, resources that would allow all students to continue their education from home, even to a partial extent, would be beneficial, and would mean that female students would not need longer to catch up upon their return to campus. However, without improved internet access and greater affordability in rural areas of Ethiopia, intervention in terms of distance education would be of limited success (Mengistie 2020).

It is also important for the colleges and the ATTSVE project to plan carefully and allocate resources to support female students' return to school to avoid perpetuating already-existing gender inequalities in education (Demise et al. 2002). This includes the provision of sanitary materials and personal protective equipment like masks. Extra tutoring and support, revision of courses covered before the closures, and extra financial support for transportation and lost income during their time at home must be provided to the students.

Furthermore, it is crucial that local governments and institutions work toward reducing SGBV through raising awareness and legal enforcement, and that they ensure that support is available to women who are survivors of SGBV or who are feeling more vulnerable to it (or both).

These results also highlight the need for Ethiopia's government to make available appropriate mental health interventions for girls and all young people during this time (Negash et al. 2020). Specific female-focused interventions are needed because of the different challenges girls and young women are facing compared to their male counterparts. Future research is needed to shed additional light on the mental health implications of COVID-19 in a student context in the Global South.

It would also be beneficial to compare and contrast the differing situations of female and male students who have had to return home because of the pandemic to further illuminate the gendered effects of the pandemic on female students.

Conclusion

The analysis of our data suggests that female students are facing significant challenges from their interrupted education, many specific to their gender, in the four key areas of negative socioeconomic consequences, inability to continue their education in the home, increased mental health issues, and increased fear of SGBV. The impact of the gendered pandemic on young women in Ethiopia is clear given these research findings. Although significant progress has been made over the last ten years, Ethiopia still has some of the lowest gender equality performance indicators in sub-Saharan Africa. The Global Gender Gap Report 2020 ranks Ethiopia at 82 out of 153 countries in terms of the scale and scope of gender disparities (WEF 2019). The qualitative data from interviews with students provides a holistic picture of multiple interconnected impacts of the pandemic on female students.

As the pandemic progresses, specific research on the impact on the education and well-being of young women in post-secondary education in Ethiopia will, potentially, increase, thus allowing greater comparison of results.

This study supports the view that young people, especially young women, are most significantly affected by the pandemic in terms of mental health effects, life interruptions such as leaving school, and financial burdens, as the International Labor Organization (2020) suggests. The members of this sex and age demographic need the most support through the development of innovative solutions, or there will be increased pressure on existing health resources.

The girls who participated in our study had many fears and uncertainties about the future, but every one of them said that she was looking forward to continuing her education. As one student said, "It is a scary disease. How can people continue to live separated from each other?" These unique student findings provide much-needed gender-focused data for the Ethiopian education system, educational institutions, and development projects including the ATTSVE project to consider, both during this pandemic and afterward as the world recovers from the effects of COVID-19.

Acknowledgments

We thank Global Affairs Canada for providing the funding for the ATTSVE project, the gender-focal staff at the four agricultural colleges for conducting some of the interviews, and especially all the young women who shared their stories with us.

Hannah Pugh (ORCID: 0000-0002-6150-171X) has worked in international development for over fifteen years and coordinated the ATTSVE development project for Dalhousie University. Her research interests include international development methodologies, gender, and youth.

Eleni Negash (ORCID: 0000-0002-8804-2744) has extensive experience with the study population through having coordinated gender-transformative activities as part of the ATTSVE project for the past five years.

Frehiwot Tesfaye (ORCID: 0000-0002-5030-4200) has worked on development, gender mainstreaming, and capacity-building for over eleven years in Ethiopia. She is currently working for the ATTSVE project as Programming Manager.

Madalyn Nielsen (ORCID: 0000-0003-2317-7047) is a master's student in Global Development Studies at Queen's University and recently completed ATTSVE-funded research on livestock businesses.

References

Agricultural Transformation through Stronger Vocational Education (ATTSVE). 2019. *Student Perceptions of Gender Based Violence at Four ATVET Colleges*. Montreal: Participatory Cultures Lab.

Beyene, Adisu, Catherine Chojenta, Hirbo Roba, Alemu Melka, and Deborah Loxton. 2019. "Gender-Based Violence among Female Youths in Educational

Institutions of Sub-Saharan Africa: Systematic Review and Meta-Analysis." *Systematic Review* 8: 32–49. https://doi.org/10.1186/s13643-019-0969-9.

Chuku, Chuku, Adamon Mukasa, and Yasin Yenice. 2020. "Putting Women and Girls' Safety First in Africa's Response to COVID-19." *Brookings*, 8 May. Retrieved 16 September 2022 from https://www.brookings.edu/blog/africa-in-focus/2020/05/08/putting-women-and-girls-safety-first-in-africas-response-to-covid-19/.

Demise, Asresash, Ruth Shinebaum, and Kassahun Melesse. 2002. "The Problems of Female Students at Jimma University, Ethiopia, with Suggested Solutions." *Ethiopian Journal of Health Development* 16(3): 257–66. Retrieved 16 September 2022 from https://www.ajol.info//index.php/ejhd/article/view/9793.

Gausman, Jewel, and Ana Langer. 2020. "Sex and Gender Disparities in the COVID-19 Pandemic." *Journal of Women's Health* 29(4): 465–66. https://doi.org/10.1089/jwh.2020.8472.

Geda, Alemayehu. 2020. "The Macroeconomic and Social Impact of COVID-19 in Ethiopia and Suggested Directions for Policy Response." Retrieved 16 September 2022 from https://www.researchgate.net/publication/340938630_The_Macroeconomic_and_Social_Impact_of_COVID-19_in_Ethiopia_and_Suggested_Directions_for_Policy_Response.

"Gender Roles in Ethiopia." 2013. *EthiopiaForum*, 21 November. Retrieved 16 September 2022 from https://ethiopiaforum.wordpress.com/2013/11/21/gender-roles-in-ethiopia.

Gilbert, Marius, Giulia Pullano, Francesco Pinotti, Eugenio Valdano, Chiara Poletto, Pierre-Yves Boëlle, Eric D'Ortenzio, Yazdan Yazdanpanah, Serge Paul Eholie, Mathias Altmann, Bernardo Gutierrez, Moritz Kraemer, and Vittoria Colizza. 2020. "Preparedness and Vulnerability of African Countries against Importations of COVID-19: A Modelling Study." *The Lancet* 395(10227): 871–77. https://doi.org/10.1016/S0140-6736(20)30411-6.

IASC (Inter-Agency Standing Committee). 2020. "Addressing Mental Health and Psychological Aspects of COVID-19 Outbreak." 17 March. Retrieved 5 November 2022 from https://interagencystandingcommittee.org/iasc-reference-group-mental-health-and-psychosocial-support-emergency-settings/interim-briefing-note-addressing-mental-health-and-psychosocial-aspects-covid-19-outbreak

ILO (International Labour Organization). 2020. "World Employment and Social Outlook—Trends 2020." Retrieved 5 November 2022 from https://www.ilo.org/global/about-the-ilo/newsroom/news/WCMS_734454/lang--en/index.htm

Kaparounaki, Chrysi, Mikaella Patsali, Danai-Priskila Mousa, Eleni Papadopoulou, Konstantina Papadopoulou, and Konstantinos Fountoulakis. 2020. "University Students' Mental Health amidst the COVID-19 Quarantine in

Greece." *Psychiatry Research* 290: 113–27. https://doi.org/10.1016/j.psychres.2020.113111.

Liang, Leilei, Hui Ren, Ruilin Cao, Yueyang Hu, Zeying Qin, Chuanen Li, and Songli Mei. 2020. "The Effect of COVID-19 on Youth Mental Health." *Psychiatric Quarterly* 92: 841–52. https://doi.org/10.1007/s11126-020-09744-3.

Mengistie, Tilahun Adamu. 2020. "Impacts of COVID-19 on the Ethiopian Education System." *Science Insights Education Frontiers* 6(1): 569–78. http://dx.doi.org/10.2139/ssrn.3626327.

Negash, Assegid, Matloob Ahmed Khan, Girmay Medhin, Dawit Wondimagegn, and Mesfin Araya. 2020. "Mental Distress, Perceived Need, and Barriers to Receive Professional Mental Health Care among University Students in Ethiopia." *BMC Psychiatry* 20: 125–36. https://doi.org/10.1186/s12888-020-02602-3.

Ornell, Felipe, Jacqueline Schuch, Anne Sordi, and Felix Kessler. 2020. "Pandemic Fear and COVID-19: Mental Health Burden and Strategies." *Brazilian Journal of Psychiatry* 42(3): 1–16. https://doi.org/10.1590/1516-4446-2020-0008.

Peterman, Amber, Alina Potts, Megan O'Donnell, Kelly Thompson, Niyati Shah, Sabine Oertelt-Prigione, and Nicole van Gelder. 2020. "Pandemics and Violence against Women and Children." *Centre for Global Development*, 1 April. Retrieved 16 September 2022 from https://www.cgdev.org/publication/pandemics-and-violence-against-women-and-children.

Starr, Lisa, and Claudia Mitchell. 2018. "How Can Canada's Feminist International Assistance Policy Support a Feminist Agenda in Africa? Challenges in Addressing Sexual Violence in Four Agricultural Colleges in Ethiopia." *Agenda* 32(1): 107–18. https://www.tandfonline.com/doi/full/10.1080/10130950.2018.1427692.

UN (United Nations). 2013. "Advancing Gender Equality: Promising Practices." Retrieved 16 September 2022 from https://www.sdgfund.org/sites/default/files/MDG-F_Case-Studies_front.pdf.

UN (United Nations) Ethiopia. 2020. "Socio-Economic Impact of COVID-19 in Ethiopia." 15 June. Retrieved 16 September 2022 from https://ethiopia.un.org/en/49388-un-socio-economic-assessment-covid-19-ethiopia.

Wenham, Clare, Julia Smith, and Rosemary Morgan. 2020. "COVID-19 is an Opportunity for Gender Equality Within the Workplace and at Home." *BMJ* 369: 1546. https://doi.org/10.1136/bmj.m1546.

WHO (World Health Organization). n.d. "Coronavirus." Retrieved 16 September 2022 from https://www.who.int/health-topics/coronavirus#tab=tab_3.

———. 2020. "Listings of WHO's Response to COVID-19." 29 June. Retrieved 16 September 2022 from https://www.who.int/news-room/detail/29-06-2020-covidtimeline.

WEF (World Economic Forum). 2019. *Global Gender Gap Report 2020*. 16 December. Retrieved 16 September 2022 from https://www.weforum.org/reports/gender-gap-2020-report-100-years-pay-equality.

Yeung, Nelson, Joseph Lau, Kai Chow Choi, and Sian Griffiths. 2017. "Population Responses during the Pandemic Phase of the Influenza A(H1N1)pdm09 Epidemic, Hong Kong, China." *Emerging Infectious Diseases* 23(5): 813–15. https://dx.doi.org/10.3201/eid2305.160768.

CHAPTER 7

Exploring the Psychosocial Experiences of Women Undergraduates in Delhi, India, during the COVID-19 Pandemic

Richa Rana, Poonam Yadav, and Shreya Sandhu

Introduction

The COVID-19 pandemic is of unprecedented and increasing concern for the world's population. The Indian education system, particularly the institutions and stakeholders of higher education, has felt its impact. With the announcement of the first official lockdown on 24 March 2020, the country decided to shut its schools and colleges, so classes have either been postponed or moved online, even though higher education institutions are ill-equipped to deal with virtual learning (Talidong and Toquero 2020) and are facing a host of challenges in the wake of other issues that the COVID-19 lockdown is bringing to the surface. Higher education institutions (HEIs) were prompted to establish management approaches regarding the pandemic to encourage positive health behavior among students (Akan et al. 2010). This entire situation has had a significant influ-

Notes for this section can be found on page 133.

ence on the psychosocial experiences of Indian undergraduate students who have had to limit themselves to the boundaries of their homes. This is because most students in India continue to live with their parents while attending college, especially if they are enrolled in an HEI in the same city. This is partly because parents sponsor their children's education for some years after schooling and because of cultural norms that give preference to cohabitation with one's family. Many students reported anxiety and stress not only because of COVID-19 itself, but also because of being trapped at home with their families. We aimed to capture the experiences of these college students, since girls and women in general and female undergraduates in particular are niche groups whose concerns are not usually voiced in the discourse on the current pandemic.[1]

It is not the first time that the world is experiencing the effects of widespread illness that has brought unforeseen challenges to its inhabitants, especially girls and women. E. Sara Davies and Belinda Bennett (2016) highlight the challenges faced by women and girls during the Ebola and Zika epidemics. They discuss the relationship between school closure and disturbed learning, on the one hand, and early pregnancy, on the other, during the Ebola outbreak, and the "conspicuous invisibility of women" (Harman 2016, cited in Davies and Bennett 2016: 1043) during the Zika outbreak. However, the impact of epidemics on girls and girlhood remains a relatively unexplored field of study, particularly, perhaps, in relation to the challenges faced by Indian women undergraduates and the adaptive patterns they have employed.

A World Bank Group policy report (de Paz et al. 2020) entitled *Gender Dimensions of the COVID-19 Pandemic* shows that women and girls are affected in particular ways by infectious disease outbreaks like COVID-19, and that some face more negative impacts than men do. For example, girls in some middle- and low-income countries are expected to take on more household and family care duties, and this leaves them with less time for learning at home. The prevalent social and gendered norms in India and elsewhere, and the bargaining power of men vis-à-vis women in the household, determine how balanced the distribution of household and care duty is, but it is most likely to lead to a reduction in time devoted to study for girls and women.

Patriarchal social norms determining access to assets related to land use, inheritance, or finance also need to be considered in this context, along with the prevalent traditional social and gendered norms that affect the coping strategies and decision-making processes of young women. For example, given the closure of schools and the economic difficulties related to the pandemic, families may adopt coping strategies that lead to girls being at higher risk of early marriage and pregnancy.

Young Women and Education in India

Despite the extensive research and government investment in the so-called modernized education system in India—in which importance is given to universalization, access, and equity, according to Krishna Kumar (2010)—scant attention has been paid to the voices and experiences of young Indian women undergraduates. Studies of college-level undergraduate women in India have revolved around four primary areas: college as a site of temporary freedom for girls and women and as a critical time for them; the role of college-based friendship in the making of girlhood; college education as a bridge to girls' marriage for their parents; and the role of the patriarchy and sociocultural dominance in the internalization and rationalization of gendered thought, space, and time (Kirk 2005; Kumar 2010; Patel 2017). Girls' lives and education in contemporary India continue to be shaped by cultural forces deeply anchored in history (Kumar 2010). These forces, along with traditional practices, can be traced back to ancient India, as Uma Chakravarti (1999) reminds us. This structural framework includes the sociolegal devices that regulate perceptions and decisions on matters as significant as the appropriate age for marriage, the eligibility of women for economic independence, and their social status. We argue that the current pandemic has exacerbated the effects of these social and cultural forces in molding girls' lives and their experiences.

We are interested in the many forms of subordination faced by young women, especially those from lower socioeconomic backgrounds, as they navigate formal education in India. Salient norms around gender shape parental decision-making, as do critical considerations around economic investment, marriage alliances, and the associated opportunity costs, such as the loss to parents of the unpaid domestic labor of girls who are not educated (Mukhopadhyay et al. 1994). Furthermore, education is often imagined as a basis for consolidating feminine accomplishments and "improving [girls'] capacity to be effective mothers, wives, and household workers" (Dyson 2014: 58). However, the perspectives of young women themselves rarely form the center of analysis in studies of young people and higher education in India.

In India, girlhood is a highly structured and controlled phase of socialization during which a girl's rights and freedom are regulated according to the patriarchal social fabric. Karuna Chanana (2001: 37) argues that

> [t]he growth and development of women's education in India are caught in two simultaneous processes. On the one hand, the state policy and public discourse on education put a premium on the need to promote education among girls and women to generate positive forces at the macro-level. On the other, the micro-level forces rooted in the family, the kin group and culture determine the educational policies, programs and ability of girls and women to access them. Therefore, it is not possible to view women's education without reference to their social context, which is rooted in culture, religion and the "patrifocal family structure and ideology."

This gives young women a disadvantage as far as accessing and completing a college education is concerned. Our study looked at the experiences of women undergraduates in relation to their struggles and concerns during the COVID-19 pandemic in the new enforced online teaching and learning environment. The University of Delhi (a public university) responded to the COVID-19 pandemic by shifting classes online using various media like WhatsApp and video calls through Zoom and Google Meet, and by making course content and notes available to students through college apps and the uploading of lectures onto Moodle and YouTube. Concerning assessment, first- and second-year students are graded based on their performance in an internal assessment, and final-year students have been asked to appear for an examination. After months of speculation, the University Grants Commission and the University of Delhi decided to conduct the third-year bachelor's exam in September. The indecisiveness about the dates, the lack of technical support, vagueness about the format, and much more has left the students anxious. This anxiety is the focus of our study, as we tried to understand and explore the nature of the women undergraduates' psychosocial experiences during the pandemic. We focused on how already-present socioeconomic inequalities intersect with the gendered space and time in which this pandemic has confined these women undergraduates to their family homes. The research aimed to unveil the nature of the academic anxieties, psychological distress, and social struggles the young women undergraduates faced, along with the coping strategies they adopted during the pandemic.

Method

We used the snowball sampling technique to select four participants referred to here by the pseudonyms Savi, Pahal, Yasti, and Adya, all of whom were between eighteen and twenty-one years of age and were studying humanities and social sciences in four affiliated colleges for women at the University of Delhi, and with whom we conducted in-depth interviews. Savi and Pahal belong to the lower-middle class and Yasti and Adya to the middle class. Savi belongs to a scheduled caste,[2] and Pahal and Adya to a general category.[3] Also, these three women are Hindus while Yasti is Muslim. These young women are in different years of their three-year undergraduate courses.

In-depth interviews, crucial for capturing people's voices and stories (Hennink et al. 2020), were based on detailed interview guidelines and enabled us to build one-on-one rapport with the participants. Depending on the participants' linguistic comfort and availability, we conducted interviews in English or Hindi at specified times. We conducted two to three interviews to enable us to obtain in-depth information from each participant. All interviews were conducted by the authors online over Zoom (audio and video calls), with the unique context of India and its prevalent gender norms being kept in mind, and were recorded. At the beginning of the first interview, we introduced participants to the research topic, told them that the calls would be recorded, and assured them of the confidentiality of any information they imparted to us. We asked those who agreed to participate for their written consent. To maintain confidentiality, we have used pseudonyms throughout.

For Virginia Braun and Victoria Clarke (2006: 79), thematic analysis, to which we subjected our data, is "a method for identifying, analyzing and reporting patterns (themes) from within [it]." It is a flexible method suitable for theory-driven (deductive) as well as data-driven (inductive) research approaches. We used a primarily inductive form of thematic analysis, and we followed the six-phase process outlined by Braun and Clarke (2006) for conducting such thematic analysis. During the first phase we transcribed the interviews and translated the Hindi ones into English, which helped to familiarize us all with the data. The second phase was devoted to generating initial codes following several close readings of the interview transcripts inductively while keeping the aims of our research in mind. We applied the codes to shorter sentences as well as to longer paragraphs. These codes were further refined through constant engagement with the data. During the third phase we collated initial codes under broader themes that captured their content to facilitate our search for themes. During the fourth phase, we undertook a process of refinement by checking whether themes worked with coded extracts. We involved the entire data set in a review of the themes. This refinement of themes also helped us to ensure coherence and discreteness within and between the themes. Phase five was devoted to identifying the individual story of each theme, as well as the overall story held together by all the themes. This helped us define and name themes. During the sixth phase we selected the specific examples of themes necessary to produce this chapter.

Findings

We analyzed young women's experiences during this pandemic by drawing on the literature on past pandemics and how they affected women's access to, and continuation of, education. Girls and women have been recognized as a vulnerable group in many domains during this coronavirus outbreak (Hall et al. 2020). Katarzyna Burzynska and Gabriela Contreras (2020) assert that during it, some parents who assign a lower value to girls' education might not provide their daughters with a second chance to become educated when it ends. Further, because of the closure of educational institutions, the current situation may dampen the already-achieved progress of young women students, especially in developing countries. The anxiety and uncertainty faced by the young women in our study was palpable, as we go on to show.

Academic Anxieties and Student Struggle

Although the literature establishes that there are gender-based differences in education, especially higher education, for young women in India, there is negligible research on young women's struggles to access education through online media. Our interviews uncovered anxieties related to online classes, internal assessments, exams, and other academic matters among the research participants. Concerns ranged from small technical issues to teachers being unresponsive to students' queries online. Savi, who is pursuing an undergraduate degree in a language course, told us about many of the issues that she has faced while attending online classes. She explained,

> Ma'am, if we have like a batch of forty, then first there are a lot of technical issues, and if we want to say anything about the disturbance then we have to go and check the chat box whether someone's audio is muted or not. Also, many students are not available at the same time, some are not able to join, and some don't know how to join.

Even during the interview session, Savi was experiencing network issues. She has to go to a particular spot on her terrace where there is better video quality, and this makes her invisible in classroom discussions. Maria E. Salinas (2020) and Andrew Perrin and Erica Turner (2019) report similar kinds of technology-related challenges experienced by Black, Latino, and Hispanic students, who, in the absence of Wi-Fi and traditional broadband facilities at home, have to rely on smartphone internet or travel to McDonalds, the library, or a public hotspot to complete their academic assignments. Adya, who is in her second year of a bachelor's degree in geography, spoke about how the teachers had been exerting pressure on her and her fellow students in practical classes to complete their assignments, and said that the teachers had not given them timely feedback, which is a reasonable expectation in a practical class.

Pahal, who is in her third year, mentioned that they had still not received any explicit instructions from the university regarding their exams. She was seriously concerned because the exams had been postponed, and this led to a lot of confusion and anxiety. When asked about her final-year exams, she replied, "Ma'am, today also like . . . they are saying that they are not sure when they should organize those exams."

This state of confusion regarding examinations and the attainment of a degree affects future goals and actions. This is especially true for young women from developing countries like India, where a substantial number of patriarchal values and social norms (de Paz et al. 2020) already confine their time in higher education to rigidly specific stipulated years, and where many parents understand higher education to be merely a CV for marriage, as Viresh Patel (2017) reminds us. Under the so-called protection principle that works under the control of patrilineal kin (Chanana 2001), young women are socialized to internalize, confirm, and enact the patriarchal values that promise to protect them economically, emotionally, and physically. Therefore, for many of them, the idea of even having a choice to study in the future is frightening, never mind the possibility of rebelling.

It is clear that our findings support Stidham Kelli Hall et al.'s (2020) assertion that girls and women constitute a vulnerable group in many domains and that their vulnerability is exacerbated by COVID-19. Undeniably, anxieties related to their academic lives have emerged as the most common form of mental illness in women undergraduates. Han Qi and his colleagues' (2020) investigation into the pervasiveness of anxiety among Chinese adolescents during COVID-19 also substantiates our results. Their findings suggest that strict measures, including lockdown, the shutdown of academic institutions, and the cancellation of various events, put adolescents at risk of anxiety. In such an uncertain time, girl students report greater worry and a higher risk of anxiety.

Negotiating Freedom and Choices

For each undergraduate whom we interviewed, attending college or being physically present there had different meanings. For these young women, uncertainty about the reopening of college and the resumption of traditional classes, which involve meeting with college peers and friends, fills them with anxiety. Adya said,

> We are students. We don't have a habit of staying at home for a long duration and now it's been three and a half months at home. There was a time that I used to think that nobody understands me, at least from home. You can have calls, even the video calls, but you really need a person in a physical sense to tell them about your things and so going out really makes a difference for a moment.

In Adya's narrative, her reference to "we" explicitly reflects her heightened need for peer-group belonging. Engagement with a peer group is highly significant during this phase of life, since it serves as an opportunity to acquire unique skills and experiences in collective spaces (Brown 1990; Rubin et al. 1998, cited in Kiuru et al. 2007). For girls, the meaning of friends and peer groups is different from their meaning to boys. For example, girls' peer groups are more intimate, are tightly knitted (Benenson 1990), and lean toward trusting relationships (Brendgen et al. 2001). Moreover, with their friends, girls indulge in greater self-disclosure (Buhrmester 1990). Since Indian culture places great significance on parental consent for making friends and for meeting and interacting with peers, parents are becoming stringent with these rules during the lockdown and, as Patel (2017) observes, parents' permission has greater significance for young women than for young men. Additionally, for women undergraduates, this restriction on their freedom is threatening (Drennan 2018).

Other participants also expressed similar concerns. For them, going to college signifies freedom to study, to hang out, to meet people, to participate in protests, to travel solo, and to engage in many more behaviors. College gave Savi an opportunity to travel solo, unguarded by any male member of her family; for her, this was an exciting experience. With the closing of college during COVID-19 she has lost her chance at freedom, and with it her agency to exercise this freedom. She said, "In the back of the mind there is a lingering tension that when there was college there was some joy in our life. Going to college daily, traveling daily. And for me they were mainly solo trips."

Since she has been confined to her home, the discourse surrounding women's safety and security has socialized Savi into believing that her locality is unsafe for going out alone after dark. Social media and family members constantly reiterate this, and she consensually agrees, and even tried to convince us that the city becomes unsafe once darkness falls. Only when she goes to college does she feel that she has the choice to be on her own, and this is what she most misses now. Her current understanding of time and safety indicates a tendency toward believing that she will come to harm in the dark, and this may well turn out to be a self-fulfilling prophecy.

Although venturing out to college and for other related activities with friends gives a sense of freedom to young women, freedom is still a negotiated category. Most research on girls and young women, especially that which focuses on education and work opportunities, refers to narratives that highlight the success stories of girls' newfound freedom and opportunities. But we need to understand the complexity of this freedom in the Indian context, especially since the experience varies depending on one's situatedness in the sociocultural milieu. "Freedoms are not straightforward, nor equally available" (Charlton 2007: 122). We noted that students were not given the freedom, even, to choose their own college subjects. For example, our research participants found that their parents did not readily trust their choice of subject for undergraduate study. Pahal's choice to pursue a BSc in Home Science was not accepted initially by her parents. They brought in her elder brother and discussed with him in great detail the pros and cons of her opting for this subject, and then they finally agreed to her choice. She recounted how neither she nor any elder sibling were consulted when her brother chose his undergraduate subject. She felt that her parents did not believe that she was capable of making such a big decision by herself.

Sociocultural, Economic, and Psychological Struggles

Pahal felt that the current COVID-19 situation has resulted in parents marrying off their daughters, since there are fewer expenses and a much smaller dowry involved. Citing a case from her neighborhood, she explained,

> There is a girl I guess of my age only, and she has got married in this COVID. I have seen her working, but I was really shocked, like what happened suddenly that she has to get married this time only . . . So, well there might be more [girls], and their parents might be thinking that there is no point in educating them further . . . so it's better to get them married. Marriage can be organized by calling fifty people, and there'll be a less[er] financial burden over parents.

Since these gendered experiences of women undergraduates are embedded in sociocultural factors such as caste, tribe, and class (Chanana 2000), the COVID-19 pandemic, in affecting families' economic situation, can have devastating consequences for young women. Families of women students coming from the lower end of the hierarchy have come to expect them to marry early, primarily through arranged matches.

These undergraduate women expressed concerns regarding their greater contribution to the household and to care work since they have been confined to their homes. Before the pandemic struck, most of these young women would have gone home after finishing their classes and meeting their academic work responsibilities, and would not have been expected to contribute much to household work. The situation changed and, for our participants, the pandemic-induced lockdown appeared to have reversed the progress made by women in general through their decades of unrelenting struggle for economic empowerment and being allowed out of the house.

Young women are also witnessing the effects of the economic slowdown caused by this pandemic. Pahal mentioned that along with her studies, she used to give paid extra classes before the lockdown started, but this came to a halt, affecting her financial independence, which will have consequences for her self-sponsoring her college education. She explained,

> After 12th standard only, I have been an independent girl financially also . . . but this situation has created a scenario in which I am sitting at home twenty-four hours, and there is no source of income. All my savings are gone like that. So, I am not financially stable right now.

129

For Pahal, the importance of work lies in making sure she can contribute to her family's income and be self-reliant in realizing her higher education aspirations. But since her father's income has been reduced by the lockdown, she feels anxious about both the financial condition of her family and her ability to pay for her higher education.

Psychological Issues

Yasti's daily routine is "just a lot of monotony right now." She added,

> I am a little bit disappointed in myself because I thought that I'll be productive starting June, but I have not been able to do that . . . I feel like there is no deadline in this lockdown, so there is nothing to look forward to.

In addition, because there is no certainty regarding when the situation will be over, the students lack motivation and there is nothing to look forward to on a daily basis, so even though Yasti is engaged in two internships, she still feels unproductive. Her daily routine during the lockdown seems futile to her.

Coping Strategies

A recent psychological wellness guide on COVID-19, produced especially by Emory University for families with college students at home, asserts that "[c]ollege students are accustomed to a level of autonomy and independence that is difficult to lose when returning home" (Department of Psychiatry COVID-19 Response 2020: 1). Simultaneously, they may experience isolation, grieve for the loss of their college experiences, and face conflicts with parents. The American Psychological Association (2020) has also considered the issue of students' coping with stress related to COVID-19.

We found that young women are using diverse coping strategies depending on their needs, socioeconomic class, and time frames. They know that they must employ coping mechanisms if they are to survive the COVID-19 lockdown. The uncertainty and ambiguity attached to COVID-19 has impacted the daily schedules and life patterns of these young women. Additionally, it has presented new challenges to, and changes in, their lived social reality.

Something that all the participants mentioned was their communication with their friends through calls, video chats, texts, and so on, and the fact that this has helped them get through these difficult times. Like Adya, all our respondents are maintaining peer relationships through social media and telephone conversations, and they are scheduling virtual meetings with their friends. Some of these young women have engaged themselves in doing things around the house and have also indulged in various hobbies and interests to offset the stress and deal with the loneliness. Savi told us about how she had started helping her mother by cutting up vegetables and dusting the house. In Pahal's case, the loss of earning power led to a state of struggle, confusion, and tension in the early months of the pandemic. But after some time she showed resilience and found a new job and has been keeping herself busy. However, Yasti's work in two internships gives her little relief and she experiences boredom. Savi said,

> In college, we have a lot of societies and many foundations which advertise various competitions on their online platform[s], so I have joined those. Also, I write something on my own. Also, I am working as a content writer for a foundation as well.

She added, "I try to help my mother in household work." Her engaging in stereotypically feminine work like chopping vegetables and dusting the house might offer a glimpse of her conformity to patriarchal structures, or it may simply be the only way she can help her mother. Deniz Kandiyoti's (1988) notion of patriarchal bargaining is worth considering here. She suggests that women can decide to conform to patriarchal demands for emotional, psychological, or financial gain. For Savi, the coping strategy of helping her mother may give her emotional or psychological satisfaction.

Conclusion

Our research study focused on exploring the nature of the psychosocial issues faced by young women undergraduates during COVID-19 and on highlighting the coping strategies they use. Drawing on information about the socialization of young women and the patriarchal fabric of Indian society, we have shown how already-existing socioeconomic inequalities intersect with the imposed confinement of these women undergraduates. They all face academic anxieties related to the delaying of exams and to problems accessing and continuing with online classes as they struggle to complete their education. Although divided by socioeconomic and other cultural markers, all the women undergraduates are somewhat similarly placed in relation to what might be called a new digital divide that has been created by the pandemic-induced lockdown. They all miss being physically present in college, and they all face sociocultural and economic struggles, including the loss of income and the fear of being unable to return to college after the pandemic has come to an end. Most feel that the pressure to get them married off will build up, as parents view this pandemic as an opportunity to have a low-cost wedding. On a more personal level, these young women also reported feeling unproductive, demotivated, hopeless, and lonely during this period. This pandemic has left these young women longing for real time with their friends, venturing out, attending college, and going to lectures. It has left them feeling shut off behind closed doors, and they aspire to freedom.

This chapter has revealed that the mental health of these women undergraduates is of concern during this pandemic. Anxiety related to their academic lives, to the loss of income, and to the increased fear of losing out on educational opportunities in a country that prioritizes boys' education is obvious. They are suffering from the lack of contact with their peer groups, and they fear getting trapped into early marriages given the dominant patriarchal values of their society. Those from a lower socioeconomic and more conservative background are at even greater risk. The negative impact of the pandemic on the economy and the resultant unemployment and slowdown not only puts limitations on their mobility, it also threatens their further education.

Finally, this study helped us to recognize the experiences of young women in the context of the current political and economic environment of a developing nation like India. Here, young women are expected to adhere to traditional cultural values, but at the same time, they want to be educated and financially independent. We have attempted to highlight the lived experience of young women students during this pandemic and show how it affects their already-gendered lives in the Indian social context.

It is crucial to acknowledge that this research has exposed how young women undergraduates are battling differently with psycho-socio-economic entrapments related to COVID-19; it will be interesting to see how this pandemic-induced gender disparity in access to, and continuation of, education will be addressed in future.

Acknowledgments

We extend warm thanks to our editors Claudia Mitchell and Ann Smith, whose insightful and detailed comments and suggestions helped us to improve this chapter. We thank our research participants, who gave their valuable time to this study, and we thank our mentor, Dr. Arvind Kumar Mishra, for his insightful comments and suggestions.

RICHA RANA is a Research Scholar at the Zakir Husain Centre for Educational Studies, Jawaharlal Nehru University, New Delhi, India. Her research interests include intersectionality, gender identity, and achievement motivation in education.

POONAM YADAV is a Research Scholar at the Zakir Husain Centre for Educational Studies, Jawaharlal Nehru University, New Delhi, India. Her research foci include social cognition, social identity, group processes, attribution, and emotion.

SHREYA SANDHU is a Research Scholar at the Centre for Studies in Sociology of Education, Tata Institute of Social Sciences, Mumbai, India. Her interests include academic culture, neoliberalism, and education reform policies.

Notes

1. We have used the terms "girls" and "young women" interchangeably since, in Indian culture, females in the age group between eighteen and twenty-one years are generally considered to be young women, but we understand that this is not the case in other countries.
2. The scheduled castes are officially designated groups of people in India. In modern literature, these are sometimes referred to as Dalits, a word that means "broken" or "scattered."
3. The general category, defined by default, refers to those who do not require the benefit of an affirmative action policy on the grounds of their social background, or are not considered to require such a benefit.

References

Akan, Hulya, Yesim Gurol, Guldal Izbirak, Sukran Ozdalti, Gulden Yilmaz, Ayca Vitrinel, and Osman Haryan. 2010. "Knowledge and Attitudes of University Students toward Pandemic Influenza: A Cross-Sectional Study from Turkey." *BMC Public Health* 10: 413. https://doi.org/10.1186/1471-2458-10-413.

American Psychological Association. 2020. "Coping with COVID-19-Related Stress as a Student: With Schools around the Country Closed, Students are Facing Unprecedented Change." Retrieved 21 September 2022 from https://www.apa.org/topics/covid-19/student-stress.pdf.

Benenson, Joyce F. 1990. "Gender Differences in Social Networks." *Journal of Early Adolescence* 10(4): 472–95. http://doi.org/10.1177/0272431690104004.

Brendgen, Mara, Dorothy Markiewicz, Anna Beth Doyle, and William Michael Bukowski. 2001. "The Relations between Friendship Quality, Ranked-Friendship Preference, and Adolescents' Behavior with Their Friends." *Merrill-Palmer Quarterly* 47(3): 395–415. https://doi.org/10.1353/mpq.2001.0013.

Brown, B. Bradford. 1990. "Peer Groups and Peer Cultures." In *At the Threshold: The Developing Adolescent*, ed. Shirley S. Feldman and Glen Elliott, 171–96. London: Harvard University Press.

Buhrmester, Duane. 1990. "Intimacy of Friendship, Interpersonal Competence, and Adjustment during Preadolescence and Adolescence." *Child Development* 61(4): 1101–11. https://doi.org/10.2307/1130878.

Burzynska, Katarzyna, and Gabriela Contreras. 2020. "Gendered Effects of School Closures during the COVID-19 Pandemic." *The Lancet* 395(10242): 1968. https://doi.org/10.1016/S0140-6736(20)31377-5.

Braun, Virginia, and Victoria Clarke. 2006. "Using Thematic Analysis in Psychology." *Qualitative Research in Psychology* 3(2): 77–101. https://doi.org/10.1191/1478088706qp063oa.

Charlton, Emma. 2007. "'Bad' Girls versus 'Good' Girls: Contradiction in the Constitution of Contemporary Girlhood." *Discourse: Studies in the Cultural Politics of Education* 28(1): 121–31. https://doi.org/10.1080/01596300601073739.

Chakravarti, Uma. 1999. "Beyond the Altekarian Paradigm: Towards a New Understanding of Gender Relations in Early Indian History." In *Women in Early Indian Societies*, ed. Kumkum Roy, 72–81. New Delhi: Manohar.

Chanana, Karuna. 2000. "Treading the Hallowed Halls: Women in Higher Education in India." *Economic and Political Weekly* 35(12): 1012–22. https://www.jstor.org/stable/4409055.

———. 2001. "Hinduism and Female Sexuality: Social Control and Education of Girls in India." *Sociological Bulletin* 50(1): 37–63. https://www.jstor.org/stable/23620149.

Davies, Sara E., and Belinda Bennett. 2016. "A Gendered Human Rights Analysis of Ebola and Zika: Locating Gender in Global Health Emergencies." *International Affairs* 92(5): 1041–60. https://doi.org/10.1111/1468-2346.12704.

de Paz, Carmen, Miriam Muller, Ana Maria Munoz Boudet, and Isis Gaddis. 2020. *Gender Dimensions of the COVID-19 Pandemic*. Washington, DC. World Bank. Retrieved 21 September 2022 from https://openknowledge.worldbank.org/handle/10986/33622.

Department of Psychiatry COVID-19 Response. 2020. *COVID-19 Psychological Wellness Guide: Families with College Students at Home*. Atlanta, GA: School of Medicine, Emory University. Retrieved 21 September 2022 from https://med.emory.edu/departments/psychiatry/_documents/tips.families.college.students.home.pdf.

Drennan, Vasundhara Sirnate. 2018. "Is It Possible Some Women Don't Want to Be Free of Patriarchy?" *The Hindu*, 2 February. Retrieved 21 September 2022 from https://www.thehindu.com/thread/arts-culture-society/is-it-possible-some-women-dont-want-to-be-free-of-patriarchy/article22635214.ece.

Dyson, Jane. 2014. *Youth, Agency and the Environment in India*. Cambridge: Cambridge University Press.

Hall, Stidham Kelli, Goleen Samari, Samantha Garbers, Sara E. Casey, Dazon Dixon Diallo, Miriam Orcutt, Rachel T. Moresky, Micaela Elvira Martinez, and Terry McGovern. 2020. "Centring Sexual and Reproductive Health and Justice in the Global COVID-19 Response." *The Lancet* 395(10242): 1175–77. http://doi.org/10.1016/S0140-6736(20)30801-1.

Hennink, Monique, Inge Hutter, and Ajay Bailey. 2020. *Qualitative Research Methods*. Delhi: Sage.

Kandiyoti, Deniz. 1988. "Bargaining with Patriarchy." *Gender and Society* 2(3): 274–90. https://www.jstor.org/stable/190357.

Kirk, Jackie. 2005. "Reclaiming Girlhood: Understanding the Lives of Balkishori in Mumbai." In *Seven Going on Seventeen: Tween Studies in the Culture of Girlhood*, ed. Claudia Mitchell and Jacqueline Reid-Walsh, 135–47. New York: Peter Lang. http://www.jstor.com/stable/42978696.

Kiuru, Noona, Aunola Kaisa, Jukka Vuori, and Jari-Erik Nurmi. 2007. "Role of Peer Groups in Adolescents' Educational Expectations and Adjustment." *Journal of Youth and Adolescence* 36: 995–1009. http://doi.org/10.1007/s10964-006-9118-6.

Kumar, Krishna. 2010. "Culture, State and Girls: An Educational Perspective." *Economic and Political Weekly* 45(17): 75–84. https://www.jstor.org/stable/25664388.

Mukhopadhyay, Carol Chapnick, and Susan C. Seymour. 1994. "Introduction and Theoretical Overview." In *Women, Education, and Family Structure in*

India, ed. Carol Chapnick Mukhopadhyaya and Susan C. Seymour, 1–33. Boulder, CO: Westview Press.

Patel, Viresh. 2017. "Parents, Permission, and Possibility: Young Women, College, and Imagined Futures in Gujarat, India." *Geoforum* 80: 39–48. https://doi.org/10.1016/j.geoforum.2017.01.008.

Perrin, Andrew, and Erica Turner. 2019. "Smartphones Help Blacks, Hispanics Bridge Some—but Not All—Digital Gaps with Whites." *Pew Research Center*, 20 August. Retrieved 7 November 2022 from https://www.pewresearch.org/fact-tank/2021/07/16/home-broadband-adoption-computer-ownership-vary-by-race-ethnicity-in-the-u-s/#/

Qi, Han, Rui Liu, Xu Chen, Xiao-Fei Yuan, Ya-Qiong Li, Huan-Huan Huang, Yi Zheng, and Gang Wang. 2020. "Prevalence of Anxiety and Associated Factors for Chinese Adolescents during the COVID-19 Outbreak." *Psychiatry and Clinical Neurosciences (PCN)* 72(10): 555–57. https://doi.org/10.1111/pcn.13102.

Salinas, Elena Maria. 2020. "Without Wi-Fi, Low Income Latino Students Resorted to Doing Homework in Parking Lots to Access Public Hotspots." *CBS NEWS*, 17 July. Retrieved 21 September 2022 from https://www.cbsnews.com/news/low-income-latino-communities-digital-divide-coronavirus-pandemic/?s=09.

Talidong, Karen Joy B., and Cathy Mae D. Toquero. 2020. "Philippine Teachers' Practices to Deal with Anxiety amid COVID-19." *Journal of Loss and Trauma* 25(6/7): 573–79. https://doi.org/10.1080/15325024.2020.1759225.

PART III
Vulnerabilities

CHAPTER 8

Lockdown and Violence against Women and Children
Insights from Hospital-Based Crisis Intervention Centers in Mumbai, India

Anupriya Singh, Sangeeta Rege, and Anagha Pradhan

Introduction

The COVID-19 pandemic is still unfolding, and its full impact is yet to be realized. However, global experience from the HIV, Ebola, and Zika epidemics suggests that pandemics, like other disasters and humanitarian crises, affect women more adversely because of the interactions between and among several preexisting and newly added vulnerabilities. One of the most noted impacts of pandemics is the increase in domestic violence and in intimate partner violence (IPV) against women and girls. Pandemic-related food shortages, economic crises, uncertainty about the future, and psychological stress from isolation and quarantine are known to increase the frequency and intensity of violence against women and children (VAW/C). Data from several countries shows a manifold increase in the incidence of VAW/C during the COVID-19 pandemic lockdown

Notes for this section can be found on page 153.

(Peterman et al. 2020). A rapid assessment by UN Women in Europe and Central Asia found that during the present crisis women's psychological and mental health has been affected more than men's and that between 20 and 40 percent of women did not know where to seek help (UN Women 2020). The contraction of health services and restricted mobility resulting from the breakdown of transport services further reduces survivors' access to essential services, such as psychological support, as well as to contraceptives and post-exposure prophylaxis.

The adverse effects of epidemics, and of this pandemic, on adolescent girls are more complex. Adolescent girls face violence specific to their age and gender (Ellsberg et al. 2017), as well as the consequences of the stay-at-home policy, which include emotional stress and anxiety about the future, exposure to parental violence, disrupted education, forced early marriage, and the deprivation of peer and other support services (Peterman et al. 2020). Violence against women (VAW) is known to be associated with a wide range of adverse physical, sexual, and mental health impacts (Rege and Bhate-Deosthali 2018). A surge in unwanted pregnancy among adolescent girls, mostly resulting from sexual violence following the Ebola epidemic in Africa, was found to be associated with the closure of schools and increased exposure of girls to abusers as they took on the role of caregivers to the family (UNFPA 2015).

Health systems have a crucial role to play in ensuring an effective response to women and girls reporting violence, since a well-organized and sensitive health system can facilitate disclosure of such violence as well as providing care. Health systems are also often the first port of call for women and girls facing violence (WHO 2013). However, global experience from previous epidemics shows that when health systems are overwhelmed with epidemic management, routine essential service delivery may be affected, and this can result in non-epidemic-related, preventable morbidity and mortality (UN Women 2020). COVID-19 has placed an immense burden on health systems and health providers but, despite this, actions related to care and psychological first aid for survivors can help mitigate some of the consequences of violence. In relation to epidemics, the World Health Organization (WHO) guidelines underline the health system's responsibility to ensure the provision of high-quality essential services that foster in the population trust in the health system and that sustain appropriate health-seeking, even during an epidemic (WHO 2020). These guidelines recommend exploring the possibility of gender-based violence (GBV) in all health-seeking contact interviews, including those that are part of prenatal care, and also emphasize making information available to women and adolescent girls, as well as services that help to mitigate the health-related effects arising from IPV, GBV, and sexual violence, and, in general, ensuring a response to the medical, psychological, and social needs of survivors of such violence.

In India, the National Family Health Survey (Government of India, Ministry of Health and Family Welfare 2017) is the only source of data on a national level on the prevalence of IPV. It states that almost one-third of women who have ever been married (31 percent) have experienced spousal physical, sexual, or emotional violence inflicted by their current husband (for currently married women) or most recent husband (for formerly married women), while 24 percent had experienced at least one of these forms of violence in the twelve months preceding the survey. Several accounts point to an increase in calls to helplines dealing with violence against women and children during the lockdown (Nigam 2020).

While the lockdown in India was announced on 24 March 2020, directives for the implementation of a list of essential services were announced by the Ministry of Health and Family Welfare (MoHFW) and the Ministry of Women and Child Development (MoWCD) well after a month into the lockdown. This list directed all hospitals to continue the provision of uninterrupted care for women and child survivors of violence, including appropriate referrals to support services.

The on-the-ground reality in India showed that the public health system was overwhelmed with COVID-19 case management and lacked the preparedness for the provision of essential services, including those for survivors of violence. Although the MoHFW directive mentioned the need to engage the private sector in states facing a shortfall of public health facilities, there is no evidence of any uptake by private providers. On the contrary, media reports expressed concerns related to the private health sector in terms of overcharging, insisting on COVID tests irrespective of health problems, and reducing or completely shutting down non-COVID health-related services. There are several anecdotal accounts of the denial of maternal health services having led to maternal morbidities and mortalities (Prasad et al. 2020). Additionally, access to safe abortion services was affected in both public and private healthcare facilities (Ipas Development Foundation 2020), and maternal mortality is estimated to increase by 52 percent over the next year (Global Financing Facility 2020). Despite directives issued by the MoWCD for all offices engaged in VAW response services (Government of India, Ministry of Women and Child Development 2020), several services, such as one-stop centers, shelter homes, child welfare services, and offices of protection officers, were not available.

One of the first responses to VAW/C came from the Municipal Corporation of Greater Mumbai when it declared that Dilaasa centers offer essential services and must continue to do so during the lockdown as part of outpatient departments providing psychosocial services to women and children facing violence.[1] Each has a team of two counselors, two auxiliary nurse midwives, and a data entry operator. At Dilaasa centers, survivors of violence are provided with psychological support through empowerment counseling, emergency shelter in the hospital, police aid and legal intervention, and medical and medicolegal support. Dilaasa counselors liaise with other support agencies such as the Child Welfare Committee (a district-level autonomous body set up under the Juvenile Justice Act (2015) to assist children in need of care and protection), Protection Officers (appointed by the State Department of Women and Child Development to liaise between the violence survivor and the judiciary system), the District Legal Services Authority (which ensures that those who cannot afford legal fees are provided with lawyers free of cost), government-run shelter homes, and special cells (located inside police stations) for women and children to facilitate comprehensive care for them. During the lockdown, Dilaasa centers continued to provide services to women who sought them personally or via telephone.

Some positive examples of state response have also been noted during the lockdown and ongoing pandemic, ranging from declaring hospital-based crisis intervention centers as emergency services to strong messages from political leaders that VAW/C will not be tolerated and announcements from district-level administrators that abusive partners will be sent to institution-based quarantine facilities (Bhate-Deosthali 2020). The divisional bench of Jammu and Kashmir High Court took *suo moto* cognizance of the increase in VAW during the pandemic and said that "all courts will treat cases of domestic violence with urgency and proceed with the matters in accordance with the Circulars issued regarding the procedure to be followed ensuring social distancing" (Rege and Shrivastava 2020).[2]

Efforts were made at Dilaasa centers to move from face-to-face counseling to telephone support for survivors of VAW/C during the COVID-19 lockdown. Recognizing that women may not have privacy even if contacted on safe phone numbers, guidance was provided on how to initiate telephone conversations even if abusers were around. These entailed enquiring about the survivor's and her family's health and relief requirements

(Rege and Shrivastava 2020). The Centre for Enquiry into Health and Allied Themes (CEHAT) also operated a twenty-four-hour helpline for survivors across India.

In this chapter, based on the experiences of survivors who sought help at Dilaasa centers during lockdown, we discuss the challenges faced by adolescent and young women survivors in seeking help, as well as those faced by counselors in providing it because of the lockdown.

Methodology

Dilaasa centers were approached by 180 women and girl survivors of GVB between lockdown and the time of writing (March to June 2020). Adolescent girls and young women aged between ten and twenty years accounted for 17 percent (31/180) of survivors. We present details of their experiences in this chapter. Survivors older than twenty were not included in the data analysis we report on in this chapter.

While twenty of the thirty-one survivors only contacted the helpline, eleven reached the hospital and, subsequently, a Dilaasa center. Of the twenty telephone contacts, four were calls from survivors, three from parents, and two from support agencies, while the rest were calls from counselors contacting girls and women survivors registered with Dilaasa who could not access the center physically because of the lockdown.

Other survivors reached the hospitals and Dilaasa centers despite stringent lockdown. Of these eleven women and girls, seven sought healthcare for the termination of pregnancy, prenatal care, or the delivery of babies that resulted from sexual violence or consensual sex between minors, while four, accompanied by the police, were admitted for medico-legal examination—two girls who had run away from home and two minors who had had consensual sex.

Counselors maintain documentation for all survivors who seek help, including details about the nature of the violence experienced, pathways to the crisis center, the individual survivor's expectations of the counselor, the intervention provided, and specific challenges faced by survivors because of the lockdown. This has been an established practice in Dilaasa centers since their inception. The data is maintained in hard copies and transferred to Excel format by a team of data entry operators and researchers in consultation with counselors. The team members who are not directly involved in the provision of crisis counseling services sign a confidentiality agreement in relation to the intake forms and data. All publications related to data are then reviewed by the institutional ethics committee and scientific review committee. In this chapter we draw on these records.

Profile of the Girls and Women Who Sought Services during Lockdown

All except one of the nineteen adolescent survivors aged between twelve and seventeen were unmarried. The twelve young women survivors were aged between eighteen and twenty. Of these, two were in live-in relationships and one was married. Fourteen survivors, all new cases, sought help from a Dilaasa center for the first time during lockdown. Most survivors (twenty-eight of thirty-one) belonged to economically marginalized groups with family breadwinners engaged in unskilled or semiskilled occupations in the informal sector. The parents of the other three girls worked as professionals in the organized sector. Of these girls and young women, twenty-six were survivors of sexual violence and the remaining five were survivors of domestic violence.

Findings

In this section, we present the impact of lockdown on adolescent girls and young women in relation to the barriers they faced in accessing services and the efforts made by counselors to respond to their immediate needs, facilitate access to services, and stop the violence to which they were being subjected.

Increased Vulnerability to Abuse from Family

Incest and Lack of a Support System

When she called the helpline, eighteen-year-old Nitya disclosed that she was a victim of incest.[3] She spoke hesitantly about having been raped by her father over the past four years. The frequency of abuse had increased during the lockdown. Her mother had been a mute spectator and Nitya had not been able to disclose this to any other family member or friend. Her feelings of loneliness, helplessness, and anxiety increased and resulted in her being disconnected from the outside world. The closure of schools and the inability to meet friends who had provided her with a coping mechanism made her call the helpline and seek support for the first time. She was scheduled to go abroad for her higher education and had hoped that the relocation would end the abuse. The pandemic, with its online education and its sealing of international borders, threatened her plans. The counselor validated her sense that this was a difficult time and suggested that she might need to think of alternative options. She rejected the suggestion of making a complaint to the police despite all the efforts of the counselor to ensure that she was protected and did not lose access to her house or to financial support. Options such as speaking to at least one trusted person about the ongoing abuse, temporarily moving in with a friend, and speaking to her father in the presence of a supportive person were also discussed. Nitya disclosed to the counselor that she had tolerated years of abuse and felt that she could deal with it for a few more months. This was the first time she had talked about her experience to an outsider, and it was important for her to feel the nonjudgmental acceptance inherent in the fact that someone trusted her without blaming her. The counselor continued to speak to Nitya, who finally said that she would disclose the abuse to a close friend and think about moving in with her.

Inappropriate Touching by a Brother Who Was Also a Minor

Niyoti, who was twelve, had been disrobed and inappropriately touched by her fifteen-year-old brother. This was the first episode of violence that she had experienced. Her parents, essential services providers, would leave home early and return late in the evening. The closure of schools left her unsupervised at home with her brother. Niyoti was confused by the experience and found the helpline number on social media. She told the counselor that she knew it was wrong, but she liked the touch and felt guilty for feeling pleasure. She feared being judged by her parents and so did not want to disclose this to them. The counselor validated her feelings and discussed the bodily changes associated with adolescence, stressing the importance of differentiating between sexual pleasure and unsafe touch. The counselor also discussed ways of keeping herself safe if she ever found herself alone with her brother and encouraged her to speak to her parents to ensure that the abuse was not repeated.

Domestic Violence by a Father and Fear of Losing Shelter

Stay-at-home orders placed young girls like eighteen-year-old Priya at risk of abuse. Priya and her sister have an extremely abusive father. He does not allow them to use mobile phones, delays paying college fees, and constantly threatens to throw them out of the house if they do not comply with his rules. They are under his constant vigilance and are criticized for wearing Western attire and makeup. With the lockdown underway, the violence intensified. Priya was locked in a room and denied food when she questioned her father's abusive behavior. She was unable to get out of her house and contacted the helpline for support. The counselor discussed different strategies, such as involving neighbors who could negotiate with her father and change his ways, but because he was a politically influential person neighbors did not want to engage with him. It was critical to get Priya out of the house, so the counselor suggested involving the police. The police went to her house and asked her father to release her from her room. Since she had disclosed that her grandparents lived in the same building (and are equally abusive), the counselor liaised with the police to ask the father to move in with his parents and have the sisters live with their mother.

Nonrecognition of Work-from-Home Commitments

Parveen, a young working professional who is the main earner in her family, had been facing abuse from her brother and her mother. Lockdown forced her to work from home. Increased housework coupled with her loss of earnings had made her mother irritable and she was not supportive of Parveen's work. She expected Parveen to do housework and was unable to comprehend that working on a computer constitutes working from home. Parveen's office work had increased, so she asked her brother to take up some of the household chores. He became violent and tried to slap her. When the constant abuse became unbearable Parveen contacted the helpline, because she found it impossible to stay under the same roof as her mother and brother. The counselor discussed different strategies, such as involving housing committee members to stop the abuse, since moving out during lockdown was not possible. But Parveen then located a friend who was willing to house her, so the counselor facilitated safe passage for her with the help of the police.

Increased Tensions and Vigilance by Parents

The closure of schools trapped adolescents at home. Separation from her peers, having to share household chores, and the constant vigilance of her parents drove sixteen-year-old Jaya to run away from home. Worried about her safety, her parents filed a police complaint that led to their tracing her. The police brought her to the hospital for medical examination to rule out sexual assault. When the Dilaasa counselor comforted her in the privacy of the counseling department, Jaya disclosed that the constant nagging of her mother had led her to run away. She revealed that they live on the fringes of a forest area and that she went to the forest and sat there until she was located by the police. The counselor validated her feelings of frustration and encouraged her to discuss with her parents the stress she was facing. It was also critical for the counselor to discuss with Jaya her physical safety and the risks involved in being by herself in a forest. She was encouraged to contact the helpline when she felt stressed or wanted to unburden herself. She was counseled into communicating with her mother, since it was important for her to discuss the impact of lockdown on her, her fears and insecurity, and her need to be reassured.

Aggravation of Threats and Harassment of a Rape Survivor

Smita is a sixteen-year-old survivor of sexual violence. She had registered a police complaint against the abuser before the lockdown was imposed and the abuser was arrested. During lockdown, Smita and her family were verbally abused, blamed, and pressured by the abuser's relatives to withdraw the case. Smita's father received no support from the police, and the increase in threats, along with the complete lack of support from anyone, led the family to phone a Dilaasa counselor. The counselor contacted the investigating officer, informed him about the abuse faced by the survivor and her family, and urged him to provide immediate assistance. Intervention by Dilaasa helped mobilize police support and repeated reprimands by the police helped put a stop to the verbal abuse the family had been facing. Since family members had to approach the police physically, counselors also addressed concerns about exposure, the possibility of infection, and precautionary measures to prevent their contracting COVID-19.

Disruption of Government Services and Barriers to Access to Care

Access to Abortion Services

As the focus of hospitals shifted to a COVID-19 response, sexual and reproductive health services among others were invariably deprioritized.

This was evident in the case of twenty-year-old Meeta, a young woman who came to a hospital requesting an abortion when she was eight weeks pregnant. The hospital turned her away and said that she should come back after the lockdown was lifted. Dilaasa counselors had to intervene and explain the impact it would have on her if she waited any longer, and they requested that a medical abortion be provided. The doctors insisted on a battery of tests that were not indicated for medical abortion and would delay it. Medical abortion in India is allowed up to nine weeks into pregnancy according to the MoHFW guidelines (Government of India, Ministry of Health and Family Welfare 2013). In order to prevent further delay, an NGO service provider was located to avoid having Meeta travel during lockdown and to ensure quick service.

The pregnancy of Seema, a fourteen-year-old rape survivor, was diagnosed to be of twenty weeks' duration. Indian law allows medical termination of pregnancy post-twenty weeks of gestation only through a court order. Seema and her parents were desperate but could not leave home since the police enforced the lockdown restrictions on any travel from home. It was the counselors who negotiated with the police and organized transport that allowed Seema to reach a public hospital for an examination. Dilaasa counselors liaising with a lawyer to present her case to the court and seek an order of termination of pregnancy finally resulted in her being given the required service.

Despite directives of the MoHFW declaring sexual and reproductive health services as essential, Seema's case points to their non-implementation, since it was only following the intervention of a trained counselor that she, like many others, could be given the required medical services.

Access to a Shelter Home

Gaining access to a shelter home proved to be a challenge for Pooja, a seventeen-year-old rape survivor who was seven months pregnant. She lived with her mother, a single parent dependent on her extended family for financial and social support. During the lockdown extended family members feared stigmatization by neighbors and members of the community, so Pooja was asked to leave home. Shelter homes denied her admission, citing a lack of quarantine facilities mandated by the government directive. Later, they insisted on a negative COVID-19 test. Dilaasa counselors had to intervene and after several phone calls and negotiation with an entire chain of command, Pooja was accepted into a shelter facility.

Extended Stay in a Shelter Against the Wishes of a Young Girl and Her Parents

A thirteen-year-old rape survivor, Rita, whose pregnancy was detected in her third trimester, was admitted by her parents to a hospital for the delivery of her baby. Rita and the newborn were discharged from the hospital and, following the procedures of the Child Welfare Committee (CWC), both were moved to a shelter home. According to the procedures, Rita's parents were expected to be brought in to relinquish the baby for adoption. With the sudden announcement of the lockdown, however, CWC members stopped coming to the shelter home. Adoption procedures were put on hold. Rita was stuck there. Since her parents had lost their livelihood, they were desperate to return to their native home and wanted the shelter home to release their daughter. When repeated pleas to the shelter home authorities failed, Rita's parents approached Dilaasa in a desperate bid to get their daughter back. Interventions in this instance were lengthy, since shelter homes had no guidance on how to hand back a child; the CWC had this authority, and they could not meet to complete the procedures because of the lockdown. It was only after much negotiation that the shelter relented, and Rita was released to her parents.

Dealing with Economic Stress from the Loss of Livelihood

Five survivors who had sought Dilaasa services disclosed that lockdown resulted in their parents losing employment in the informal sector, and that this resulted in a food crisis for their families. The counselors addressed the immediate need by connecting them with NGOs engaged in relief work.

Closure of Courts and Police Apathy toward Violence against Women

The complete shutdown of the courts and the refusal by the police to record complaints added to the emotional trauma of Ayesha, a seventeen-year-old rape survivor who was forced by her family to marry her abuser to protect what is known as family honor. The police refused to protect her despite her having reported physical and emotional violence. When she called the helpline in acute distress, several calls and follow-up actions led to her getting a complaint recorded and moving to a safe place.

Discussion

Given the background of reports of increased numbers of cases of violence against women, the reduction in the number of cases registered with hospital-based Dilaasa centers needs special consideration. In the first two months of lockdown, five of the eleven hospitals where Dilaasa centers are located were declared COVID-dedicated facilities, and most noncritical services were suspended to avoid the spread of infection. Additionally, the once-safe havens for accessing VAW services for survivors were now high-risk places for contracting COVID-19 or other infections, and this could explain the reduction in cases of VAW registered at these Dilaasa centers.

A decrease in hospital-based obstetric care was also noted during the Ebola epidemic in 2015 (UNFPA 2015). Such reduced use of healthcare during epidemics is a result of the fear of infection and associated stigma, restricted mobility, and trust in the health system becoming eroded. Economically marginalized families may delay health-seeking activity to avoid out-of-pocket medical costs in the face of an economic crisis (WHO 2020). This was seen in the case of a young survivor, thirteen-year-old Reena, whose family, fearing infection, treated her persistent abdominal pain with painkillers at home for weeks. This pain was later diagnosed as related to her advanced pregnancy, the result of sexual violence. Reena might be seen as representative of all those young girls who might not have been able to reach a health facility despite physical symptoms resulting from abuse.

Of the thirty-one survivors discussed here, three had reached hospital in their second trimester for an abortion. The barriers and anxieties experienced by unmarried, pregnant Indian girls, trapped in a social culture and legal framework that denies adolescents the sexual rights and agency to make sexual reproductive health decisions (Jain and Tronic 2019; Jejeebhoy et al. 2010; Kalyanwala et al. 2010), were intensified during the lockdown (Jain and Tronic 2019). Healthcare providers that are unsympathetic to their situation and insistent on parental consent do not help either (Ayyavoo et al. 2018). The conversion of public health facilities to COVID-19 care centers, the shutdown of private sector facilities because of their unwillingness to remain open, the nonavailability of healthcare providers, and the lack of protective gear further hampered girls' access to safe abortion care (Ipas Development Foundation 2020).

The lack of clear protocols and guidance for the CWCs, shelter homes, and one-stop centers impeded survivors' access to support. Unreasonable demands such as a compulsory negative COVID-19 test for shelter admission and mandatory quarantine at institutions led to the denial of services for survivors. Those approaching Dilaasa centers could access services because of the efforts of dedicated counselors who negotiated barriers on their behalf.

The duration of lockdown, the fear of infection, inadequate supplies, boredom and frustration, and inadequate information are well-documented stressors during quarantine (Brooks et al. 2020). Additionally, those with weaker economic status who suffer loss of income show higher levels of depression and stress (Peterman et al. 2020; WHO 2020). Mental health professionals have predicted an increase in anxiety, depression, and self-harm during and post-pandemic, while a recent Indian survey has shown a 20 percent increase in mental health conditions during lockdown (Kumar and Nayar 2020). Quarantine, isolation, restrictions on mobility, deprivation of social support, and exposure to uncertainties common to quarantine are known to cause restlessness, boredom, frustration, and, at times, violence among children and adolescents (ibid.). There is an urgent need to ensure psychological support for adolescents during these and other times of crisis (Guessouma et al. 2020).

Helplines managed by trained psychologists are known to be effective for getting mental health support to those who may not be able to access it physically (Sriram et al. 2016). With social distancing, quarantine, and lockdowns being the only strategies for the control of the COVID-19 pandemic, survivors were encouraged to use digital and technology-based services, including helplines and web-based applications. While global experience shows adolescents being more comfortable using these means, their usefulness in the Indian context, especially for adolescent girls and young women from socioeconomically disadvantaged groups who have limited access to mobile phones and the internet, as well as the required privacy, remains limited (Nigam 2020). A patriarchal society, gendered access to technology, and higher vigilance toward girls and young women may pose a barrier to the use of telephone support systems for Indian girls when their abusers are in close proximity to them.

Conclusion

The lockdown compounded the vulnerabilities of survivors of violence. The experiences of adolescent girls who sought support at Dilaasa centers during the lockdown are representative of the plight of many who may not have been able to seek services. The urgency of the interventions needed by all these girls proves the value of the decision to declare Dilaasa centers as an emergency service. The location of Dilaasa centers in hospitals played a valuable role, as did the adoption of alternative strategies for contacting all those who had been registered at the departments, and a 24/7 helpline. Functioning in times of crisis, the Dilaasa teams ensured the availability of services and liaised with many government agencies to ensure that young girls received the necessary services. However, the lockdown also exposed the lack of guidelines and protocols for state service providers such as shelter homes and legal service authorities, who could have played a pivotal role in comprehensive service provision. Going forward, it is critical to create a plan for the preparedness of systems across different departments responsible for preventing and mitigating the impact of violence on women and girls. Clearer guidelines regarding the functioning of support services during emergencies and better monitoring of the services available to survivors of violence need to be prioritized.

Acknowledgments

We acknowledge the dedication of Dilaasa teams who continue to provide support to the survivors of violence during the most trying times of the COVID-19 pandemic.

Sujata Ayarkar helped with the compilation and preliminary analysis of data for this chapter. Dr. Padma Bhate-Deosthali, Senior Advisor to CEHAT, reviewed the early drafts and provided useful recommendations.

ANUPRIYA SINGH is the Senior Research Officer at the Centre for Enquiry into Health and Allied Themes (CEHAT), a non-profit working on health and human rights, and is engaged in intervention with survivors of violence to provide psychosocial support. She has five years of experience in engaging with women and children facing violence.

SANGEETA REGE is the Coordinator of CEHAT and leads the organization toward research and interventions in the health concerns of marginalized people. She has eighteen years of experience in engaging with the public health sector on GBV and integrating gender concerns into medical education.

Anagha Pradhan is a Senior Research Officer at CEHAT. She has over twenty years of experience in social health research with a focus on public health systems.

Notes

1. The first Dilaasa (a Hindi word that means "reassurance") center was established in 2000 by the Municipal Corporation of Greater Mumbai (MCGM) and the Centre for Health and Allied Themes (CEHAT). In 2006, it was integrated as an outpatient department into the hospital following a positive evaluation, and in 2015 Dilaasa departments were replicated in eleven municipal hospitals under the National Health Mission, a flagship health program of the Government of India. Since 2005, the CEHAT has been the technical partner of the MCGM for building the capacity of healthcare providers and for monitoring the health-system response to violence against women.
2. See "COVID-19" (2020).
3. All names used are pseudonymous.

References

Ayyavoo, Charmila, Jayam Kanan, and Ahila Ayyavoo. 2018. "Would Abortion Services in India Benefit from Lesser Hurdles?" *Journal of Evidence Based Medicine and Healthcare* 5(4): 2890–94. https://doi.org/10.18410/jebmh/2018/591.

Bhate-Deosthali, Padma. 2020. "Responding to Violence against Women—The Shadow Pandemic during COVID-19." *The Leaflet*, 22 April. Retrieved 22 September 2022 from https://theleaflet.in/responding-to-vaw-the-shadow-pandemic-during-covid-19/.

Bhate-Deosthali, Padma, Sangeeta Rege, Poulomi Pal, Subhalakshmi Nandi, Nandita Bhatla, and Alpaxee Kashyap. 2018. *Role of the Health Sector in Addressing Intimate Partner Violence in India: A Synthesis Report*. New Delhi: International Center for Research on Women.

Brooks, Samantha K., Rebecca K. Webster, Louise E. Smith, Lisa Woodland, Simon Wessely, Neil Greenberg, and Gideon James Rubin. 2020. "The Psychological Impact of Quarantine and How to Reduce It: Rapid Review of the Evidence." *The Lancet* 395(10227): 912–20. https://doi.org/10.1016/S0140-6736(20)30460-8.

"COVID-19: J&K HC Takes Suo Moto Cognizance of Increase in Domestic Violence Cases amidst Lockdown." 2020. *The Leaflet*, 18 April. Retrieved 22 September 2022 from https://theleaflet.in/covid-19-jk-hc-takes-suo-moto-cognizance-of-increase-in-domestic-violence-cases-amidst-lockdown/.

Ellsberg, Mary, Amita Vyas, Bernadette Madrid, Margarita Quintanilla, Jennifer Zelaya, and Heidi Stöckl. 2017. *Violence Against Adolescent Girls: Falling through the Cracks?* Background paper, Ending Violence in Childhood Global Report. New Delhi: Know Violence in Childhood.

Global Financing Facility. 2020. "Preserve Essential Services during the COVID-19 Pandemic: India." Retrieved 22 September 2022 from https://www.globalfinancingfacility.org/sites/gff_new/files/documents/India-Covid-Brief_GFF.pdf.

Government of India, Ministry of Health and Family Welfare. 2013. *A Strategic Approach to Reproductive, Maternal, Newborn, Child and Adolescent Health (RMNCH+A) in India.* New Delhi.

———. 2017. *India Fact Sheet: National Family Health Survey (NHFS-4), 2015–2016.* Mumbai: International Institute for Population Studies.

Government of India, Ministry of Women and Child Development. 2020. "Operations of One Stop Centres and Women Help Lines and Designated Officials to Help Violence affected Woman due to Special Circumstances Prevailing." Retrieved 7 November 2022 from https://wcd.nic.in/sites/default/files/Advisory%20dated%2025.03.2020%20for%20OSC-WHL_0.pdf

Guessouma, Sélim Benjamin, Jonathan Lachal, Rahmeth Radjack, Emilie Carretier, Sevan Minassian, Laelia Benoit, and Marie Rose Moro. 2020. "Adolescent Psychiatric Disorders during the COVID-19 Pandemic and Lockdown." *Psychiatry Research* 291: 113264. https://doi.org/10.1016/j.psychres.2020.113264.

Ipas Development Foundation. 2020. *Compromised Abortion Access due to COVID-19: A Model to Determine Impact of COVID-19 on Women's Access to Abortion.* New Delhi.

Jain, Dipika, and Brian Tronic. 2019. "Conflicting Abortion Laws in India: Unintended Barriers to Safe Abortion for Adolescent Girls." *Indian Journal of Medical Ethics* 4(4): 310–17. https://doi.org/10.20529/IJME.2019.059.

Jejeebhoy, Shireen J., Shveta Kalyanwala, A. J. Francis Zavier, Rajesh Kumar, and Nita Jha. 2010. "Experience Seeking Abortion among Unmarried Young Women in Bihar and Jharkhand, India: Delays and Disadvantages." *Reproductive Health Matters* 18(35): 163–74. https://doi.org/10.1016/S0968-8080(10)35504-2.

Kalyanwala, Shveta, A. J. Francis Zavier, Shireen Jejeebhoy, and Rajesh Kumar. 2010. "Abortion Experiences of Unmarried Young Women in India: Evidence from a Facility-Based Study in Bihar and Jharkhand." *International Perspectives on Sexual and Reproductive Health* 36(2): 62–71. https://doi.org/10.1363/ipsrh.36.062.10.

Kumar, Anant, and K. Rajasekharan Nayar. 2020. "COVID 19 and its Mental Health Consequences." *Journal of Mental Health* 30(1): 1–2. https://doi.org/10.1080/09638237.2020.1757052.

Nigam, Shalu. 2020. "COVID-19, Lockdown and Violence against Women in Homes." *SSRN*, 29 April. Retrieved 22 September 2022 from https://papers.ssrn.com/sol3/papers.cfm?abstract_id=3587399.

Peterman, Amber, Alina Potts, Megan O'Donnell, Kelly Thompson, Niyati Shah, Sabine Oertelt-Prigione, and Nicole van Gelder. 2020. *Pandemics and Violence Against Women and Children*. CGD Working Paper 528. Washington, DC: Center for Global Development. Retrieved 22 September 2022 from https://www.cgdev.org/sites/default/files/pandemics-and-vawg-april2.pdf.

Prasad, Vandana, B. Subha Sri, and Rakhal Gaitonde. 2020. "Bridging a False Dichotomy in the COVID-19 Response: A Public Health Approach to the 'Lockdown' Debate." *BMJ Global Health* 5(6): 1–5. http://dx.doi.org/10.1136/bmjgh-2020-002909.

Rege, Sangeeta, and Padma Bhate-Deosthali. 2018. "Violence against Women as a Health Care Issue: Perceptions and Approaches." In *Equity and Access: Health Care Studies in India*, ed. Purendra Prasad and Amar Jesani, 286–302. New Delhi: Oxford University Press.

Rege, Sangeeta, and Surbhi Shrivastava. 2020. "Coping with the 'Shadow Pandemic': Responding to Violence against Women during COVID-19." *Sexual Violence Research Initiative (SVRI)*, 20 May. Retrieved 22 September 2022 from https://svri.org/blog/coping-%E2%80%98shadow-pandemic%E2%80%99-responding-violence-against-women-during-covid-19.

Sriram, Sujata, Aparna Joshi, and Paras Sharma. 2016. "Telephone Counselling in India: Lessons from iCALL." In *Counselling in India*, ed. Sujata Sriram, 201–16. Singapore: Springer. https://doi.org/10.1007/978-981-10-0584-8_11.

UNFPA (United Nations Population Fund). 2015. *Rapid Assessment of Ebola Impact on Reproductive Health Services and Service Seeking Behaviour in Sierra Leone*. Freetown. Retrieved 7 November 2022 from https://reliefweb.int/sites/reliefweb.int/files/resources/UNFPA%20study%20_synthesis_March%202025_final.pdf

UN Women. 2020. "Gender Assessments in Europe and Central Asia Reveal Pandemic's Devastating Impact on Women." 21 July. Retrieved 22 September 2022 from https://www.unwomen.org/en/news/stories/2020/7/news-europe-and-central-asia-gender-assessments-reveal-pandemics--impact-on-women.

WHO (World Health Organization). 2013. *Responding to Intimate Partner Violence and Sexual Violence Against Women: WHO Clinical and Policy Guidelines*. Geneva.

———. 2020. "Maintaining Essential Health Services: Operational Guidance for the COVID-19 Context: Interim Guidance." 1 June. Retrieved 22 September 2022 from https://apps.who.int/iris/handle/10665/332240.

CHAPTER 9

The Impact of COVID-19 on Child Marriage in India

Gayatri Sharma and Ayesha Khaliq

Introduction

The COVID-19 pandemic has devastated families across the globe. As a result of COVID-19, up to ten million more girls are now at risk of becoming child brides (UNICEF 2021). Since all girls are not positioned equally, some will suffer more. Experience from the Ebola crisis strongly suggests that girls will be disproportionately affected, particularly those among the poorest and most socially marginalized groups (Girls Not Brides 2020). Economically weaker countries have been less successful in withstanding the pandemic. India was particularly vulnerable since government expenditure on healthcare and education has reduced over the years, thereby increasing the gap between those who can afford private education and healthcare and those who cannot. Between 2019 and 2020, India spent only 3.1 percent of its gross domestic product on education and 1.26 percent on healthcare (Khadria and Thakur 2020; Mondal 2021). Those who are less able to access education and healthcare are more vulnerable to

---

Notes for this section can be found on page 170.

death, financial insecurity, dropping out from education, child marriage, child labor, and child trafficking.

In March 2020, India imposed one of the strictest lockdowns in the world, and this had disastrous consequences for poor people who lacked the savings required to survive without a work-related income in cities across India. The lockdown was followed by the revelation that a religious gathering of the Tablighi Jamaat (an Islamic missionary movement) in New Delhi in mid-March 2020 had led to a large spike in the coronavirus cases reported in India. This revelation came at a time when Hindu-Muslim relations were already strained. Several news channels published fake news ostensibly showing Muslims deliberately spreading the coronavirus. Religious tensions, which were already high in India, were exacerbated and cases of discrimination toward Muslims in relation to the denial of healthcare and the refusal to accept their services were reported.

The social impact of the marginalization of Muslims was first felt when Muslim women had difficulty in accessing medical services. Cases were reported from Rajasthan and Jharkhand of pregnant Muslim women being denied such services and the subsequent death of a baby (Angad 2020; Iqbal 2020). A hospital in Uttar Pradesh required Muslims to have evidence of a negative COVID-19 test result before they could receive treatment (Agrawal 2020). In Gujarat, a hospital was reported to be segregating Hindu and Muslim patients (Ghosh and Dabhi 2020). A surge in atrocities against Dalits was also reported during the first wave.[1] The concept of physical distancing was twisted to strengthen notions of untouchability—a form of social ostracism and segregation directed against Dalits. Although this is prohibited by the Constitution, it is still extant, and the pandemic led to its increased practice along with other forms of caste-based discrimination. For example, *Times Now* reported that in Jharkhand, "Five Brahmins lodged at [a] quarantine facility refuse[d] to eat food prepared by SC cooks" ("Jharkhand" 2020).

Girls who belong to Adivasi families are normally at higher risk of being married off early because of their lack of access to education and employment opportunities. Adivasis (Indigenous/tribal groups) primarily live in remote forest fringe areas. The pandemic compounded the problem because schools remained closed and access to livelihood options became more difficult to secure. Furthermore, Indigenous people living in these areas are more vulnerable to the impact of climate change. Heavy flooding in Assam, West Bengal, and Bihar coincided with the 2020 pandemic, leading to further distress for Indigenous communities and greater likelihood of girls being subjected to forced or early marriage.

Since the Indian economy contracted by a historic 23.9 percent following the unplanned lockdown in March 2020, the loss of jobs and livelihood translated into children being pulled out of school, girls being forced into early marriages, and an increase in child labor. When the first lockdown eased in June and July 2020, child marriages spiked, marking a 17 percent increase from the previous year (Bhandare 2020). According to the *Times of India* ("Government Intervened" 2020), CHILDLINE, a national helpline, intervened in nearly 5,584 cases related to child marriage during the 2020 lockdown. A study conducted by the Centre for Catalyzing Change (2020) reported that in Jharkhand, Chhattisgarh, Odisha, and Bihar, 8 percent of respondents came across incidents of child marriage in their neighborhood that had occurred since the beginning of the pandemic, and two-thirds of adolescents reported that their family members were planning their marriage; the proportion was higher among girls.

Child marriage has significant detrimental ramifications for girls, and the pandemic has made matters much worse. In line with this, this chapter aims to examine the role of COVID-19 in exacerbating the conditions contributing to a rise in child marriages in India, and proposes recommendations for developing a comprehensive response to prevent the number of child marriages from escalating. Our qualitative research methodology relied on a desk-based analysis of existing materials. Information was acquired from published literature, journals, media articles, and research papers for an in-depth analysis aimed at understanding the factors that contribute to child marriage in India, as well as their consequences and their impact on girls' development and well-being.

Reverse Migration

Within a few days of the start of the twenty-one-day lockdown announced on 24 March 2020, thousands of migrant workers gathered at the bus station in Delhi in the hope of reaching home. Unable to find transport, casual workers formerly employed in Delhi, Gurgaon (Haryana), Punjab, Gujarat, Mumbai (Maharashtra), and Tamil Nadu walked home to their native villages and towns in Uttar Pradesh, Odisha, Bihar, and Jharkhand. As factories and workplaces closed down, people who were dependent on daily wages ran out of savings. The Supreme Court directed the central and state government to send migrant workers back to their homes in special trains only in June, more than two months after the lockdown was implemented. It is unclear how many workers migrated back to their homes in rural areas, but based on census estimates of the number of migrants who enter urban areas annually for work, it is estimated that about twenty-three million workers migrated back to rural areas as a result of COVID-19 (Kundu 2020). According to the World Bank (2020), the lockdown in India has had an impact on the livelihoods of a large proportion of the country's nearly forty million internal migrants. While government and NGOs did provide basic necessities in camps to those who did not return home, many had to take out loans to survive. This is most likely to result in an upsurge in child marriage.

In April 2021, as the second wave of the pandemic set in and a new set of lockdowns was imposed, migrant workers again left metropolitan cities to return to their villages. Although workers were warned to prepare for the second stage of lockdown, the damage caused by the first lockdown had not yet been overcome. Since the rural economy (which is dependent primarily on agriculture) cannot absorb the growing influx of workers, growing impoverishment in rural areas is a cause for concern. Rural areas cannot absorb the influx of labor in productive work without steps being taken by the state and central governments to generate employment, so child marriages are very likely to increase among migrant workers who find it financially difficult to educate their children.

Women Power Connect held focus group discussions during the 2020 and 2021 lockdowns with grassroots organizations working in the states of Jharkhand and Rajasthan on ending child marriage. According to their unpublished findings, reverse migration in Jharkhand played a significant role in this practice. With men returning and girls remaining at home, parents and families arranged for girls to be married to returnees. Since expenses were low in lockdown weddings, parents had no difficulty arranging these marriages. In Rajasthan as well, reverse migration has contributed to an increase in child marriage in areas that experience a high rate of out-migration.

Discrimination against Muslims

Religious tensions are contributing to the growing marginalization of Muslims in India. The Citizenship Amendment Act (CAA) of 2019 ensures Indian citizenship to all religious community migrants from Pakistan, Afghanistan, and Bangladesh, except Muslims. Since the National Registration of Citizens requires proof of citizenship, Muslims fear the loss of their Indian citizenship. Protests against the CAA in 2019 led to riots in New Delhi in which both Hindus and Muslims lost their lives. Growing marginalization translates into a lack of access to services, impoverishment, violence, and, consequently, higher rates of child marriage.

Following the Tablighi Jamaat incident, the national media in India promoted the idea that Muslims had deliberately planned the event to spread the virus in India. The hashtag "Corona-jihad" was flashed on news channels such as Zee News and Republic TV. Since people found it hard to differentiate between Muslims and Tablighis, all Muslims were seen as potential carriers of the virus. Fake news shots of Muslim vendors spitting on vegetables and on police officials were spread by local news channels and the print media, and this led to a massive increase in Islamophobia. This manifests in refusal to accept groceries from Muslim delivery workers, discrimination between Hindu and Muslim patients, and denial of medical care to pregnant Muslim women.

According to Astitva, an NGO in western Uttar Pradesh, women belonging to marginalized communities (Dalits and Muslims) faced an increase in domestic violence, loss of income, and child marriage (Salim 2021). Media reports highlighted the demand to boycott Muslim economic activities, and this had drastic ramifications for women. With an increase in hatred against this maligned community, Muslim women faced difficulties in accessing services and support, such that even if the rates of child marriage do not go up among Muslim families, the stigma of being seen to be carriers of the virus and the subsequent marginalization will put Muslim child brides at heightened risk of sexually transmitted disease, mental health problems, and restricted access to maternal healthcare.

An Overview of Child Marriage in India

Official data has shown a trend toward improvement in cases of child marriage across India since 2015. According to data from the National Family Health Survey 4 (2015–16), 26.8 percent of girls were married before the legal age of eighteen (Government of India, Ministry of Health and Family Welfare 2016)—a dramatic improvement over the situation in 2005/2006, when almost half of all girls were married before the age of eighteen. According to the National Commission for Protection of Child Rights (2018), girl child marriages are highest among the Scheduled Tribes and Scheduled Castes. According to this report, in Bihar, Gujarat, and Telangana child marriage rates are high among the Other Backward Castes (those that are educationally or socially disadvantaged).

In order to address the root cause of child marriage and prevent cases from rising, it is important to understand why child marriages occur in the first place, and how the pandemic will further exacerbate these root causes. Nancy Fraser (2003) provides a means of analyzing such complex issues; she engages in a thought experiment during which she imagines a conceptual spectrum of social divisions: at one end of the spectrum are redistribution issues (she gives the example of class differentiation), while at the other end are recognition issues (she gives the example of sexual differentiation). Between these two extremes lie more complex social divisions, at the edges of which both recognition and redistribution issues, like gender and race, for example, intersect. We try to understand where child early and forced marriage (CEFM) in India fits on this spectrum so as to identify solutions and the priorities that policymakers should insist upon, and we return to Fraser's work later in this chapter.

In the course of our work on child marriage, we have learned that the reasons behind early child marriage differ from state to state and region to region. Child marriage rates are far higher in rural areas than in urban areas because there are fewer opportunities for education and work for women in the former. The factors responsible for the prevalence of child marriage, despite prohibition, vary according to caste, class, religion, tradition, social norms, coercion, and economic status, but the most significant factor is poverty coupled with gender inequality and the low value associated with girls and women in India.

Factors Contributing to Child Marriages in India

Poverty and Lack of Education

Girls are considered a financial liability since they are perceived to be financially dependent on male members of the family; marrying them early is considered a viable option. The patriarchal mindset that favors boys over girls is embedded in Indian society; when given a choice, a family would rather spend its resources on education and health for boys than for girls. Child marriage, therefore, is seen to be a way of reducing the cost inherent in a girl's education. In turn, the lack of good quality education available for girls that could motivate them to remain in school or help them acquire a job or marketable skills contributes to the vicious cycle of poverty. Poor-quality school education is not geared toward skills-building and is a major contributor to CEFM. Parental illiteracy is also a major factor behind the prevalence of child marriage. Parents with little or no education do not understand the consequences of early marriage for their daughters and are unaware that it is a violation of a child's basic human rights.

Control over a Girl's Sexuality and Fear of Violence Against Women and Girls

Parents often fear the sexual autonomy of girls and see it as leading to pre-marital sex and pregnancy out of wedlock. Early marriage paves the way for the transfer of the control of a girl's sexual and reproductive life to her husband and in-laws (Girls Not Brides 2015). With the closure of schools and the disruption in education caused by the pandemic, parents are more worried about controlling their daughters' sexuality and thus resort to marrying them off early to preserve their family honor. In a conservative society, the social stigma associated with a pregnancy before marriage is greater than that associated with child marriage. The widespread notion of family honor coerces families into marrying their daughters early so as to preserve the girls' virginity. Child marriages provide a way of arranging a girl's marriage before she is mature enough to exercise her right to choose. Furthermore, what are known as love marriages (as opposed to arranged ones) have less social acceptability, particularly when the bride and groom belong to different caste groups or religions.

Dowry

The practice of dowry is widely prevalent in India; the bride's family pays the groom in cash or gifts upon marriage. The older the daughter is, the fewer her suitors and the more her parents then have to pay to get a match. Families, therefore, prefer to have their daughters married at a young age so as to reduce the cost of the dowry. The restrictions put in place during the pandemic have given poor families an opportunity to perform marriage ceremonies at a lower cost and with fewer people. This has been a major driving force for CEFM during the lockdown period.

Inadequate Implementation of Laws

The implementation of laws prohibiting child marriage has not proved effective. The enforcement of the Prohibition of Child Marriage Act (PCMA) of 2006 is weak in India. An adequate budget has not been allocated by states to the implementation of the PCMA, and this has led to overburdened Child Marriage Prohibition Officers (CMPOs), some of whom do not even know what their roles and responsibilities are, according to Oxfam Indian and Women Power Connect (2018). At discussions organized by Women Power Connect in Jharkhand, the Protection Officers (appointed to deal with cases of domestic violence) were also tasked with the responsibility of preventing child marriage. The overburdening of these officers has led to a situation in which they are improperly trained and do not know how to deal with cases of child marriage.

Religious, Social, and Cultural Practices

In Rajasthan, custom plays a large role in perpetuating child marriage, along with the fear of sexual violence against girls that pushes families to marry them off early. For example, the customary practice of *Gauna*, which allows for the consummation of a child marriage only once the girl has reached maturity, is a cover-up for the solemnization of early marriages. In fact, *Gauna*, while disallowing early consummation of the marriage, encourages child marriage since the child bride is promised to a particular groom. The custom of *Mrityu Bhoj* in Rajasthan, which decrees high expenditure on food at funerals, also encourages child marriage, since families combine a funeral with a wedding in order to save costs. A high prevalence of sexual violence in Rajasthan, including rape and sexual harassment, leads to further child marriage as well, since marriage provides a form of security to girls by supposedly protecting them from sexual violence perpetrated by a stranger.

In 2016, among both Hindus and Muslims, 25 percent of women were married by the age of 15.5 years and 50 percent were married by that of 17.5 years, according to Srinivas Goli (2016). In the case of Dalits and Adivasis, 25 percent of women are married by 15.5 years of age. There is no evidence that child marriage is higher among Muslims in India than it is among Hindus. However, Goli suggests that since Muslim Sharia law allows for early marriage, there is a perception that child marriage is more common among Muslims.

The Impact of COVID-19 on Girls in India

The impact of COVID-19 on girls in India has been disastrous for a number of reasons. The first is the interruption of education and the move to online learning in 1.5 million schools in India, which has affected 247 million children (Sharma 2021), since not everyone has been able to adjust to this new normal. According to Meeta Sengupta and P. Krishnakumar (2018), the Digital Empowerment Foundation has reported that 30 percent of India's population lags behind in the measurement of basic literacy, and it is thrice that for digital literacy. Girls have less access to smartphones and the internet than boys do, so they are more likely than boys to drop out of online schooling, with the result that their early marriage becomes far more likely.

The second reason is the collapse of the health system in India given the huge increase in COVID-19 patients. Girls have found it difficult to access hospitals for reproductive healthcare or for abortions. Getting married has been an easier solution to an unwanted pregnancy than facing the stigma of such an event outside of marriage.

The increase in domestic violence is the third reason. During the 2020 lockdown reported incidents of domestic violence increased twofold according to the National Commission for Women (NCW) (2020), which received 2,043 complaints in June 2020, the highest figure in eight months. Since families are forced to stay indoors and girls and women cannot go out and ask for help, cases of domestic violence have shot up. In some cases, girls themselves see marriage as a means of escaping a violent household. Furthermore, child marriages have increased because girls are unable to access services set up to help and support them, like healthcare NGOs, because offices are closed, and staff are working from home.

The fourth reason is the death of both parents, particularly during the second wave of COVID-19 in India, which has led to abandoned and orphaned children, many of whom are at high risk of sexual abuse and violence. Girls are more vulnerable to sexual abuse and violence than boys, and while government schemes have been announced to help children left orphaned by COVID-19, such schemes are unlikely to prevent an increase in child trafficking and child marriage, especially for girls.

As a result of COVID-19, shrinking incomes, and the diversification of funds spent on combating the virus, it is expected that more and more girls will be pulled out of school and either trafficked for marriage or sex work or married off early to ease the financial burden on the natal family.

There is no official data yet on the extent of the increase in child marriages in India, but we do know that the long-term consequences of COVID-19 will be enormous for girls.

The Legal Framework in India

The prohibition of child marriage is specifically dealt with by the Prohibition of Child Marriage Act of 2006 (PCMA), which makes the legal age of marriage eighteen for women and twenty-one for men. Personal laws follow similar age criteria for entering a valid marriage, with the exception of Muslim Sharia law, which makes the attainment of puberty for both boys and girls the minimum requirement for marriage. Child marriage can be repudiated by the Muslim girl if she was married before she was fifteen years of age according to the Dissolution of Muslim Marriages Act 1939.

The law on child marriage has its limitations in India, since the PCMA differentiates between men and women with regard to the age of marriage and does not make child marriages illegal (but only voidable at the option of either party to the marriage). Further, although the PCMA was enacted in 2006, amendments were not made in the Muslim and Hindu marriage and divorce laws to make personal laws consonant with the PCMA. Consequently, the legal framework in India contradicts itself and is in urgent need of amendment.

The Government Response to Child Marriage

The primary response of the government to control child marriage has been through the law. Aside from the PCMA, laws prohibiting the practice of giving dowry and offering protection from domestic violence indirectly relate to the prevention of child marriage. The Dowry Prohibition Act of 1961 failed to curb the practice of giving expensive gifts as a dowry at the time of a girl's marriage. Reasons for the failure of this law include growing materialism and the rise of capitalism in India, the lack of employment opportunities for women evident in the small number of employed women, and social acceptance of the custom. All this leads to few complaints being made at the time of marriage. The Protection of Women from Domestic Violence Act of 2005 (PWDVA), while used by many married women against their husbands and in-laws, is hardly used by unmarried women against their parents according to the Lawyers Collective (2013). The PWDVA can be used by unmarried women to take action and seek redress against their parents forcing them to marry, but the mindset required to take legal action against one's parents and natal family members is, for the most part, missing in India.

In the midst of the COVID-19 pandemic, the central government in India launched a high-level committee to look into the issue of motherhood and marriage at an early age. This was a welcome step since it showed the state's concern with the rising numbers of early marriages that are likely to take place, coupled with a rise in pregnancies. In August 2020, the Prime Minister made an announcement to raise the legal marriageable age of girls from eighteen to twenty-one in an effort to tackle issues of population control, early pregnancy, maternal mortality, and the lack of opportunities for girls in education. However, instead of focusing on redistribution, the task force is increasing law enforcement, although this has not succeeded thus far in curbing child marriage in India. Despite the legal age of marriage being eighteen, girls as young as twelve and thirteen are married off in rural and underdeveloped areas. The proposed change, although well intentioned, will lead only to a change in the law and will have no impact on the existing social realities of the country. This change in the age of marriage will not prevent child marriage but will lead only to a higher rate of early marriage if being twenty-one years of age becomes the legal requirement.

Consequences of the Second COVID-19 Wave in India

The impact of the second wave of COVID-19 in India became clear only toward the end of April 2021 as the death rate shot up and the health system gradually collapsed under the weight of the number of COVID patients. Since children, particularly girls, had already dropped out of school given the lockdown restrictions in 2020, the second wave will further worsen the situation. For more than a year, most children have been at home and unable to access online education. Families with daughters are finding it extremely difficult to keep them at home for any longer. For the daughters' safety and to prevent them from being exploited and abused at home, marriage is now seen as the safest option. According to Anand Chawla Noor and Ayesha Singh (2021), CHILDLINE reported a 50 percent increase in the number of calls reporting abuse during this period. The increase in elopement and the additional stigma attached to this has led parents to believe that getting their daughters married early is better than keeping them at home (Koushik 2021).

Given the severity of the second wave, girls are at heightened risk of exploitation and abuse. With incomes shrinking further and schools remaining closed, the view that a girl is a burden will gain ground again. According to UNICEF (2021), the second wave will have dire consequences for girls in terms of access to education, social protection, a lack of reproductive health services, and an increase in unwanted pregnancies and marriages. Due to the surge in COVID cases and deaths in India, the number of children who will be orphaned, abused, trafficked, and forced into early marriage will increase. Millions of children are struggling financially, and many girls are forced to engage in sex work in exchange for food and economic survival as it is.

Redistribution and Deconstruction for a Nuanced Response

Child marriage falls toward the redistribution side of Fraser's (2003) imaginary spectrum, but not to an extreme degree. Therefore, both redistribution (economic benefits for have-nots) and deconstruction (removing stigma associated with marginalized groups) are necessary to end child marriage in India.

Increasing the age of marriage to twenty-one years for women, in a country whose society views marriage as the greatest achievement for a woman, will remain a law on paper only. Although it delinks marriage from the age of consent (eighteen), it is unlikely to have any immediate impact on controlling child marriage. While schools are closed, communities and families will continue to practice child marriage irrespective of what the marriage age is. Even when schools are open, education does not easily translate into a paying job for a woman. Impoverishment, the lack of jobs linked to the contracting economy, the closure of schools, and being denied access to healthcare facilities will push families to marry their daughters early or even to sell them to traffickers.

A more comprehensive response to increasing child marriage rates in India would be, first, to identify who is most at risk. Migrant workers who have returned home to their villages in Uttar Pradesh, Bihar, and West Bengal are vulnerable since their families have already experienced a drop in income and will do so again on an even greater scale. This may well translate into early marriage being forced on girls. Uttar Pradesh and

Bihar have the highest numbers of workers who migrate to other cities, and it is reasonable to expect a surge in the number of workers returning to these two states. The financial implications lead us to suspect that early marriage will escalate here, too. West Bengal in particular is vulnerable to a surge in joblessness because the damage caused by Cyclone Amphan in May 2020 is still being felt. Girls here too are at increased risk, so the governments in these vulnerable states should remain alert to the high possibility of an increase in child marriage and child trafficking.

The urgently needed protection of children from poor households, particularly in rural areas and districts in Uttar Pradesh, Bihar, and West Bengal (and other identified vulnerable states), needs to be prioritized in government efforts. Innovative strategies need to be developed to provide education to those children, particularly girls, who do not have internet access and will not be able to attend online classes. They are at extreme risk. In Jharkhand, loudspeakers are being used to disseminate educational information, and other such strategies need to be implemented soon. Since girls are given less nutritious food to eat than their brothers even in normal times, in times of crisis, this disparity will increase. The midday meal that is provided in schools can be delivered to homes, as was done in the state of Kerala. Providing sanitary napkins to girls and providing information on hygiene and handwashing must be prioritized. While job-creation schemes are laudable, the immediate relief of food, basic education, and healthcare needs to be provided to those girls most at risk of CEFM.

According to a report in *The Print* (Tewari and Mishra 2019), the UNDP's Multi-Dimensional Poverty Index (2018) has indicated that every third Dalit and Muslim in India is multidimensionally poor. This poverty is not just about income, but includes nutrition, health, education, and assets. Official data does not show that child marriages are higher among Muslims in India or that the issue has any religious dimension to it. This situation is likely to change in the COVID-19 context as more and more Muslims face ostracism and discrimination. Muslims in the vulnerable states, particularly in Uttar Pradesh, Bihar, and West Bengal, may face an even sharper decline in income than other communities, and the government should be cautious in relation to this.

COVID-19 has proved to be doubly treacherous for the marginalized Dalits, Adivasis, and Muslims. Once cases of COVID-19 decrease and governments and NGOs are able to conduct their training and awareness-generation programs, the needs of these vulnerable categories of people will have to be prioritized, and the needs of girls, if they are to escape being married off or sold to traffickers, given even greater priority. Issues of religious discrimination cannot be politely brushed under the carpet; the social cost of such discrimination has to be discussed openly and dealt with. Deconstruction of the Muslim other will become important in NGO activities if they are to reduce stigma against the Muslim community. It is essential to bridge the distance between the government and the marginalized for effective post-COVID-19 policies. The core principles of nondiscrimination, social justice, and equality should be the basis on which rehabilitation and redistribution plans are carried out.

Conclusion

To prevent the number of child marriages from escalating, it is important to identify who is vulnerable to this practice, based on identity and economic considerations. Child protection schemes must be strengthened to eliminate child marriage and must be included in COVID-19 recovery and prevention plans. By providing cash and other economic handouts to vulnerable families and ensuring access to sexual and reproductive health services, it is possible to reduce the number of early marriages. State initiatives to prevent child marriage need to address the basic needs of those who are marginalized. Changes in the child marriage law are of secondary concern and need not be accorded priority right now. The need now is to strategize toward interventions that will bear realistic outcomes. The government has to refocus its attention and employ a gender-sensitive approach to rescue girls, particularly those coming from migrant workers' families and marginalized groups. Saving families from economic ruin will mean saving some girls, at least, from early marriage, and this is of paramount importance.

GAYATRI SHARMA is a human rights lawyer and is currently the Programme Director at Women Power Connect, a network-based NGO in India that works on various issues concerning gender and women's rights, including the prevention of child marriage. She holds an LLM degree from the University of Warwick.

AYESHA KHALIQ previously worked at Women Power Connect as a Project Coordinator. She has a keen interest in gender, child rights, policy, and inclusive social development. She holds a bachelor's and master's in Sociology from the University of Delhi and an MSc in Social Policy from the London School of Economics.

Note

1. The word Dalit translates to "oppressed."

References

Agrawal, Kabir. 2020. "UP Hospital Bars Muslim Patients Who Don't Come with Negative Test for COVID-19." *The Wire*, 19 April. Retrieved 22 September 2022 from https://thewire.in/communalism/up-hospital-bars-muslim-patients-who-dont-come-with-negative-test-for-covid-19.

Angad, Abhishek. 2020. "In Jharkhand, Pregnant Woman Told to Clean up Blood, Loses Child." *Indian Express*, April 19. Retrieved 22 September 2022 from https://indianexpress.com/article/india/in-jharkhand-pregnant-woman-says-told-to-clean-up-blood-loses-child-6368865/.

Bhandare, Namita. 2020. "Covid-19 and the Spike in Child Marriages." *Hindustan Times*, 4 September. Retrieved 22 September 2022 from https://www.hindustantimes.com/columns/covid-19-and-the-spike-in-child-marriages/story-aLS6zAq2Beoiyb4wyrfbdM.html.

Centre for Catalyzing Change. 2020. "Assessment of Issues Faced by Adolescent Girls & Boys During Covid-19 and the Lockdown." Retrieved 22 September 2022 from https://www.c3india.org/uploads/news/Youth_survey_(low_Res).pdf.

Fraser, Nancy. 2003. "Social Justice in the Age of Identity Politics: Redistribution, Recognition and Participation." In Nancy Fraser and Axel Honneth, *Redistribution or Recognition? A Political–Philosophical Exchange*, 7–109. London: Verso.

Ghosh, Sohini, and Parimal A. Dabhi. 2020. "Ahmedabad Hospital Splits COVID Wards on Faith, Says Govt Decision." *Indian Express*, 17 April. Retrieved 22 September 2022 from https://indianexpress.com/article/coronavirus/ahmedabad-covid-19-coronavirus-hospital-ward-6363040/.

Girls Not Brides. 2015. "Child, Early and Forced Marriage and the Control of Sexuality and Reproduction." 1 October. Retrieved 22 September 2022 from https://www.girlsnotbrides.org/learning-resources/resource-centre/child-early-and-forced-marriage-and-the-control-of-sexuality-and-reproduction/.

———. 2020. "COVID-19 and Child, Early and Forced Marriage: An Agenda for Action." 6 April. Retrieved 22 September 2022 from https://www.girlsnotbrides.org/documents/930/COVID-19-and-child-early-and-forced-marriage.pdf.

Goli, Srinivas. 2016. "Eliminating Child Marriages in India: Progress and Prospects." New Delhi: Child Rights Focus, Beti, and Action Aid. Retrieved 22

September 2022 from https://www.actionaidindia.org/wp-content/uploads/2018/06/Eliminating-Child-Marriage-in-India.pdf.

"Government Intervened to Stop Over 5,584 Child Marriage during Coronavirus-Induced Lockdown." 2020. *Times of India*, 27 June. Retrieved 22 September 2022 from https://timesofindia.indiatimes.com/india/govt-intervened-to-stop-over-5584-child-marriage-during-coronavirus-induced-lockdown/articleshow/76661071.cms.

Government of India, Ministry of Health and Family Welfare. 2016. "India Fact Sheet: National Family Health Survey 4 (NFHS-4), 2015–16." Retrieved 22 September 2022 from http://rchiips.org/nfhs/pdf/NFHS4/India.pdf.

Iqbal, Mohammed. 2020. "Pregnant Woman Refused Attention in Government Hospital." *The Hindi*, 5 April. Retrieved 22 September 2022 from https://www.thehindu.com/news/national/other-states/pregnant-woman-refused-attention-in-government-hospital-alleges-rajasthan-minister/article31261893.ece.

"Jharkhand: Five Brahmins Lodged at Quarantine Facility Refuse to Eat Food Prepared by SC Cooks." 2020. *Times Now*, 25 May. Retrieved 22 September 2022 from https://www.timesnownews.com/mirror-now/crime/article/jharkhand-five-brahmins-lodged-at-quarantine-facility-refuse-to-eat-food-prepared-by-sc-cooks/596825.

Khadria, Binod, and Narender Thakur. 2020. "GDP in Education or Education in GDP?" *Economic and Political Weekly* 55(49). Retrieved 22 September 2022 from https://www.epw.in/journal/2020/49/letters/gdp-education-or-education-gdp.html.

Koushik, Janardhan. 2021. "Tamil Nadu: Amid Covid-19 Lockdown, Nilgiris Witnessing Rise in Cases of Child Marriages, Sexual Abuse." *Indian Express*, 1 May. Retrieved 22 September 2022 from https://indianexpress.com/article/india/tamil-nadu-amid-covid-19-lockdown-nilgiris-witnessing-rise-in-cases-of-child-marriages-sexual-abuse-7298115/.

Kundu, Sridhar. 2020. "At Least 23 Million Migrants Are Returning to India's Villages: Can the Rural Economy Keep Up?" *Scroll.in*, 25 May. Retrieved 22 September 2022 from https://scroll.in/article/962804/at-least-23-million-migrants-are-returning-to-indias-villages-can-the-rural-economy-keep-up.

Lawyers Collective. 2013. "Staying Alive: Monitoring and Evaluation Reports." Retrieved 22 September 2022 from http://www.lawyerscollective.org/wp-content/uploads/2012/07/Staying-Alive-Evaluating-Court-Orders.pdf.

Mondal, Dibyendu. 2021. "India Spends Just 1.26 Percent of GDP on Public Healthcare." *Sunday Guardian Live*, 2 January. Retrieved 22 September 2022 from https://www.sundayguardianlive.com/news/india-spends-just-1-26-gdp-public-healthcare.

National Commission for Women. 2020. "Increase in Domestic Violence against Women." *Press Information Bureau*, 22 September. Retrieved 22 September 2022 from https://pib.gov.in/Pressreleaseshare.aspx?PRID=1657678.

NCPCR (National Commission for Protection of Child Rights). 2018. "India Child Marriage and Teenage Pregnancy." *Young Lives*, 18 September. https://www.younglives.org.uk/sites/default/files/migrated/India%20Report.pdf.

NFHS (National Family Health Survey). 2015–16. "Key Findings from NFHS 4." Retrieved 7 November 2022 from http://rchiips.org/nfhs/pdf/NFHS4/India.pdf.

———. 2019–20. "Key Findings from NFHS 5." Retrieved 7 November 2022 from http://rchiips.org/nfhs/NFHS-5_FCTS/India.pdf .

Noor, Anand Chawla, and Ayesha Singh. 2021. "The Covid Generation: Children Stare at a Grim and Desperate Future." *New Indian Express*, 25 April. Retrieved 22 September 2022 from https://www.newindianexpress.com/magazine/2021/apr/25/the-covid-generationindias-children-stare-at-a-grim-and-desperate-future-2293506.html.

Oxfam India, and Women Power Connect. 2018. "Mapping and Identifying Gaps in Support Services Addressing Domestic Violence and Child Marriage: Bihar, Jharkhand, Chhattisgarh, Odisha and Uttar Pradesh"(unpublished report available on request from the authors).

Salim, Mariya. 2021. "How Marginalised Women in India Bore an Extra Burden of Covid-19 'Shadow Pandemic.'" *IPS News*, 1 March. Retrieved 22 September 2022 from http://www.ipsnews.net/2021/03/marginalised-women-india-bore-extra-burden-covid-19-shadow-pandemic/.

Sengupta, Meeta, and P. Krishnakumar. 2018. "A Look at India's Deep Digital Literacy Divide and Why It Needs to Be Bridged." *Financial Express*, 24 September. Retrieved 22 September 2022 from https://www.financialexpress.com/education-2/a-look-at-indias-deep-digital-literacy-divide-and-why-it-needs-to-be-bridged/1323822/.

Sharma, Milan. 2021. "Closure of 1.5 Million Schools in India Due to Covid-19 Pandemic Impacts 247 Million Children." *India Today*, 5 March. Retrieved 22 September 2022 from https://www.indiatoday.in/education-today/news/story/closure-of-1-5-million-schools-in-india-due-to-covid-19-pandemic-impacts-247-million-children-1775892-2021-03-05.

Tewari, Ruhi, and Abhishek Mishra. 2019. "Every Second ST, Every Third Dalit and Muslim is Poor, Not Just Financially: UN Report." *The Print*, 12 July. Retrieved 22 September 2022 from https://theprint.in/india/every-second-st-every-third-dalit-muslim-in-india-poor-not-just-financially-un-report/262270/.

UN (United Nations). 2021. "India's New COVID-19 Wave is Spreading like 'Wildfire,' Warns UN Children's Fund." *UN News*, 7 May. Retrieved 22 September 2022 from https://news.un.org/en/story/2021/05/1091512.

UNICEF (United Nations Children's Fund). 2021. "COVID-19: A Threat to Progress Against Child Marriage." *UNICEF*. Retrieved 22 September 2022 from https://data.unicef.org/resources/covid-19-a-threat-to-progress-against-child-marriage/.

World Bank. 2020. "COVID-19 Crisis through a Migration Lens: Migration and Development." Retrieved 22 September 2022 from https://openknowledge.worldbank.org/bitstream/handle/10986/33634/COVID-19-Crisis-Through-a-Migration-Lens.pdf?sequence=5&isAllowed=y.

Chapter 10

The Impact of the COVID-19 Pandemic on Child Domestic Workers in Ethiopia

Annabel Erulkar, Welela Tarekegne, and Eyasu Hailu

Background

Child domestic work, the most common form of child labor globally, is considered a kind of modern-day slavery (Black 2002; UNICEF 1999). There are an estimated 17.2 million child domestic workers in the world, and the vast majority are girls (ILO 2012). Domestic work keeps children out of school, confined to the home, socially isolated, and burdened with excessive domestic duties (Black 2002). Their movements and how they spend their time are strictly controlled by their employers. Younger domestic workers are often preferred by employers since they are easier to control and manipulate, and they demand little or no pay (HRW 2006).

Domestic work is done by many girls in Ethiopia, especially those who migrate from rural to urban areas. In a study of nearly ten thousand young people in six regions, 37 percent of working urban girls were found to be engaged in domestic work (Erulkar et al. 2010) that is characterized by extremely low pay or no pay at all, and in which the working hours and work burdens make the occupation exploitive in many cases. The same study found that among adolescent women who were rural-to-urban migrants, 67 percent entered the world of work as domestic workers. A study in Addis Ababa found that domestic workers work an average of sixty-four hours per week for a mean monthly wage of USD 6 per month (Erulkar and Mekbib 2007). A significant number of former domestic workers, the vast majority of whom are female, report being sexually abused in the context of work. Furthermore, emerging studies indicate that domestic workers are at significantly higher risk of nonconsensual sex compared to their counterparts who are not engaged in domestic work (Erulkar and Ferede 2009). In addition, migrant girls who are new to the city frequently find positions as domestic workers through job-placement brokers who act as go-betweens and place prospective workers in families seeking house help. Recent research among brokers in Ethiopia found that they can be both supportive of newly migrating girls and also exploitive. A number of brokers admitted to sexually abusing migrant girls before placing them in homes as domestic workers (Erulkar 2020).

Under the Labor Law in Ethiopia, children under the age of fifteen are prohibited from working and those aged fifteen to seventeen are considered young workers. They may work a maximum of seven hours per day and are prohibited from working before 6:00 a.m. and after 10:00 p.m. They may not work on rest days or public holidays and are prohibited from specified dangerous forms of work, such as mining and working in quarries, electric power plants, or sewers and tunnels (Federal Negarit Gazette of the Federal Democratic Republic of Ethiopia 2019). Domestic work, however, is not governed by the Labor Law but by the 1960 Ethiopia Civil Code. The Civil Code gives domestic workers relatively little protection and allows their work conditions to be regulated "by the conscience of the employers" (Gebremedhin 2016: 41). In addition, Ethiopia has not ratified the International Labour Organization (ILO) 2011 Domestic Workers Convention No. 189, which includes minimum labor standards for these workers.

The first case of COVID-19 was identified in Ethiopia in mid-March 2020. By the end of July 2020, Ethiopia was home to over fifteen thousand cases, with the vast majority located in the country's capital city, Addis Ababa (Worldometer 2020). In early April, the Ethiopian government declared a State of Emergency that included the closure of schools, the banning of large gatherings and sports events, a reduction in the allowable number of passengers on public transport, and the prohibition of reducing the workforce or the termination of workers who were governed by the Labor Law, among others (Embassy of the FDRE, UK 2020).

The Biruh Tesfa for All Program for Marginalized Girls in Ethiopia

Biruh Tesfa for All is a program that operates for extremely marginalized and disadvantaged girls in poor urban areas of Ethiopia. Its design was based on the results of research conducted in very poor and slum areas (Erulkar et al. 2006; Erulkar and Mekbib 2007). The program addresses life skills and the deficits in the lives of the most marginalized girls, including the lack of access to education. It provides safe spaces for these girls, offers them adult mentors, and fosters friendship networks. Through the program, adult female mentors are recruited from low-income project communities and trained to facilitate sessions on basic education and life skills. Following training, mentors recruit girls for this program by going house-to-house in their neighborhoods to identify ten- to nineteen-year-old girls who are out of school. By applying the recruitment criterion of targeting female adolescents who are out of school, the project captures many girls who are in domestic servitude, as well as girls with disabilities. House-to-house recruitment methods also allow mentors to negotiate girls' involvement in the program, especially with gatekeepers, such as employers of domestic workers, who may resist their taking part. Once recruited into groups, girls meet in local facilities, including government schools after hours, that serve as safe spaces. Where needed, facilities are improved and renovated to be accessible to girls with disabilities. Once in safe space groups, girls receive informal education, learn life skills, and are given referrals for other services. Previous evaluations have found that the program is associated with significant improvements in friendship networks, knowledge of HIV and AIDS, the use of HIV-related and other health services, and improved literacy and numeracy (Erulkar and Medhin 2017; Erulkar et al. 2013; Temin and Heck 2020). From 2006 to 2016, the program reached over seventy-five thousand child domestic workers, rural-to-urban migrants, and girls with disabilities in many urban centers of Ethiopia (Erulkar and Medhin 2017).

Founded in 2018, Biruh Tesfa for All works as a follow-on to the earlier Biruh Tesfa project, with emphasis on achieving measurable improvements in literacy and numeracy and increased focus on inclusive education

Figure 10.1. A mentor teaches girls in Addis Ababa about hygiene. Photo: Zeleman Productions.

that is high quality, effective, and sustainable. Previous Biruh Tesfa projects used community-based mentors exclusively. However, Biruh Tesfa for All engaged a mix of lay mentors and recent graduates of teacher training colleges in order to ensure that literacy and numeracy goals for girls in the project were met. The project now includes a mix of teachers and mentors, in about a one-to-four ratio. In addition, the project includes focused accommodation of girls with disabilities by providing assistive aids and inclusive teaching for girls with special needs. Based on registration data, half of all Biruh Tesfa for All participants have never been to school, two-thirds were migrants to the area, and one-quarter self-identified as child domestic workers who, on average, reported doing seventy-eight hours of domestic work per week. In February 2020, new safe space girls' groups had recently started meeting in three project cities in Ethiopia—Addis Ababa, Bahir Dar, and Shashamene. The following month, in March 2020, the groups were suspended because of the COVID-19 pandemic and school closures in Ethiopia. As a result of this, project researchers designed a descriptive, qualitative study to understand the impact of the COVID-19 pandemic on child domestic workers in the program.

Methods

This is a qualitative study that collected information from project beneficiaries and mentors in the Biruh Tesfa for All program. In-depth interviews with beneficiaries and mentors took place over the telephone to avoid face-to-face contact in order to mitigate the risk of COVID-19 transmission.

Interviews took place with respondents in all three project sites in Addis Ababa, Bahir Dar, and Shashamene. In all, twenty-four in-depth interviews divided equally among the sites (eight in each) and between beneficiaries and mentors were undertaken. While Biruh Tesfa for All beneficiaries are aged from ten to nineteen, we interviewed only girls in the fifteen-to-nineteen age range. We excluded those aged ten to fourteen because of the ethical issues involved in interviewing populations who are very young and who are already extremely vulnerable, such as child domestic workers. In our experience, ethical review committees do not approve of interviewing vulnerable adolescent children.

We developed a discussion guide for the interviews. Topics included asking respondents to describe their communities; to indicate their knowledge of COVID-19; to discuss any preventative measures or changes in behavior as a result of the pandemic; and to talk about the impact of the pandemic on themselves, their communities, other girls in the program, or other girls like them generally. We also solicited suggestions for improvements to the program and on how to support beneficiaries and mentors in the context of the pandemic.

Selection for interviews was meant to be somewhat representative of beneficiaries and mentors in the program and to reflect their overall profile, based on registration data reflecting their age, migration, and (dis)ability status. Research staff for this study analyzed the demographic profile of beneficiaries and mentors using registration data for the project. Site-based program officers were given guidance on selecting respondents based on different profiles including age, education, migration, and (dis)ability. They were instructed not to select the best-performing beneficiaries or mentors and not to contact respondents themselves, in case their involvement led to biased responses during the interviews.

Selected respondents were contacted by female research staff by telephone to request the interview. The initial call was used to explain the research, obtain informed consent or assent, and obtain permission to tape-record the telephone interview. We obtained informed consent from young women who were eighteen or nineteen and underage girls who were emancipated minors (those living away from parents or guardians). Among underage girls living with their parents or guardians, we obtained informed consent from the parent or guardian and assent from the respondent. On the day of the scheduled interview, the respondent was asked if she had any additional questions about the interview or tape recording. If needed, the interviewer readministered informed consent or assent over the phone, certifying the respondent's verbal consent to be interviewed with the interviewer's own signature. The interviewer asked the respondent to locate a quiet place for the interview, out of earshot of household members and away from other background noise. The interview itself took between forty-five and sixty minutes.

During the call, the interviewer took handwritten notes that were later fleshed out using the tape recording, thus allowing the documentation of verbatim quotes. While conversations were in Amharic, all interview notes and documented responses were transcribed into English. Transcripts were analyzed to identify themes and patterns that emerged from the data, with illustrative quotations being used to highlight overarching themes. When direct quotations are used, the respondent category and location are cited; all names used are pseudonyms. Tape recordings were erased following completion of the transcription. Following the institution's policy on the storage of data, interview transcriptions will be retained on password-protected computers for five years, accessible to only a small number of study staff. The research received review and approval by the institution's ethical review board.

Results

Knowledge and Practice Related to COVID-19

The Biruh Tesfa for All program is implemented in very poor urban slum areas. When asked to describe their communities, mentors and girls alike described living conditions as crowded and unhygienic, with housing constructed with impermanent material. At the same time, many respondents remarked on the mutual support and cohesion of residents in these areas.

> It's an overly crowded neighborhood. People are mostly daily laborers here. They make their income day by day. Homes are usually mud houses. About fifty people live in a single compound here. It's a very challenging area to live here, especially for your health. But I love that people think of each other here. People are

there for you in good and bad times. We are always there for one another. I don't like that people are not very clean here. I wish my community was more sanitary and wish people disposed of trash properly. (Mahlet, mentor, Addis Ababa)

Both mentors and girls alike reported significant levels of knowledge about COVID-19 and expressed concern about protecting themselves from the virus. All respondents mentioned the importance of wearing a mask, frequent handwashing and sanitizing, physical distancing, and avoiding crowded places. Respondents mentioned learning about COVID-19 mainly from media sources—radio and television—but also mentioned learning from other community members, and from their mentors and social media, although this was, however, also described as an unreliable source of information.

All respondents mentioned taking measures proactively to protect themselves, to the greatest extent possible. Given their economic circumstances, many respondents were forced to continue working, even if it put them at risk. Girls and mentors reported being the most afraid of contracting COVID-19 when on public transport or in a crowded market. Respondents noted that people who are poor face far more challenges regarding protecting themselves from COVID-19 than do those who are relatively better off, because they need to go on working.

> Rich people have locked their doors and stay at home. They have everything they need. However, poor people don't have basic needs. The poor have to work. They are vulnerable to the virus. If poor people decide not to go out from home, how can they live? They have to leave the home. (Frehiwott, beneficiary, Bahir Dar)

For Fatuma, a mentor in Shashamene, "People are so poor they don't even have water to wash their hands, let alone soap. People are aware of the virus, but they cannot protect themselves from it. The reason for it is economic[s]."

The crowdedness of living conditions made prevention of COVID-19 extremely difficult. In particular, social distancing was said to be impossible because of the living conditions in these low-income communities. As Helen, a mentor in Addis Ababa, put it,

> In our culture, social distancing is very hard, but I believe that to stop this virus, social distancing is very important. Regularly washing our hands is very important as well, we all live very close to one another so we should all wash our hands constantly. Most people earn a living by renting rooms in their homes. Let alone in one compound, many of us live together in one house. Our homes are extremely overcrowded so keeping our distance is nearly impossible.

While all respondents said that they themselves practiced precautionary measures against the virus, there was variation in opinions about whether their communities were practicing prevention adequately. To some extent, respondents from Addis Ababa described more adherence to prevention guidelines than respondents from the other two cities. This is probably because most COVID-19 cases are found in the nation's capital. Some felt that community members were adhering to protective guidelines, while others felt that members of their communities did not take prevention seriously.

> Most people make fun of you when you wear a mask. They make you feel guilty about protecting yourself. They catcall and harass people for protecting themselves ... To tell you the truth many people don't even wear masks ... They only wash their hands when they eat. We shouldn't eat together anymore like we used to but people still eat together. People don't protect themselves here because they believe the virus is a myth. They don't think God would ever do this to Ethiopia. Even if it's here, it won't kill us. That is what people believe. (Abeba, mentor, Bahir Dar)

> There is no prevention here. A lot [of] people aren't protecting themselves; I wouldn't be surprised if it spread here. A lot of people neglect the severity of the virus because they think the virus is a scam. They take the issue to religion and think that God won't let them be infected. (Aysha, beneficiary, Shashamene)

Some respondents described what has become known as COVID fatigue, since members of their communities relaxed precautionary measures as the pandemic went on. Abaynesh, a beneficiary in Bahir Dar, said,

> At the beginning when the virus came up, people were somehow worried, but not anymore. People have now forgotten the virus and consider that it no longer exists ... Very few people protect themselves from the virus or consider [protection] important ... They even say that the virus does not exist.

Impact of COVID-19 on Child Domestic Workers

All girls and mentors described the economic impact of the pandemic on their personal situations. Many lost their jobs or had their incomes reduced substantially. Girls who relied on petty trade saw a dramatic decline in their business and income. Girls who had recently migrated from rural areas were described as being particularly vulnerable to the economic downturn brought about by the pandemic. Being new to the city, they were unaccustomed to life there, were socially isolated, and lacked safety nets, family, and other sources of social support. As Emebet, a mentor in Addis Ababa, put it,

Whatever the age, migrant girls will be economically challenged. They do not have a support system in the city most of the time, and they will have a hard time to have even one meal a day. Before Corona, many of them would stand outside of hotels and get leftovers from the hotel, but now the hotels are out of business and many are closed, and they might even be scared to eat leftovers now because of the virus.

Many girls in domestic work were extremely hard hit. Most domestic workers in the Biruh Tesfa for All program are recent migrants living away from parents and working for other low-income families in the project area. Most are live-in domestic workers who are provided with accommodation or shelter, as well as food, as part of their employment. Given that housing in such areas is generally very modest and limited, accommodation often amounts to a mattress in a corner of the living room or on the kitchen floor. As such, girls housed by their employers who lose their jobs are without accommodation and other sources of support.

During the pandemic, many residents in low-income areas lost their jobs or remained at home. As a result, their domestic workers were also let go, either because their employers could not afford to pay them or because household members remained homebound and were therefore able to assume domestic duties in the home. In addition, domestic workers were dismissed because they were perceived to increase the risk of contracting COVID-19.

Kidist, mentor, Bahir Dar, explained,

> Let me tell you about a girl that comes here to wash clothes. I asked her recently why she stopped her other job and she said they fired her because they got scared that she'd bring the virus. The girl also said her former employer has all her kids in the house and out of school now, so they can help her with the household chores. The girls would rather stay unpaid and in the same home because they know no one will hire during this time . . . By the way, the employers of these girls are not well off or rich people. They are just desperate people who need someone to look after their children because they have to work as well. They pay them very low wages. So now when financial constraints arise because of Corona, I have no doubt in my mind that these employers will have to let the girls go.

According to Helen, a mentor in Addis Ababa,

> I saw another girl a while back and she told me that two girls that she knows have been fired because the employers said they can't afford to pay them anymore. The majority of the girls we have [in the program] are maids. I saw one girl as well and she looked so bad. She looked so dirty; her hair was a mess. She looked really bad. You know, when the employers are not doing well, they take

it out on the girls. This girl I am telling you about looked so bad. You could tell she was out of it. She looked hungry as well.

For Genet, a beneficiary in Shashamene,

> A lot of us have been fired because people don't want to risk getting the virus from us, so I am sure girls are struggling. For instance, in the house where I used to work, none of them are working anymore so they fired me. I have been trying to find employment elsewhere and I haven't been able to find anything. I sent my sister back to our family [in the rural area] because I didn't want her to go hungry here with me. I'm contemplating going back myself because I can't pay rent anymore.

Because most domestic workers rely on their employers for a place to live, many prefer to endure any abuse rather than lose their accommodation during the pandemic. Some of the girls said that they would prefer to stay at work even if they were not paid, while mentors hoped that girls could withstand abuse and not being paid so that they could remain housed during the pandemic.

Yordanos, a mentor in Addis Ababa, said,

> When life stresses the employers, they take it out on the girls. These girls don't have the time or resources to protect themselves from this virus . . . When the employers let the girls go, because they can't afford to pay them anymore, girls head to the streets . . . So, even when they're being treated badly and not getting paid, they take the abuse and stay with their employers. Because of the current environment, these girls stay even when they're being starved, beaten and abused.

Among domestic workers who retained their jobs, many reportedly had to risk contracting COVID-19 rather than members of the household doing so. Girls were reportedly sometimes not given the means to protect themselves, such as masks or soap. In addition, while domestic workers were previously confined to the household, during the pandemic they were sent out to do errands in the community and risk infection themselves.

We learned from Rahel, a mentor in Bahir Dar, that

> employers will definitely not get their maids masks. They will probably tell them to wear a scarf but will not get them the protective equipment at all. People think of domestic workers as less than human. Employers only think of themselves. So, I think domestic workers will be the ones who get the virus first because of the lack of concern for their safety from their employers.

And Bayssa, a mentor in Shashamene, said,

> I noticed how even my neighbors started sending just the domestic worker out to run all the errands and would keep themselves and their kids indoors. Little did they know that if the girl is infected, they'll catch the virus too. Instead of doing that, employers should take equal care of their workers, they should educate [them] and let the girls know about ways they can protect themselves from the virus.

Some girls returned to their rural areas of their own volition or at the request of their parents when news of the pandemic initially spread. Many girls reportedly traveled home for *Fasika* (Easter) in April and never returned. Some of the domestic workers who were dismissed had no choice but to return to their rural areas. Some dreaded having to go back because they were accustomed to life in the city. Gete, a beneficiary in Shashamene, exclaimed,

> I don't want to go back to my hometown. I don't want to drink river water after drinking tap water. The people I used to work for were really nice, but we couldn't make it work and I had to leave. It hurt me psychologically.

The rates of COVID-19 infection are higher in urban areas of Ethiopia. Many mentors claimed that parents in the rural areas might not welcome back their daughters, for fear that they would bring the virus with them. Some explained that girls who return to the rural areas during the pandemic will be ostracized by society because of the transmission risk that people believe an urban resident represents. Many mentors also mentioned the risk of girls being forced to marry if they returned to rural areas.

Abebe, a mentor in Bahir Dar, expressed her concern, saying,

> Going back to their families will be difficult because most rural people think the virus is in the city so they will not accept them if they go back. They will think they brought the illness with them. I think this will damage their mental health. The rural people will isolate these girls.

Mahlet, a mentor in Addis Ababa, said,

> So, I was talking to one of the girls before the session started and she told me that she's from Amhara region . . . I asked her why she came here, and she told me she fled an arranged marriage. She said she used to beg when she first got to Addis Ababa and now she washes clothes for half the day and begs for the other half. So now, if this girl has to go back to her hometown, there is no question that she will be married off by her family.

Mentors presumed that, if they are not forced to marry, many of the girls who relocated to the rural areas will return to cities once the pandemic is over.

The suspension of the Biruh Tesfa for All girls' groups highlighted how critical the safe space gatherings were in the lives of domestic workers, recent migrants, and other marginalized girls. Virtually all the girls interviewed expressed the desire to resume attending the girls' groups. Many spoke of the program allowing them to make friends, have recreation time, and have a break from the grueling nature of their work. Many said that, in addition to building much-needed skills, the project gave them hope. For Emebet, a mentor in Addis Ababa,

> During our time together, I noticed they [beneficiaries] would come to the safe spaces early and sit and play together before us mentors arrived. They would do each other's hair, they would speak together in their language, they would exchange information about how their employers treat them and the kind of homes they are in. I remember seeing the sadness in their eyes when it was time to go home. Now, this escape is gone, and their employers are bitter and anxious during this time. So, just imagine how they must be feeling right now.

Conclusion

Child domestic workers are among the most marginalized and disadvantaged girls and young women in Ethiopia and globally. This large but overlooked group of girls is generally made up of recent migrants from rural areas, on their own with little in the way of support networks, and with low levels of education or no education whatsoever. In many Ethiopian settings, they are reliant on employers for virtually all their basic needs, including food and shelter, in addition to their meagre incomes. The conditions of their work in some households are exploitive, abusive, and tantamount to modern slavery, yet they enjoy few protections under existing laws.

The COVID-19 pandemic has negatively affected communities globally, especially those that are most disadvantaged. In Ethiopia, girls in domestic work are already at risk and vulnerable in many different ways that have only been amplified by the pandemic. Girls and young women who have managed to retain their jobs as domestic workers are frequently pushed to the front lines of the pandemic, forced to circulate in densely populated communities as they run essential household errands like buying food, while their employers remain confined to the home.

Many domestic workers described in this study have lost their jobs in the context of the pandemic, resulting in an instantaneous loss of income as well as of a place to live. Finding another job during the pandemic is exceedingly difficult. Some may be welcomed back by their families in rural areas and prefer to remain there during the pandemic, away from urban epicenters. Others risk an arranged, forced marriage if they return, or face being stigmatized and perceived as bringing the virus to their rural communities. Those who choose to stay in the city may end up living on the street or in other unsafe conditions. Previous research has suggested that domestic work is a slippery slope and feeder occupation to commercial sex work (or commercial sexual exploitation) (Population Council 2018). Although such cases were not reported in this study, transitioning to commercial sexual exploitation may be one of the survival strategies such girls resort to at this time.

Prevention and support programs for child domestic workers are critical, but remain small-scale and scattered, unlikely to reach the millions of marginalized girls who are absorbed into domestic work. The COVID-19 pandemic and its impact on girls and young women in domestic work underscore the importance of targeted, evidence-based programs for special categories of marginalized girls who are not easily reached by mainstream programs. Biruh Tesfa for All is an example of an evidence-based, large-scale initiative that addresses the needs and realities of such girls. The program is designed to build girls' protective assets, such as friendship and mentoring networks; access to entitlements such as health and social services; communication skills; basic literacy and numeracy; financial literacy and life skills; and to address barriers to participation by engaging employers and other gatekeepers. Just as importantly, beneficiaries and mentors from this study described such programs as giving child domestic workers hope and a positive outlook for a better future.

Since the suspension of Biruh Tesfa for All safe space groups, the program is now reengaging with beneficiaries. Beneficiary girls initially took part in remote learning sessions for several months. During this time, beneficiaries were provided with workbooks and homework assignments by their mentors. Mentors later collected and corrected homework, providing feedback during the exchange of workbooks, as well as new assignments. During these exchanges, girls were also provided with personal protective equipment such as masks, hand sanitizer, soap, and some basic foodstuffs. While remote learning did not allow for intensive teaching and learning based on physical interaction in the classroom, it ensured that the program remained engaged and in contact with beneficiary girls. Ultimately, small group meetings resumed and included precautions such as physical distancing, mask-wearing, and the use of hand sanitizer. In

Figure 10.2. A Biruh Tesfa For All beneficiary does a job to benefit herself and her peers. Photo: Zeleman Productions.

addition, mentors started conducting periodic follow-up of girls, or welfare check-ins, and the program has hired counselors in each project site, offering girls counseling services either in person or by phone. Currently, 8,475 girls are taking part in the Biruh Tesfa for All program.

Acknowledgments

This project was made possible by funding via aid from the UK government. The contents are the sole responsibility of the authors and do not necessarily reflect the views of the UK government. We are grateful to our collaborators, the Ethiopian Ministry of Education, Humanity and Inclusion (the NGO formerly known as Handicap International), and Plan International. Many staff from the Population Council, Ethiopia, contributed to this study. Yetenayet Akalehiywot supported the logistics of the study and gave us valuable ideas and contributions. Program Officers Habtamu Demele, Bisrat Getaneh, and Mohammed Seid assisted with the identification of respondents for the study. Tigist Solomon helped with the interview process. Finally, we are most grateful to the girls and mentors of the Biruh Tesfa for All program for sharing their ideas and experiences, and without whom this research would not have been possible.

Annabel Erulkar is Country Director in the Population Council's Ethiopia office and a social scientist specializing in child protection and girls' health and development. She heads projects related to child marriage, child labor, migration, and trafficking.

Welela Tarekegne is Program Officer for Ethics and Child Protection at the Population Council, Ethiopia. She works on the safeguarding of children in the Biruh Tesfa for All project and ensures compliance with safeguarding policies and guidelines.

Eyasu Hailu is Research Officer at the Population Council's Ethiopia office. He undertakes data collection, supervision, analysis, cleaning, and report production.

References

Black, Maggie. 2002. *Child Domestic Workers: Finding a Voice*. London: Anti-Slavery International.

Embassy of the Federal Democratic Republic of Ethiopia (FDRE), UK. 2020. "Ethiopia Declares State of Emergency to Curb Transmission of Coronavirus." 14 April. Retrieved 29 September 2022 from https://www.ethioembassy.org.uk/ethiopia-declares-state-of-emergency-to-curb-transmission-of-coronavirus/.

Erulkar, Annabel. 2020. "Characteristics of Brokers in Relation to the Migration of Girls and Young Women in Ethiopia." Research brief. Addis Ababa: Population Council.

Erulkar, Annabel, and Abebaw Ferede. 2009. "Social Exclusion and Early, Unwanted Sexual Initiation in Poor Urban Settings in Ethiopia." *International Perspectives on Sexual and Reproductive Health* 35(4): 186–93. https://doi.org/10.1363/ipsrh.35.186.09.

Erulkar, Annabel, Abebaw Ferede, Worku Ambelu, Woldemariam Girma, Helen Amdemikael, Behailu GebreMedhin, Berhanu Legesse, Ayualem Tameru, and Messay Teferi. 2010. *Ethiopia Young Adult Survey: A Study in Seven Regions*. Addis Ababa: Population Council and UNFPA.

Erulkar, Annabel, Abebaw Ferede, Woldemariam Girma, and Worku Ambelu. 2013. "Evaluation of 'Biruh Tesfa' (Bright Future) HIV Prevention Program for Vulnerable Girls in Ethiopia." *Vulnerable Child and Youth Studies* 8(2): 182–92. https://doi.org/10.1080/17450128.2012.736645.

Erulkar, Annabel, and Girmay Medhin. 2017. "Evaluation of a Safe Spaces Program for Girls in Ethiopia." *Girlhood Studies: An Interdisciplinary Journal* 10(1): 107–25. https://doi.org/10.3167/ghs.2017.100108.

Erulkar, Annabel, and Tekle-Ab Mekbib. 2007. "Invisible and Vulnerable: Adolescent Domestic Workers in Addis Ababa, Ethiopia." *Vulnerable Child and Youth Studies* 2(3): 246–56. https://doi.org/10.1080/17450120701487857.

Erulkar, Annabel, Tekle-Ab Mekbib, Negussie Simie, and Tshai Gulema. 2006. "Differential Use of Adolescent Reproductive Health Programs in Addis Ababa, Ethiopia." *Journal of Adolescent Health* 38(3): 253–60. https://doi.org/10.1016/j.jadohealth.2005.03.026.

Federal Negarit Gazette of the Federal Democratic Republic of Ethiopia (FDRE). 2019. *Labour Proclamation No. 1156/2019*. Addis Ababa: FDRE.

Gebremedhin, Mussie. 2016. "Procrastination in Recognizing the Rights of Domestic Workers in Ethiopia." *Mizan Law Review* 10(1): 38–72. https://doi.org/10.4314/mlr.v10i1.2.

Human Rights Watch (HRW). 2006. "Swept under the Rug: Abuses Against Domestic Workers around the World." *Human Rights Watch*, 27 July. Retrieved 29 September 2022 from https://www.hrw.org/report/2006/07/27/swept-under-rug/abuses-against-domestic-workers-around-world.

International Labour Organization (ILO). 2012. *Child Domestic Work: Global Estimates 2012*. Geneva: ILO International Programme on the Elimination of Child Labour (IPEC).

Population Council. 2018. *Domestic Work and Transitions to Commercial Sexual Exploitation: Evidence from Ethiopia*. Research brief. Addis Ababa.

Temin Miriam, and Craig Heck. 2020. "Close to Home: Evidence on the Impact of Community-Based Girl Groups." *Global Health Science and Practice* 8(2): 300–24. https://doi.org/10.9745/GHSP-D-20-00015.

UNICEF. 1999. *Child Domestic Work*. Innocenti Digest 5. Florence.

Worldometer. 2020. "Worldometer: Coronavirus Ethiopia." Retrieved 29 September 2022 from https://www.worldometers.info/coronavirus/country/ethiopia.

CHAPTER 11

The New Normal for Young Transgender Women in Thailand
Unspoken Gender-Based Violence in the Time of COVID-19

Rapeepun Jommaroeng, Sara Hair, Cheera Thongkrajai, Kath Kangbipoon, and Suda Bootchadee

Introduction

On 11 March 2020, the World Health Organization's Director-General, Dr. Tedros Adhanom Ghebreyesus, announced that COVID-19, a novel coronavirus, had spread to the extent that it "could be characterized as a pandemic" (WHO 2020). As of 10 July 2020, Thailand had recorded 3,202 cases of COVID-19 and fifty-eight related deaths (WHO Health Emergency Dashboard 2020). On 4 April 2020, a nightly curfew was imposed; everyone had to be at home between 10 p.m. and 4 a.m. The COVID-19 pandemic has resulted in lockdowns, limitations on movement, and international travel restrictions, all of which have been meant to contain the spread of the virus. Newly published articles (see, for ex-

Notes for this section can be found on page 203.

ample, Pfefferbaum and North 2020) state that the impact of COVID-19 may be far-reaching and may have a detrimental effect on the well-being and safety of individuals and communities, given the possibility of being stigmatized, the lack of medical resources, and significant economic loss and subsequent feelings of isolation and confusion. Pfefferbaum and North have also suggested that this impact might include the demonstration of harmful behaviors by people who have COVID-19 as well as in the wider population, with concurrent negative mental health outcomes.

Disasters have been characterized as "extreme natural events that are outside our control," while those affected have been described as "victims of a maleficent nature" (Spurway and Griffith 2016: 471). However, other studies have positioned disasters as events that occur "as a result of structural issues that exist within communities [and] that result in a disproportionate level of vulnerability for specific groups" (King et al. 2019: 460), such as Transgender Women (TGW) and girls. Of course, women and girls in general regularly face violence in Thailand, even when disasters have not occurred.

Rena Janamnuaysook et al. (2015) note that of 202 transgender research survey participants, 21 percent had experienced sexual abuse or violence at least once in their lifetimes. The mixed-methods exploration by Myra Betron (2009), which included twenty-seven TGW from Thailand, found that the vast majority (89 percent) had experienced one or more forms of violence within the past year: twenty-one (78 percent) had experienced emotional violence; nine (33 percent) had experienced physical violence; and sixteen (59 percent) had experienced sexual violence. Much of the existing literature indicates that girls and woman are at a higher risk of emotional and physical abuse after instances of disaster (Campbell et al. 2016; Enarson et al. 2007; First et al. 2017; Parkinson 2019; Rao 2020). One example is the rape of sixty-eight survivors of the 2010 earthquake in Haiti whom Doctors Without Borders treated in one area within a month (Institute for Justice and Democracy in Haiti 2010). There is no single identifiable reason for the increase in violence following a disaster; intersecting components including homelessness, unemployment, increased substance use, trauma, grief, stress and loss, and confined accommodation were identified by female survivors of Australia's 2009 "Black Saturday" bushfires as possible reasons (Parkinson and Zara 2013).

It has been well documented that when disasters occur, those who live in poverty or come from lower socioeconomic backgrounds have fewer resources, less choice, and more logistical constrictions (Enarson et al. 2007; True 2013). Periods of disaster often leave women and girls who are already poor in a worse economic position, as Elaine Enarson et al. (2007) point out. Chaman Pincha and Hari Krishna (2008) provide one such example in exploring the impact of the 2004 tsunami in India for *aravanis* (nonbinary people), noting that while they were from low socioeconomic backgrounds prior to the disaster, their economic and social vulnerability was increased as a result.

TGW in Thailand often have limited access to employment opportunities as a direct result of discrimination based on their gender expression and identity (Cameron 2006; Nemoto et al. 2016). While as Scott Berry et al. (2012) note, TGW may be employed as hairdressers, cooks, sex workers, models, dancers, performers, hostesses, and waitresses, those particularly vulnerable to the financial impacts of COVID-19, according to Jack Burton (2020), are those employed in the informal economy, such as sex workers and those who work in massage parlors, bars, and karaoke venues. This is because most of these workers are excluded from government financial relief stimulus packages (UNAIDS 2020) and may not have other rights or entitlements, as Marc Theuss et al. (2014) note. Internationally, TGW are a "very high burden population for HIV" (Baral et al. 2013: 214). In their systematic review and meta-analysis of the literature on prevalence, the frequency of HIV was found to be 12.5 percent (in the range of 5.1 to 19.9 percent) for Thai TGW. Preliminary research (see MacCarthy et al. 2020) has identified the significant impact of COVID-19 on sexual minority men and TGW in the US. Sarah MacCarthy et al. (ibid.) undertook a study that included thirty-six Latinx sexual minority men and sixteen Latinx TGW, and the participants reported that 23.1 percent had increased their alcohol consumption, 67.3 were having sleep difficulties, and 78.4 percent were having mental health difficulties. Within the sample, 34.6 percent stated that their medication attention was lower, and TGW indicated that there were delays in accessing hormones and gender-affirming procedures. Furthermore, it was also noted that of the eighteen participants who were using pre-exposure prophylaxis (PrEP), 33.3 percent had disrupted access to this medication.

The overarching aim of this study was to explore how COVID-19 had an impact on the different facets of the lives of TGW, specifically their access to employment, use of government services and aid, help-seeking for health issues, and decision-making about sexual relationships. Preliminary questions investigated each participant's income, educational level, and employment details to obtain further insight into their current situation. These were followed by open questions that helped unpack the impact of COVID-19. We used probing questions to clarify, seek additional depth, and discuss specific experiences in greater detail.

Methods

We conducted the data collection for this study in July 2020. Following Gina Higginbottom et al. (2013) and Pranee Liamputtong (2013), we identified the participants using purposive sampling, since this allowed us to select participants who possessed information and experiences that were relevant to our research. In line with the model offered by Pranee Rice and Douglas Ezzy (2000), in-depth interviews were used to obtain thick and deep explanations of the experiences of the participants. This allowed for a clearer understanding of how COVID-19 had had an impact on their lives. The interviews took place over two weeks from early to mid-July 2020 and were conducted via Line, Skype, or Zoom because of the COVID-19 pandemic restrictions, but also because of the different locations of the participants. The majority (n = 19) of the interviews were conducted in Thai and were typically an hour long. The participants provided informed consent to audio-recording of the interviews, which were then transcribed verbatim. All authors contributed to the design of the interview guide. All the researchers involved in the study were members of the Lesbian, Gay, Bisexual, Transgender, Intersex, and Queer (LGBTIQ) community, and the majority (n = 4) held insider status as Thai citizens who had worked extensively in their communities to further the rights of LGBTIQ people. Familiarity with the community and a high degree of experience in undertaking research in this context can be identified as a significant strength of the researchers' contribution to this chapter.

Ethical clearance for the project was obtained from the Ethical Review Committee of the Faculty of Public Health, Mahidol University, Thailand. Since the research team anticipated that the participants might become upset or distressed, contingency plans were included in the ethical protocol for easy access to the Rainbow Sky Association of Thailand for counseling and additional assistance. Strict adherence to the protocol and the intentional design that allowed for breaks and the presence of a support person meant that these possibilities did not occur.

Participants

The key informant group was comprised of young TGW who ranged in age from eighteen to twenty-five. Most of the participants were students, who came, typically, from the middle class. Within the student group there were only a few who were from lower socioeconomic backgrounds; it was these students who explained that they were having economic problems since losing their part-time employment as a result of COVID-19. Two participants who identified as students were recent graduates who had already begun working. Others worked as cabaret dancers or in night entertainment sectors in Pattaya and were less educated than the graduates since they had started working immediately after completing secondary school. All the cabaret dancers had been working in the industry for less than a year; they said that they had worked in factories and as salespeople, waitresses, cashiers, and bartenders prior to employment in the entertainment sector.

Analysis

We conducted a thematic analysis using the six stages articulated by Virginia Braun and Victoria Clarke (2006). We began by actively reading the research transcripts in an attempt to identify relationships and meaning. We developed preliminary codes and arranged portions of the data into sections. We reviewed the preliminary codes and combined similar codes into central themes. We reviewed these themes critically to ensure that they represented the data accurately, and we then named the themes, defined and reviewed them, and analyzed each portion. All the authors reviewed the themes and the coding to increase the rigor of the analysis.

Results

Five key themes emerged during the interviews: the negative economic impact of COVID-19; increased tensions in self-quarantine; discrimination in online learning; the dissolution of relationships as a result of COVID-19; and difficulty in accessing hormone treatment.

Economic Impact and State Aid

The Frustrated Dancers

Unsurprisingly, the participants who were more vulnerable to the economic impacts of COVID-19 were TGW who were less educated, from lower socioeconomic backgrounds, and working in the entertainment industry. This last aspect reflected the fact that when COVID-19 reached Thailand, many cities that relied heavily on the income from tourism were shut down. The cabaret dancers had lost their jobs because their theaters had closed. All the cabaret dancers reflected that before COVID-19, their lives had been improving because they had managed to find employment in prestigious cabaret theaters. They had been earning a significant salary in their previous roles—between THB 11,000 and 20,000 (approximately USD 350 and 650) per month on average. A number of the participants supplemented this income by working additional jobs in bars after finishing their shifts in the theaters. This income also allowed them to afford the hormone treatment necessary to feminize their physical appearance and enabled them to send money back to their families. All the cabaret dancer participants expressed their disappointment in having their employment terminated, since working in cabaret shows was what many called the "dream of [my] life," and they had worked hard to retain their employment in this role. Ping, a 23-year-old from Buriram province, said,

> It's been my dream job since I was young. I used to write an essay when I was in Grade 4 that I wanted to be in the cabaret show or a designer—something like this and I could do it. I have reached my dream but not for long, and now there is COVID-19. Then, I had to stop and will try again when there is no longer COVID-19. I'll resume my dream again.

When COVID-19 struck Thailand, many of the shows stopped. Some of the participants still attended rehearsals for a few weeks, but some lost their jobs as soon as the state of emergency was announced and the curfew was introduced. Many of the participants working in Pattaya, stressed, upset, and feeling that they were starting all over again or that they had lost all progress made toward their goals of working as cabaret dancers, decided to return to their home provinces. Jenny, a 21-year-old from Loey province, said,

> I've kept thinking about this. Why is my life like this? Why have I ended up where I started . . . back to be[ing] a 7-Eleven staff [member].[1] I used to work at the cabaret show, which is my highest dream. Now, I have to start my life all over again. I feel so frustrated.

The economic constraints of COVID-19 meant that the cabaret dancers were saving as much money as they could, and this often meant living in their family homes. The dancers entered new forms of employment, such as selling street food and working at the night market or at 7-Eleven. They said that they would prefer to work in their own businesses rather than in factories or what they called "hard jobs," as Ping explained:

> From what I've seen, those who are in the cabaret business turned themselves into entrepreneurs. For example, the star of Tiffany Show, she's now selling products at the market. Most of her friends also turned to become entrepreneurs, selling things. People working in the cabaret shows are good-looking, they definitely wouldn't go to work in factories because it's hard work.

While a number of respondents tried to find new jobs in the Pattaya area, many were unsuccessful. Jenny had been hired at a 7-Eleven but stated that the salary was half what she used to earn and that she was struggling to cover her expenses, pay her debts, and still send money home to her family. She said, "I used to give 2,000 to 3,000 Baht to my family, now it is only 1,000 Baht."

June, a 23-year-old from Mahasarakham province, described the difficulty of finding a new job during the COVID-19 pandemic when she said that

> [o]ther[s] still try to find [a] new job in their hometown but as the economy is getting worse, finding a job is very hard. The problem is not linked to their gender. Everyone, males and females, [is] also facing the same situation. But they think that some people still have prejudice and discriminate against transgenders.

June also stated that trying to find a job outside of the entertainment or sex industry was difficult given the prevalence of current stereotypes and stigmas. She explained, "Transgender women are more unlikely to find jobs due to stigmatization. We are stereotyped to be in the cabaret show or work in Pattaya to do that kind of [sex] work." The cabaret dancers were still hopeful that after the pandemic they would be rehired in their previous positions.

The Students

Students who described themselves as being from the middle class did not face as many economic difficulties as did their cabaret dancer peers. Some had additional support from their parents, but others could not rely on this support since their parents worked in lower-paid positions as farmers, street vendors, and drivers. The parents of Patty, a 22-year-old fourth-year student from Petchabun province in Chula, sell food in their village. As a result of COVID-19, their earnings have been reduced by 50 percent, and they are not able to send her any money. Patty lost her part-time job as a makeup artist and hairdresser. She said,

> When there [was] COVID-19, all my work schedules were canceled, which were tremendous. It was the income that would have made me independent without asking for money from my parents. Now that it's been canceled indefinitely, it's been very shocking, very shocking indeed. For this income, I could have bought anything, hormone[s], purses, shoes, clothes. My parents usually send me weekly stipends but they're not a lot. Now, they cannot do it regularly because [their] income has [also] been reduced. With my current study, I have to use a lot of money to complete my assignment [as a project]. Some of my friends were in trouble and had to find the money.

Some of these participants worked as makeup artists, hairdressers, or wedding organizers, so they were financially self-reliant before COVID-19 struck, and this had a significant impact on their ability to support themselves. Patty explained,

> When COVID came, it is all gone, all events have been canceled. I used to earn 5,000 to 8,000 Baht, sometimes even up to five digits. With this money I could buy clothes, bags, shoes, and hormones. I didn't have to ask my parents. It is all gone so I have to ask my mom to support me for my rent, my living cost[s].

COVID-19 also represented an opportunity for some participants. Yaya, a twenty-year-old from Bangkok, started her own online business. She decided to sell chili paste online to earn money to help support her family. She explained,

> I like cooking, so I decided to try. It's a recipe from my aunt who came from Isan, northeastern Thailand. In Bangkok there are a lot of people from Isan and good Jaew Bong [fermented fish chili paste] is hard to find. So, I decided to make [it]. I sell it for 30 Baht per box. I gave it to my aunt, and she sold it for 35 Baht. It is [a] small business, but it is going well. I plan to make something else too, try other recipes.

The student participants also stated that social distancing had had a negative impact on their studies and everyday life. Many stated that they had lost motivation and enthusiasm and that online classes made it difficult to follow the course. Other students faced more practical difficulties, like not possessing suitable devices to connect to the internet or having a limited understanding of technology. Many students applied for a scholarship or other funding to support themselves during the COVID-19 pandemic.

Government policy required universities to give THB 5,000 to students who were in financial difficulty, but those who were struggling said that this was not enough. The students suggested that the universities should reduce their fees by 30 to 50 percent since they were not using on-campus facilities.

Tensions during Self-Quarantine

Fourteen days of self-quarantine was required for all participants who returned to their hometowns during the COVID-19 pandemic. All the cabaret dancers experienced quarantine in their own homes; some were confined to a room in their family home, and this resulted in tension and stress. Many of the participants were afraid of being infected with COVID-19. June said,

> I had incoming money in my pockets every day. Now, not at all, but only expenses. It's stressful, actually very stressful. I've got myself medications because I thought that I had migraines and I think it's depression, perhaps. I have been thinking in a loop over and over. I stay alone. At first, I barely left the room. I'm usually a very serious person. I think a lot all the time. When I just got back home, I had a fever and I thought that I actually had COVID-19 because there was another person in my neighborhood who actually had it. I was afraid that I would have been infected as well. And there is the stuff about work, so I felt stressful. I think I have stress as well.

There was an overarching lack of understanding from some family members as to why the TGW were not outside and working during this period. For those who had more strained relationships with their families, these deteriorated while they were in the home. Jenny explained,

> My dad does not understand why I only stay at home. But actually, I work online with my smartphone. I'm not close to my dad, but more to my mom. She understands me more. Now that I'm at home, he's not that okay and keeps asking me why I don't go out to work. We don't talk to each other much.

Those who had positive relationships with their family members were welcomed home, and this allowed them to spend time with relatives. These families demonstrated an understanding of the situation in which the TGW found themselves and the impact of COVID-19 on them.

The cabaret dancers faced questioning from neighbors about whether they were sick or affected by COVID-19 because they had returned from Pattaya, which is a tourism hub. Ping described her feelings of being observed during her quarantine when she said, "During the quarantine at home, I felt like people looked at me because my house is a grocery store."

Jenny described her neighbors' fear that she would transmit COVID-19 to them, saying, "My neighbor asked me why I came back home. They were afraid that I would pass on the virus."

Discrimination during Online Learning

In the student group, there were a few individuals who faced discrimination on the basis of their gender identity and expression, despite the shift to online forms of learning. Jade, who is a nineteen-year-old first-year university student from Samutprakarn province, wanted to wear a female uniform, but a number of professors in her faculty said that they did not agree with her decision. During the opening ceremony and orientation, which was broadcast via Zoom, Jade was openly chastised by a professor in the presence of her peers. She explained,

> I went to talk to professors in my department, [saying] that I would like to wear female uniform. She asked, "Why [do] you want to do that?" I said I wanted to be [a] woman. I want to be a teacher and my gender has nothing to do with how I teach. The professor said that it is too much, and asked why I request[ed] this, it is too soon because I am just in first year. She said that there were a lot of processes, the welcoming of new students and the training in a school. She added, "You have to wear male clothing. And do you know clothing is not as important as studying? Do you know that our university is so open to people like you, to be able to wear female clothing in [the] graduation ceremony?" I was shocked with her answer. She said that my request was not appropriate.

Subsequently, Jade posted photographs of herself wearing the female uniform on social media. Her actions were seen as controversial by the wider transgender community on the internet and provoked a reaction from the involved professor. Jade explained,

> The professor talked about my case in [a] Zoom meeting. There were thirty students in this section. She said, "Why did you do this?" She blamed me [for] what happen[ed] [on] social media because I plan[ned] to make a complaint to the president of [the] university.

Despite the shift to online learning by many universities, discrimination is pervasive and has continued. Rules on uniform are still in effect at many Thai universities, and the rules about which uniform can be worn are based on binary conceptualizations of sex and gender. Transgender students often have to wear the uniform of the sex to which they were assigned at birth when on campus and when using university facilities. They are considered male and have Mr. as their title.

Love in the Time of COVID-19

For many couples, COVID-19 created instant long-distance relationships, since travel was restricted and couples faced additional barriers to meeting face-to-face. A number of participants had broken up with their partners as a result of the economic impacts of COVID-19, and because long-distance relationships were perceived as being difficult to maintain. As Yaya stated about a friend, "It is because [of] the distance, they didn't have time to spend together, and her boyfriend was really addicted to online games. So, they broke up." This left some participants in an even worse economic position, as Jenny explained,

> It is because of COVID-19 that he left me, and left me with his debt . . . We bought a house together but because of this COVID-19, my boyfriend dumped me. He went back to his home, leaving with all the debts to only me.

Additionally, Jenny's boyfriend of six months had left her to return to his home and to his ex-girlfriend, with whom he had a child. She said,

> We were disconnected. I saw the photo of his girlfriend. They lived together. One day he was gone. He probably got back to his ex-girlfriend, who they had a kid together. . . . If there had [been] no COVID, we would have continued to date . . . Once the COVID-19 came, we went separate ways. Actually, we still love each other but we had to part. When he left, he didn't tell me at all. I was trying to probe whether he already ha[d] a wife and kids so that I [could] make up my mind.

The ending of relationships because of COVID-19 left some of the TGW chatting online with other men, including *farang* (foreigners). Despite the pressures resulting from the pandemic, many participants persevered and tried to maintain online relationships with their intimate partners. Engaging in sexual relationships became less frequent for the participants since many were living with their parents and avoiding going out and hosting parties during this time.

Access to Healthcare and Hormone Treatment

The TGW who experienced negative impacts from COVID-19 said that purchasing hormones had become difficult. Already living with parents, these young women were using the last of their money to cover their costs for the next three to four months. Jenny, who was able to find a position at a 7-Eleven, stated that her income was not sufficient to cover her costs in addition to buying hormones. She said,

> At the moment, I don't have much money. I can't afford hormones. And I don't normally use [them] anyway. I will use [them] when I can really afford [them]. When I was [in] Grade 10, I could save the money for 1,000 Baht. I could buy hormones for two months. Then again [in] Grade 12, I could buy them for two months. Now that I'm working, I take hormones from time to time but not frequently. Now, let alone with the hormones, I can't even afford food.

Most of the participants stated that they were stressed and worried about the impact of COVID-19. The cabaret dancers said that they had experienced depression, and some were so concerned about their futures that they cried every day. Many said that they experienced an increased number of migraines and headaches. The stressors for students were amplified since they were often trying to balance studying from home and managing financially. The consumption of cigarettes increased for many participants, since they were stressed at home, but alcohol use decreased because the curfew meant that TGW could not go out and party with friends. Some had stopped drinking alcohol because they could no longer afford it, while others drank more alcohol because they had free time that was spent with friends or partying at home instead. As 21-year-old Kath from Chiang Mai province stated,

> I wanted to go out so much but when everything closed, I didn't go out at all. I wanted to party a lot. It was very boring. But the good side was I could take some rest. Healthwise, it was a good thing because I didn't get to drink alcohol at all. My face would look a little plump because I drink too much beer, sometimes almost every day in a week. But for this, I felt my face [was] smaller and my skin [was] actually brighter. But COVID-19 has made me smoke a lot more [laughing] because it's stressful. Now, I almost smoke two packets per day.

Discussion

While the impacts of COVID-19 have been widespread and significant for most communities worldwide, before the outbreak of the COVID-19 pandemic, TGW were already stigmatized and discriminated against, and this resulted in limited economic opportunities. The impact of this outbreak has put them in a more difficult situation, since they have gone from economic independence to economic desperation. For TGW from low socioeconomic backgrounds or for those who are already living in precarious positions, relying on income from tourists, life has become exponentially more difficult. Progress made toward life goals has seemingly dissipated and for many, alternative and less lucrative careers have been sought as a matter of necessity. This affects their access to health services, and, in turn, their mental health and social well-being. Access to proper transgender healthcare has shifted from being difficult to almost nonexistent.

Reliance on family for assistance and physical distance in interpersonal and intimate relationships have also resulted in the deterioration of connections for some, which may have wide-reaching impacts on the dynamics of the family in the future and the amount of support that may be given to TGW. Since Thailand is a collectivist community in which the family is often the primary source of support for TGW rather than the government, such changes may be far-reaching and significant. The state quarantine has not only affected economic lives but has also resulted in the separation of many couples who still have no legal status because their union is not recognized in law. As expected, the discrimination based on sexual orientation and gender identity employed by educational gatekeepers that was evident even before the pandemic continues to exert its influence, albeit through digital platforms such as Zoom and the monitoring of social media.

It is evident that the outbreak of COVID-19 has detrimentally affected many aspects of the lives of TGW in Thailand. It is most likely that their lives will have changed forever. The current movement working on human rights for these TGW is focused mostly on their sexual orientation and gender identity. It is surely time to consider a more inclusive approach in relation to human rights that does not exclude them. This has raised an important question for policymakers, health practitioners, and social workers in respect to how their policies and programs should be designed and redesigned, and how resources should be reallocated to cater to the needs of TGW, which have changed because of COVID-19, and to ensure that they are not excluded. This research also demonstrates the significant resilience and flexibility of TGW living in Thailand, who have, in some instances, made significant life and personal changes to adjust to their communities' new normal.

Acknowledgments

We thank all the transgender participants who made this study possible.

RAPEEPUN JOMMAROENG is a lecturer in the Department of Community Health, Faculty of Public Health, Mahidol University. He is also an LGBTIQ activist in Thailand with research interests in sexual orientation and gender identity, violence against women, girls, and LGBTIQ people, and HIV and AIDS.

SARA HAIR was awarded an Australian Postgraduate Award in 2015 to undertake her doctoral research, which explored how older transgender women in Thailand construct, understand, and experience aging. She has strong interests in aging, disability, sexuality, and gender diversity.

CHEERA THONGKRAJAI is a lecturer in the Department of Sociology and Anthropology, Chiang Mai University. She has expertise in research with the Thai transgender community.

KATH KANGPIBOON is a lecturer in the Faculty of Social Administration, Thammasat University. She is also a transgender activist who has been promoting trans rights in Thailand.

SUDA BOOTCHADEE is the Human Rights and Equality Promotion Program Manager at the Rainbow Sky Association of Thailand. She is pursuing her master's degree in Public Administration at Chulalongkorn University.

Note

1. 7-Eleven is a chain of convenience stores.

References

Baral, Stefan, Tonia Poteat, Susanne Strömdahl, Andrea L. Wirtz, Thomas E. Guadamuz, and Chris Beyrer. 2013. "Worldwide Burden of HIV in Transgender Women: A Systematic Review and Meta-Analysis." *The Lancet: Infectious Diseases* 13(3): 214–22. https://doi.org/10.1016/S1473-3099(12)70315-8.

Berry, Scott, Maria Escobar, and Heather Pitorak. 2012. "'I'm Proud of My Courage to Test': Improving HIV Testing and Counselling among Transgender People in Pattaya, Thailand." Arlington, VA: AIDSTAR-One. Retrieved 29 September 2022 from https://www.psi.org/publication/im-proud-of-my-courage-to-test-improving-hiv-testing-and-counseling-among-transgender-people-in-pattaya-thailand/.

Betron, Myra. 2009. *Screening for Violence Against MSM and Transgenders: Report on a Pilot Project in Mexico and Thailand*. Washington, DC: Futures Groups, USAID. Retrieved 29 September 2022 from https://pdf.usaid.gov/pdf_docs/PNADU587.pdf.

Braun, Virginia, and Victoria Clarke. 2006. "Using Thematic Analysis in Psychology." *Qualitative Research in Psychology* 3(2): 77–101. https://doi.org/10.1191/1478088706qp063oa.

Brawley, Scott, J. Dinger, C. Nguyen, and J. Anderson. 2020. "Impact of Shelter in Place Orders on PrEP Access, Usage and HIV Risk Behaviours in the United States." Paper presented at the 23rd International AIDS Conference, Online, 6–9 July.

Burton, Jack. 2020. "Thai Government Screws Sex Workers over 5,000 Baht Stimulus." *The Thaiger*, 1 April. Retrieved 29 September 2022 from https://thethaiger.com/coronavirus/thai-government-screws-sex-workers-over-5000-baht-stimulus.

Cameron, Liz. 2006. "Sexual Health and Rights: Sex Workers, Transgender People and Men Who Have Sex with Men: Thailand." Washington, DC: Open Society Institute. Retrieved 29 September 2022 from http://www.hivpolicy.org/Library/HPP001169.pdf.

Campbell, Doris, Jacquelyn C. Campbell, Hossein N. Yarandi, Annie Lewis O'Connor, Emily Dollar, Cheryl Killion, Elizabeth Sloand, Gloria B. Callwood, Nicole M. Cesar, Mona Hassan, and Faye Gary. 2016. "Violence and Abuse of Internally Displaced Women Survivors of the 2010 Haiti Earthquake." *International Journal of Public Health* 61(8): 981–92. https://doi.org/10.1007/s00038-016-0895-8.

Enarson, Elaine, Alice Fothergill, and Lori Peek. 2007. "Gender and Disaster: Foundations and Directions." In *Handbook of Disaster Research*, ed. Havidan Rodriguez, Enrico Quarantelli and Russell Dynes, 130–46. New York: Springer.

First, Jennifer, Nathan First, and Brian Houston. 2017. "Intimate Partner Violence and Disasters: A Framework for Empowering Women Experiencing Violence in Disaster Settings." *Affilia* 32(3): 390–403. https://doi.org/10.1177/0886109917706338.

Hammoud, Mohamed, Lisa Maher, Martin Holt, Lousia Degenhardt, Fengyi Jin, Dean Murphy, Benjamin Bavinton, Andrew Grulich, Toby Lea, Bridget Haire, Adam Bourne, Peter Saxton, Stefanie Vaccher, Jeanne Ellard, Brent Mackie, Colin Batrouney, Nicky Bath, and Garrett Prestage. 2020. "Impact of Physical Distancing Due to COVID-19 on Sexual Behaviours and HIV Pre-Exposure Prophylaxis (PrEP) Use among Australian Gay and Bisexual Men: Implications for Trends in HIV." Paper presented at the 23rd International AIDS Conference, online, 6–9 July.

Higginbottom, Gina, Jennifer Pillay, and Nana Boadu. 2013. "Guidance on Performing Focused Ethnographies with an Emphasis on Healthcare Research." *The Qualitative Report* 18(9): 1–16. https://doi.org/10.46743/2160-3715/2013.1550.

Institute for Justice and Democracy in Haiti, MADRE, TransAfrica Forum (TAF), University of Minnesota Law School, and University of Virginia School of Law. 2010. *Our Bodies Are Still Trembling: Haitian Women's Fight against Rape*. Boston: Institute for Justice & Democracy in Haiti (IJDH) and Lawyers' Earthquake Response Network (LERN). Retrieved 29 September 2022 from https://reliefweb.int/sites/reliefweb.int/files/resources/2AFAD9E18B0B66604925776E000646D1-Full_Report.pdf.

Janamnuaysook, Rena, Jesada Taesombat, and Kath Khangpiboon. 2015. "The Social Experiences of Trans People in Thailand." In *Transrespect versus Transphobia: The Social Experiences of Trans and Gender-Diverse People in Colombia, India, the Philippines, Serbia, Thailand, Tonga, Turkey and Venezuela*, ed. Carsten Balzer/Carla LaGata and Jan Simon Hutta, 44–53. Berlin: Transrespect versus Transphobia. Retrieved 29 September 2022 from https://transrespect.org/wp-content/uploads/2015/08/TvT-PS-Vol9-2015.pdf.

King, Julie, Nicole Edwards, Hanna Watling, and Sara Hair. 2019. "Barriers to Disability-Inclusive Disaster Management in the Solomon Islands: Perspectives of People with Disability." *International Journal of Disaster Risk Reduction* 34: 459–66. https://doi.org/10.1016/j.ijdrr.2018.12.017.

Liamputtong, Pranee. 2013. *Qualitative Research Methods*. South Melbourne: Oxford University Press.

MacCarthy, Sarah, Max Izenberg, Joanna Barreras, Ron Brooks, Ana Gonzalez, and Sebastian Linnemayr. 2020. "Rapid Mixed-Methods Assessment of COVID-19 Impact on Latinx Sexual Minority Men and Latinx Transgender Women." *PLoS ONE* 15(12): e0244421. https://doi.org/10.1371/journal.pone.0244421.

Nemoto, Tooru, Taylor Cruz, Mariko Iwamoto, Karen Trocki, Usaneya Perngparn, Chitlada Areesantichai, Sachiko Suzuki, and Colin Roberts. 2016. "Examining the Sociocultural Context of HIV-Related Risk Behaviors among Kathoey (Male-to-Female Transgender Women) Sex Workers in Bangkok, Thailand." *Journal of the Association of Nurses in AIDS Care* 27(2): 153–65. https://doi.org/10.1016/j.jana.2015.11.003.

Parkinson, Debra. 2019. "Investigating the Increase in Domestic Violence Post Disaster: An Australian Case Study." *Journal of Interpersonal Violence* 34(11): 2333–62. https://doi.org/10.1177/0886260517696876.

Parkinson, Debra, and Claire Zara. 2013. "The Hidden Disaster: Domestic Violence in the Aftermath of Natural Disaster." *Australian Journal of Emergency Management* 28(2): 28–35. Retrieved 29 September 2022 from https://

search.informit.com.au/documentSummary;dn=364519372739042;res=IELHSS.

Pfefferbaum, Betty, and Carol North. 2020. "Mental Health and the COVID-19 Pandemic." *The New England Journal of Medicine* 383(6): 510–12. https://doi.org/10.1056/NEJMp2008017.

Pincha, Chaman, and Hari Krishna. 2008. "Aravanis: Voiceless Victims of the Tsunami." *Humanitarian Exchange Magazine* 41, 23 December. Retrieved 29 September 2022 from https://odihpn.org/publication/aravanis-voiceless-victims-of-the-tsunami/.

Power, Lisa. 2020. "COVID-19 Has Had a Major Impact on PrEP, Sexual Behaviour and Service Provision." *NAM: Aidsmap*, 9 July. Retrieved 29 September 2022 from https://www.aidsmap.com/news/jul-2020/covid-19-has-had-major-impact-prep-sexual-behaviour-and-service-provision.

Rao, Smitha. 2020. "A Natural Disaster and Intimate Partner Violence: Evidence over Time." *Social Science & Medicine* 247: 112804. https://doi.org/10.1016/j.socscimed.2020.112804.

Rice, Pranee, and Douglas Ezzy. 2000. *Qualitative Research Methods: A Health Focus*. Melbourne: Oxford University Press.

Spurway, Kim, and Thao Griffith. 2016. "Disability-Inclusive Disaster Risk Reduction: Vulnerability and Resilience Discourses, Policies and Practices." In *Disability in the Global South: International Perspectives on Social Policy, Administration and Practice*, ed. Shaun Grech and Karen Soldatic, 469–82. Cham: Springer. https://doi.org/10.1007/978-3-319-42488-0_30.

Theuss, Marc, Rapeepun Jommaroeng, and Duangsamorn Jatupornpimpol. 2014. "Thailand (2014): Female Transgender in Pattaya; Age Category Based Social Relations, and Pathways through the HIV Testing, Care and Treatment Cascade." Thailand: Population Services International. Retrieved 29 September 2022 from https://dataverse.harvard.edu/dataset.xhtml?persistentId=doi:10.7910/DVN/L1KS3Q.

True, Jacqui. 2013. "Gendered Violence in Natural Disasters: Learning from New Orleans, Haiti and Christchurch." *Aotearoa New Zealand Social Work* 25(2): 78–89. https://doi.org/10.11157/anzswj-vol25iss2id83.

UNAIDS. 2020. "Supporting Sex Workers during the COVID-19 Pandemic in Thailand." *COVID-Blog*, 7 May. Retrieved 29 September 2022 from https://www.unaids.org/en/20200507_Thai_sex_workers.

WHO (World Health Organization). 2020. "Coronavirus Disease COVID-19 Pandemic." Retrieved 7 November 2022 from https://www.euro.who.int/en/health-topics/health-emergencies/coronavirus-covid-19/novel-coronavirus-2019-ncov.

WHO (World Health Organization) Health Emergency Dashboard. 2020. "Thailand: WHO Coronavirus Disease." Retrieved 29 September 2022 from https://covid19.who.int/region/searo/country/th.

INDEX

abortion, 89–90, 141, 150
  Dilaasa support for, 148
  ENIA plan for, 42
abuse, 52, 149
  of child domestic workers, 175, 183
  during COVID-19 lockdowns, 62, 144–46, 166–67
  police intervention in, 146, 147
  social stigma of, 25, 56, 166–67
Addis Ababa, Ethiopia, 175–76, *177*, 181
Adhanom Ghebreyesus, Tedros, 23, 190
Adivasis, 6, 157–58, 163
adolescents, 53, 78, 140
  internet connectivity of, 46, 151
  rights protection systems of, 44
  shelter homes for, 47n2
Adya (pseudonym), 124, 126, 127, 131
age, gender intersectionality with, 15, 18–19
Agricultural Transformation through Stronger Vocational Education (ATTSVE), 103, 104, 112, 114, 115–16
agriculture, technical, vocational, education, and training colleges (ATVET), 5, 9, 101–2, 103, 112–13, 114
alcohol, South African ban on, 61
American Psychological Association, 130
Anwesha Joshi, Ishani, 2–3

anxiety, 123, 127
  related to online learning, 125, 131–32
aravanis (nonbinary people), 192
Argentina, 36, 38, 39, 47n2
  Buenos Aires, 4, 33–35, 45
  Childhood, Adolescence, and Young People Office in, 42, 43
  GBV in, 33–35
  Las Luciérnagas, 41–46
  National Ministry of Women, Genders, and Diversity of, 37–38, 45
Astitva (NGO), 160
ATTSVE. *See* Agricultural Transformation through Stronger Vocational Education
AUH. *See* universal child allowance
Australia, "Black Saturday" bushfires in, 191
Ayarkar, Sujata, 152

Basic Requirements and Minimum Standards Indicators in Education Institutions, in Uganda (BRMS), 75, 83n2
Bednarczyk, Anna, 99
Belinda (pseudonym), 60, 61
Bennett, Belinda, 121
Berghahn, Vivian, 9
Berghahn Books, 9
Berry, Scott, 192

Betron, Myra, 191
Bhate-Deosthali, Padma, 152
Bihar, India, 167–68
Bipat, Jenni, 59
Biruh Tesfa for All, in Ethiopia, 6–7, 176–78, 182, 185–87, *187*
Black Protest, in Poland, 95
"Black Saturday" bushfires, 191
Bonaerenses Solidarios, in Buenos Aires, 45
Bongi (pseudonym), 60, 61
Bootchadee, Suda, 203
Braun, Virginia, 124, 194
bride price, 78, 83n3
BRMS. *See* Basic Requirements and Minimum Standards in Education Institutions, in Uganda
Buenos Aires, Argentina, 4, 33–35, 45
Burton, Jack, 192
Burzynska, Katarzyna, 125

CAA. *See* Citizenship Amendment Act, in India (2019)
Cambiemos Alliance, in Argentina, 45
Canada, 10, 103
capitalism, 89, 165
care, 87–89, 91
  feminism relation to, 95–96
caregivers, 20, 25, 50, 56, 78
CARE International, 16–17, 28
case fatality rate (CFR), 29n2
Casey, Sara, 56
CEFM. *See* child early and forced marriage
CEHAT. *See* Centre for Enquiry into Health and Allied Themes, in India
Centre for Catalyzing Change, 158
Centre for Enquiry into Health and Allied Themes, in India (CEHAT), 143, 153n1
Chakravarti, Uma, 122
Chanana, Karuna, 123
Chaudhary, Anurag, 52
Chawla Noor, Anand, 166
child domestic workers, 174, 176, 177, 178, 184
  abuse of, 175, 183
  migrant workers as, 175, 181–82, 185
  unemployment of, 181–83, 185–86
child early and forced marriage (CEFM). *See* marriage
Childhood, Adolescence, and Young People Office, in Argentina, 42, 43
child labor, of adolescent girls, 53
CHILDLINE, in India, 158, 166
child marriage, 6, 156, 158, 166, 167, 169
  bride price relation to, 83n3
  family honor relation to, 162
  Gauna in, 163
  in India, 159, 160–61, 163
  pregnancy relation to, 164
  in Uganda, 75, 76
Child Marriage Prohibition Officers (CMPOs), 163
children, 23, 40–42, 47n2
  sex work of, 167
Child Welfare Committee, in India (CWC), 149
Citizenship Amendment Act, in India (2019) (CAA), 159–60
Clarke, Victoria, 124, 194
CMPOs. *See* Child Marriage Prohibition Officers
constrained spaces, 54–55, 180
contraception, 27, 39
Contreras, Gabriela, 125
The Conversation (news outlet), 76
coping strategies, for lockdown, 130–31
COVID-19, 7, 29n2, 57–58, 59, 127, 180
  Ebola epidemic compared to, 4, 15, 17
  effect on child domestic workers, 177, 185
  effect on child marriage, 6, 158, 169
  effect on education, 108–9, 112–13, 164
  effect on long-distance relationships, 200
  effect on social services, 50
  effect on TGW, 192–93, 195, 201–2

health services during, 20, 164–65
maternal mortality rates during, 26, 141
secondary harms from, 18, 27–28
second wave of, 166–67
sexual exploitation during, 22, 62–63
social inequalities reinforced by, 33
social stigma from, 60, 160
unhealthy lifestyle during, 61–62
"COVID-19 Survive and Thrive Fund," of Girl Up Initiative Uganda, 83n4
crisis, 1, 18–20, 36, 139–40, 168
child marriage during, 22
gender in analysis of, 27–28
#CuarentenaEnRedes, 38
cultural values, traditional, in India, 132
Cyclone Amphan, 168
Cynthia (pseudonym), 55, 57, 59, 61

Dalhousie Research Ethics Board Approval process, 104
Dalhousie University, 103
Dalits, 6, 133n2, 157, 163, 170n1
Davies, E. Sara, 121
decision-makers, 16, 21, 28, 122, 128
Decree 297/2020, of Argentina, 38, 41
Decree 408/2020, of Argentina, 36
defilement cases, 79, 80, 81
Defoe, Daniel, 2
Delhi, India, 5–6, 123
democracy, care relation to, 88–89
Democratic Republic of Congo (DRC), 16, 17, 20, 21–22
Ebola in, 15, 23, 28
Department of Women's Affairs, in Ethiopia, 112
Digital Empowerment Foundation, 164
Dilaasa centers, 6, 147, 148, 149, 153n1
during lockdowns, 142–43, 150, 151–52
Dinners in the Time of Pandemic, in Poland, 86–87, 91, 92, 93, 99
as response to food shortages, 88, 97–98
disabilities, girls with, 176, 177

disasters, 191–92
discrimination, 75, 199, 202
against Muslim people, 157, 159–60, 168–69
Dissolution of Muslim Marriages Act (1939), 165
Doctors Without Borders, 191
domestic obligations, 74, 77–78, 107–8, 114
gender disparities in, 15, 19, 57, 121
domestic violence, 51–52, 139, 165–66
during COVID-19 lockdowns, 69–70, 79, 164
Domestic Workers Convention No. 189, ILO, 175
dowry, 162, 165
Dowry Prohibition Act, in India (1961), 165
DRC. *See* Democratic Republic of Congo
Duda, Andrzej, 89, 90

earthquake, in Haiti, 191
Ebola epidemic, 18, 21–24, 28, 70, 76, 150
child marriage during, 156
COVID-19 compared to, 4, 15, 17
health services during, 16–17
maternal mortality rates during, 26
pregnancy during, 77, 121, 140
Ebola virus disease (EVD), Zaire strain of, 17–18
economics, 36, 159
economic uncertainty, 21, 25, 50, 129–30
education, 20, 123, 125–26, 156, 176, 180
child marriage relation to, 167
COVID-19 effect on, 108–9, 112–13, 164
domestic obligations effect on, 114, 121
gender inequalities in, 5–6, 83n1, 114–15
internet connectivity relation to, 168
marriage compared to, 129
for pregnancy, 76

INDEX

unemployment effect on, 132
Education and Sports Sector Strategic Plan, in Uganda, 70
Ejang Muzungu, Hope, 76
Emebet (pseudonym), 181–82, 185
Emergency Family Income (IFE), 36
Emory University, 130
Enarson, Elaine, 192
ENIA. *See* National Plan for the Prevention of Unintentional Pregnancy in Adolescence, in Argentina
entertainment sector, Thailand, TGW in, 194, 195–96
entrepreneurs, TGW as, 196, 197
Erulkar, Annabel, 188
Ethiopia, 107–8, 115, 174–75, 179–80
   ATVET colleges in, 5, 9, 101–2, 103, 112–13, 114
   Biruh Tesfa for All in, 6–7, 176–78, 185–87, *187*
   health services in, 109, 110
   migrant workers in, 181–82, 185
Ethiopia Civil Code (1960), 175
Ethiopia Forum (news outlet), 107
EVD. *See* Ebola virus disease
Evita Movement, in Las Luciérnagas, 45–46
Ezzy, Douglas, 193

Facebook group, for Dinners in the Time of Pandemic, 91, 92
Faculty of Public Health, Mahidol University, 193
fake news, about COVID-19, 57–58
family honor, 149, 162
farang (foreigners), 200
Fazeli, Sahar, 10
fear
   effect on menstrual hygiene, 26–27
   of GBV, 111–12
femicide. *See* gender-based violence
feminism, care relation to, 95–96
Fisher, Berenice, 88
food shortages, 88, 97–98, 149

forced marriage, 22
   of Adivasis, 157–58
   poverty relation to, 52
   after pregnancy, 112
   in rural areas, 184
   sexual violence in, 26
foreigners (*farang*), 200
Fraser, Nancy, 161, 167

Gaitán, Ana Cecilia, 4, 47
Garino, Giselle, 56
Gauna, in child marriage, 163
Gausman, Jewel, 102
GBV. *See* gender-based violence
Geda, Alemayehu, 102
gender, 16–17, 27–28, 44–45, 50, 103, 113
   age intersectionality with, 15, 18–19
   education inequalities related to, 5–6, 83n1, 114–15
gender-based violence (GBV), 6, 7, 26, 102, 111–12, 140–41
   during lockdowns, 24–25, 51–52, 53, 55–56
   social isolation relation to, 24, 105
   state support for, 34–35, 37–38, 39–40, 44–45, 46–47
gender biases, 15, 23, 27, 104
Gender Dimensions of the COVID-19 Pandemic (World Bank Group), 121
gender discrimination, 75, 199, 202
gender disparities, in domestic obligations, 15, 19, 57, 121
gender inequalities, in education, 5–6, 83n1, 114–15
Girlhood Studies (Berghahn Books), 9
girl-led narratives, 7
girls. *See specific topics*
Girl Up Initiative Uganda, 79, 83n4
Global Affairs Canada, 103
The Global Gender Gap Report (2020), 115
The Global Partnership for Education (GPE 2020), 78
Goga, Ameena, 52

210

Goli, Srinivas, 163
Gollayan, Christian, 57
Goma, DRC, 17
GPE 2020. *See* The Global Partnership for Education

Hague, Gill, 83n3
Hailu, Eyasu, 188
Hair, Sara, 203
hair salons, lockdowns closing, 58–59
Haiti, earthquake in, 191
Hall, Stidham Kelli, 126–27
Happiness (pseudonym), 55, 56, 58
harassment, verbal, 111
Harper, Caroline, 19
health services, 47n3, 78, 89, 109, 110, 156
   during COVID-19, 20, 164–65
   during Ebola epidemic, 16–17
   reproductive, 52, 147–48
   sexual, 24
   WHO recommendations for, 39, 140–41
HEIs. *See* higher education institutions
Helen (pseudonym), 180, 182–83
Heredia, Mariana, 42–43, 45
hierarchical structure, 92–93
Higginbottom, Gina, 193
higher education institutions (HEIs), 120–21, 122–23
HIV, 192
homophobia, in Poland, 90
hormone treatment, for TGW, 200–201
Horn, Amanda, 9
household chores, 20, 74, 77, 129, 146

IFE. *See* Emergency Family Income
IFRC. *See* International Federation of Red Cross and Red Crescent
ILO. *See* International Labour Organization
incest, in lockdown, 144–45
Independent (news outlet), 79
India, 120–21, 156, 164, 168, 192
   CEHAT in, 143, 153n1
   CHILDLINE in, 158, 166
   Dalits in, 6, 133n2, 157, 163, 170n1
   Delhi, 5–6, 123
   marriage in, 122, 159, 160–61, 163, 167
   migrant workers in, 158–59, 167
   Mumbai, 6, 142–43
   National Family Health Survey in, 141, 160
   New Delhi, 157, 160
   patriarchy in, 161–62
   PCMA in, 163, 165
   second wave of COVID-19 in, 166–67
   shelter homes in, 149, 150–51
   traditional cultural values in, 132
inflation, 107
Institution of Sociology, Jagiellonian University, 91, 99
International Federation of Red Cross and Red Crescent (IFRC), 70
International Labour Organization (ILO), 175
International Rescue Committee, 26
internet connectivity, 46, 102, 114, 126, 151, 168
intimate partner violence (IPV), 139
Islamophobia, in India, 160

Jagiellonian University, Krakow, 5, 91, 99
Jammu and Kashmir High Court, 142
Janamnuaysook, Rena, 191
Jenny (pseudonym), 195, 196, 198, 199, 200–201
Jharkhand, India, 159, 168
Joining Forces Coalition, 78, 81
Jommaroeng, Rapeepun, 203
A Journal of the Plague Year (Defoe), 2
June (pseudonym), 196, 198

Kampala, Uganda, 80
Kandiyoti, Deniz, 131
Kangpiboon, Kath, 203
Kapciak, Zuzanna, 91, 93, 94, 95
Kapur, Nidhi, 4, 9, 29
Khaliq, Ayesha, 169
Krakow, Poland, 5, 90, 91, 99

Krishna, Hari, 192
Krishnakumar, P., 164
Kumar, Krishna, 122
Kumar Mishra, Arvind, 133
KwaZulu-Natal, South Africa, 50

Labor Law, in Ethiopia, 175–76
Langer, Ana, 102
Las Luciérnagas, Argentina, 41–42, 43
    Evita Movement in, 45–46
    Gender Area of, 44–45
Law and Justice party, in Poland, 89–90
Lawson, Victoria, 88
LC1. *See* Local Council 1 chairperson
Lesbian, Gay, Bisexual, Transgender, Intersex, and Queer community (LGBTIQ), 193
"Lessons from Sierra Leone Ebola Pandemic on the Impact of School Closures on Girls" (*The Conversation*), 76
LGBTIQ. *See* Lesbian, Gay, Bisexual, Transgender, Intersex, and Queer community
Liamputtong, Pranee, 193
Liberia, Ebola epidemic in, 76
lifestyle, unhealthy, during COVID-19, 61–62
literacy, 162, 164, 176–77
"Living under Lockdown" (Plan International), 56
Local Council 1 chairperson (LC1), 71, 72, 73, 74, 75
    girls supported by, 76, 77
lockdowns, COVID-19, 3, 27, 132, 157, 162, 190. *See also* COVID-19
    abuse during, 62, 144–46, 166–67
    in Argentina, 36, 43
    coping strategies for, 130–31
    Dilaasa centers during, 142–43, 150, 151–52
    domestic violence during, 69–70, 79, 164
    effect on adolescent rights protection systems, 44
    effect on mental health, 94–95, 99, 151
    effect on peer groups, 127
    effect on state support, 34, 46
    effect on survivors of GBV, 6
    forced marriage relation to, 52
    GBV during, 24–25, 51–52, 53, 55–56
    hair salons closed during, 58–59
    household chores during, 129, 146
    VAW/C during, 139–40
Loskop, Networks for Change in, 8
Luweero, Uganda, 71

MacCarthy, Sarah, 192
Mahidol University, Thailand, 193
Maichew college, in Ethiopia, 103
Maria (pseudonym), 55, 57, 58
marriage, 129, 149
    child, 6, 75, 76, 83n3, 156, 158, 159, 160, 161–63, 164, 166, 167, 169
    forced, 22, 26, 52, 112, 157–58, 184
    in India, 122, 159, 160–61, 163, 167
Martha (pseudonym), 59, 60
Masaka, Uganda, 80
maternal mortality rates, 26, 141
Mednick, Sam, 23
Mengistie, Tilahun, 102
menstrual hygiene, fear of infection effect on, 26–27
mental health, 102–3, 107–8, 109–10, 114–15, 140, 201
    COVID-19 lockdowns effect on, 94–95, 99, 151
MIFUMI, 83n3
migrant workers, 158–59, 167, 175, 181–82, 185
Ministry of Education, in Argentina, 38
Ministry of Education and Sports (MoES), in Uganda, 70, 83n2
Ministry of Gender, Labor, and Social Development, in Uganda, 81
Ministry of Health and Family Welfare, in India (MoHFW), 141, 148
Ministry of Justice and Human Rights, in Argentina, 39

Ministry of Social Development, in Argentina, 39
Ministry of Women, Genders, and Diversity, in Buenos Aires, 45
Ministry of Women and Child Development, in India (WoMCD), 141–42
Mitchell, Claudia, 1–2
Moletsane, Relebohile, 7–8
MoWCD. *See* Ministry of Women and Child Development, in India
Mrityu Bhoj, 163
Mumbai, India, 6, 142–43
Municipal Corporation of Greater Mumbai, 142–43, 153n1
Muslim people, 6, 163, 165
   discrimination against, 157, 159–60, 168–69

National Commission for Protection of Child Rights, 161
National Commission for Women (NCW), 164
National Family Health Survey, in India, 141, 160
National Health Mission, in India, 153n1
National Ministry of Women, Genders, and Diversity, in Argentina, 37–38, 45
National Plan for the Prevention of Unintentional Pregnancy in Adolescence, in Argentina (ENIA), 39, 42
National Secretariat for Children and Adolescents and the Family, in Argentina (SENAF), 39
National Strategy for Girls' Education, in Uganda, 70, 75, 83n1
NCW. *See* National Commission for Women
Negash, Eleni, 116
Nejo college, in Ethiopia, 103
neoliberal system, care in, 88
Networks for Change, in Loskop, 8
New Delhi, India, 157, 160
Ngcobo, Nokukhanya, 63

NGOs, 73, 79, 83n3, 160
Nielsen, Madalyn, 116
Nombembe, Philani, 59
Nompilo (pseudonym), 56, 57, 58, 59, 61–62
nonbinary people (*aravanis*), 192
North, Carol, 191
North Kivu, DRC, 16
novel influenza A epidemic, 109–10

obstetric care, 150
Okudi, Christine Apiot, 5, 69, 82–83
Omona, Julius, 79
"191 Defilement Cases Reported in Albertine Region During Lockdown" (*Independent*), 79
online learning, 125, 131–32, 199
orphans, sexual exploitation of, 164
Oxfam Indian, 163

Pahal (pseudonym), 124, 126, 128, 129–30, 131
pandemic. *See specific topics*
parents, 122, 128, 164
   education view of, 125
   literacy of, 162
Patel, Viresh, 126
patriarchy, 27, 56, 121–23, 131, 151, 161–62
   domestic violence relation to, 52
   effect on education, 126
Pattaya, Thailand, 194, 195, 196, 198
PCMA. *See* Prohibition of Child Marriage Act, in India (2006)
peasants, in Uganda, 74, 77
peer groups, lockdowns effect on, 127
Peer to Peer Uganda (PEERU), 78
Perelmiter, Luisina, 42–43, 45
Perrin, Andrew, 126
Pew Research Center, 57
Pfefferbaum, Betty, 191
Pincha, Chaman, 192
Ping (pseudonym), 195, 196, 198
Plan International, "Living under Lockdown" report of, 56

Poland, 89, 95
    Dinners in the Time of Pandemic in, 86–87, 88, 91, 92, 93, 97–98, 99
    Krakow, 5, 90, 91, 99
police, 79, 81, 146, 147
poverty, 50, 78, 168
    disasters effect on people in, 191–92
    forced marriage relation to, 52
Pradhan, Anagha, 153
pregnancy, 26, 27, 76, 112, 162, 164
    during Ebola epidemic, 24, 77, 121, 140
prevention guidelines, in Addis Ababa, 181
Primrose Nkosi, Zinhle, 63
The Print (news outlet), 168
Prohibition of Child Marriage Act, in India (2006) (PCMA), 163, 165
Protection of Women from Domestic Violence Act, in India (2005) (PWDVA), 165–66
Provincial Agency for children and Adolescents, in Argentina, 38
Pugh, Hannah, 116
PWDVA. *See* Protection of Women from Domestic Violence Act, in India (2005)

Qi, Han, 127
quarantine, 42, 54–55, 198

Rainbow Sky Association, Thailand, 193
Rajasthan, India, 159, 163
Rana, Richa, 133
Rasul, Imran, 77
reciprocity, unpaid care work compared to, 87–88
El Refaie, Elizabeth, 3
Rege, Sangeeta, 152
relationships, long-distance, 200
Di Renzo, Laura, 62
reproductive health services, 52, 147–48
Resolution MDS 132/2020, of Argentina, 38
Rice, Pranee, 193

rural areas, 4, 50, 51–52, 56, 78, 159
    child marriage in, 166
    expectations for girls from, 111
    forced marriage in, 184
    internet connectivity in, 114

SAAPASA. *See* Southern African Alcohol Policy Alliance in South Africa
Sadleir, Emma, 57–58
Salinas, Maria E., 126
Sandhu, Shreya, 133
sanitary products, 74, 79, 113
SARS disease, 109–10
SASSA. *See* South African Social Security Agency
Save the Children, 76
Savi (pseudonym), 124, 125–26, 128, 131
school closures, 24–25, 69, 70, 75–76, 78, 102
secondary harms, 18, 19, 24, 27–28
second wave, of COVID-19, 166–67
Secretariat of Comprehensive Policies on Drugs of the Argentine Nation (SEDRONAR), 42
Sędzikowska, Alicja, 90, 91–92, 93, 95, 96
self-quarantine, 198
SENAF. *See* National Secretariat for Children and Adolescents and the Family, in Argentina
Sengupta, Meeta, 164
Senior Woman Teacher (SWT), 69, 70, 71, 72, 73, 75
    girls supported by, 74, 77, 78 79, 80–82
7-Eleven, 195, 196, 200, 203n1
sex- and gender-based violence (SGBV). *See* gender-based violence
sexual exploitation, 21, 22, 62–63, 164, 175, 186
sexual health services, 24
sexual violence, 21, 24–26, 39, 55
    child marriage relation to, 163
sex work, 167, 186
SGBV. *See* gender-based violence

shadow pandemic, 25–26, 52
Sharia law, of Muslim people, 163, 165
Sharma, Gayatri, 169
Sheik, Ayub, 63
shelter homes, 47n2, 149, 150–51
Sierra Leone, 24, 70, 77
SIF. *See* Social Ills Fighters
Singh, Anupriya, 152
Singh, Ayesha, 166
slum areas, in Ethiopia, 179–80
Smit, Sarah, 58
Smithers, Maurice, 61
SNNPR. *See* Southern Nations Nationalities and Peoples' Region
Social Action Ministry, in Argentina, 44
social distancing, 50, 109, 180, 197
Social Ills Fighters (SIF), 8
social inequalities, COVID-19 reinforcing, 33
social isolation, 24, 34, 38, 105
Social Sciences and Humanities Research Council, in Canada, 10
social services, 50, 97
social stigma, 169, 196, 201
  of abuse, 25, 56, 166–67
  from COVID-19 infection, 60, 160
SOPs. *See* Special Operating Procedures
South Africa, 4, 50, 56, 58, 59, 61
South African Social Security Agency (SASSA), relief grant for recipients of, 59
South Coast Herald (newspaper), 59
Southern African Alcohol Policy Alliance in South Africa (SAAPASA), 61
Southern Nations Nationalities and Peoples' Region (SNNPR), 103
Special COVID-19 Social Relief of Distress Grant, in South Africa, 59
Special Operating Procedures (SOPs), for SWTs, 71
state support, 41–42, 114–15, 192
  COVID-19 lockdowns effect on, 34, 46
  for GBV, 34–35, 37–38, 39–40, 44–45, 46–47

#stayhome, 94
Supreme Court, in India, 158–59
SWT. *See* Senior Woman Teacher

Tablighi Jamaat, in New Delhi, 157, 160
Tarekegne, Welela, 188
teacher networks, on WhatsApp, 81
Tesfaye, Frehiwot, 116
TGW. *See* Transgender Women
Thailand, 190, 191, 192, 193
  entertainment sector in, 194, 195–96
Theuss, Marc, 192
Thiara, Ravi, 83n3
Thompson, Jennifer, 10
Thongkrajai, Cheera, 203
Times Now (news outlet), 157
Times of India (news outlet), 158
transgender people, GBV against, 7
Transgender Women (TGW), 192–93, 197, 198, 202
  disasters effect on, 191
  hormone treatment for, 200–201
  in Thai entertainment sector, 194, 195–96
Transnational Girlhoods, of Berghahn Books, 9
Tronto, Joan, 88–89
Turner, Erica, 126

Uganda, 5, 70, 71, 80, 81, 83n2
  child marriage in, 75, 76
  domestic obligations in, 74, 77–78
  Girl Up Initiative in, 79, 83n4
  LC1 in, 72, 74, 75, 76, 77
  school closures in, 69, 75–76
Uganda Violence against Children in Schools (VACIS), 81, 82
Undersecretariat for Children and Youth, Las Luciérnagas, 43
unemployment, 51, 98, 132, 168
  of child domestic workers, 181–83, 185–86
UNICEF, 57, 62, 167
United Nations, 52
universal child allowance (AUH), 36

universities, 51, 52, 53, 110
University of Delhi, 123
unpaid care work, 87–88, 107–8
Uttar Pradesh, India, 167–68

vaccinations, during Ebola epidemic, 22–23
VACIS. *See* Uganda Violence against Children in Schools
VAW/C. *See* violence against women and children
Venkatesan, Sathyaraj, 2–3
violence, 191
   domestic, 51–52, 69–70, 79, 139, 164, 165–66
   gender-based, 6, 7, 24–26, 33, 37–40, 49, 105, 140–41
   sexual, 21, 24–26, 39, 55, 163
violence against women and children (VAW/C), 139–40, 142–43
voluntarism, unpaid care work compared to, 87–88

Wakiso, Uganda, 71
Walaita Soddo college, in SNNPR, 103
Wall, Sarah, 87
Walsh, Shannon, 1–2
water, during crisis, 19–20
West Bengal, India, 168
WhatsApp, 8, 38, 39, 42, 81
WHO. *See* World Health Organization

Witek, Natalia, 93, 94–95, 96
WoHFW. *See* Ministry of Health and Family Welfare, in India
women, 19, 23, 28, 102, 109, 133n1. *See also* Transgender Women (TGW)
   as caregivers, 20, 56, 78
   crisis effect on, 139–40, 168
   economic uncertainty effect on, 21
   HEI experience of, 122–23
   unpaid care work of, 87–88, 107–8
   young rural, 50–51, 53, 56, 62–63
Women Power Connect, 159, 163
"Women Win" (community-based organization), 53
Woreta college, in Ethiopia, 103
World Bank Group, 121, 159
World Health Organization (WHO), 17–18, 23–24, 39, 60, 140–41
World Vision International (2020), 5

Yadav, Poonam, 133
Yasti (pseudonym), 124, 130, 131
Yaya (pseudonym), 196–97, 200
Yesmien (pseudonym), 61, 62
Youth Policy Directorate, in Las Luciérnagas, 41–42

Zaire strain, EVD, 17–18
Zdziarska, Faustyna, 92, 97–98
Zika epidemic, 121
Zulu, Lindiwe, 59

www.ingramcontent.com/pod-product-compliance
Lightning Source LLC
Chambersburg PA
CBHW051541020426
42333CB00016B/2039